D0555512

Critical Issues in Educational Leadership Series

Joseph Murphy, Series Editor

PRINCIPAL ACCOMPLISHMENTS

How School Leaders Succeed

G. Thomas Bellamy
Connie L. Fulmer
Michael J. Murphy
Rodney Muth

Foreword by Robert Donmoyer

Teachers College, Columbia University
New York and London

Published by Teachers College Press, 1234 Amsterdam Avenue, New York, NY 10027

Library of Congress Cataloging-in-Publication Data

Principal accomplishments : how school leaders succeed / G. Thomas Bellamy . . . [et al.].
    p. cm. — (Critical issues in educational leadership series)
    Includes bibliographical references and index.
    ISBN-13: 978-0-8077-4743-8 (hardcover)
    ISBN-10: 0-8077-4743-2 (hardcover)
    ISBN-13: 978-0-8077-4742-1 (pbk.)
    ISBN-10: 0-8077-4742-4 (pbk.)
    1. School principals—United States.   2. Educational leadership—United States.
    3. School management and organization—United States.   I. Bellamy, G. Thomas.
    LB2831.92.P715 2006
    371.2'012—dc22

                                                                          2006021744

ISBN 13: 978-0-8077-4742-1 (paper)
ISBN 13: 978-0-8077-4743-8 (cloth)

Printed on acid-free paper

Manufactured in the United States of America

14   13   12   11   10   09   08   07   8   7   6   5   4   3   2   1

Contents

CHAPTER 12   **Developing Individual Knowledge
    for School Leadership**   **158**

Foreword

The possession of a specialized knowledge base is one of the things that make a profession a profession. The medical profession, for example, has fashioned such a knowledge base from the results of basic research conducted by physical scientists and the theories scientists have constructed from these results. More applied inquiry conducted within the medical field itself (e.g., randomized drug trials, epidemiological studies) also contributes to the medical profession's storehouse of knowledge. A professional knowledge base, in short, is both a practical necessity and a source of status for a field and its members.

Not surprisingly, academics within the field of educational administration have spent considerable time and energy attempting to construct a knowledge base that could both guide the work of principals and other school leaders and enhance their status and the status of the educational administration field, in general. During the middle of the twentieth century, for example, the field's so-called theory movement focused on developing empirically based social science theories that could be used by school leaders, much as engineers and physicians use empirically based theoretical knowledge about the physical world to direct their professional practice.

Theoretical knowledge was still the coin of the realm in the 1980s when the University Council of Educational Administration (UCEA) launched its Knowledge Base Project. The major difference between the theory movement of the 1960s and UCEA's Knowledge Base Project in the 1980s and early 1990s was the latter's more eclectic conception of theory. Charged with articulating the profession's knowledge base about organizations, the UCEA task force endorsed an array of sometimes contradictory organizational theories: Positivist, interpretive/constructivist, and critical theory perspectives were all enthusiastically embraced. Task force members, however, said nothing about how school leaders could manage the contradictions inherent in their eclectic approach when using the field's "big-tent" knowledge base about organizations to make actual organizational decisions.

Not surprisingly, the eclectic approach is currently out of fashion and once again the search is on for the sort of empirical knowledge that links administrators' decisions and actions with desired outcomes. As this book is going to press, for example, UCEA and Division A of the American Educational Research Association are in the process of preparing an ambitious publication that (1) catalogs all that is known (and not known) about the effects of various components of principal preparation programs and (2) charts a research agenda for the field geared to filling gaps in existing knowledge.

Past attempts to articulate a knowledge base for the educational administration field have been decidedly unsuccessful, and there is little reason to believe that current efforts—which largely mimic the thinking and strategies of the past—will be any more fruitful. The difficulty, quite simply, is that the educational administration field (and the education field, in general) differs from fields such as medicine and engineering in a number of highly significant ways.

In education, for instance, change is a constant, and context matters— a lot. To be sure, viruses can mutate and metals may behave somewhat differently in different climates, but the complexity resulting from these sorts of changes and contextual variations is minimal when compared to the contextual complexity that school leaders must confront on a daily basis. Because of this complexity, academics' empirical generalizations and theories are, at best, merely hypotheses about what is likely to happen in particular settings. School leaders must test—and continually retest—whether "what works" at the aggregate level will "work" in the often-changing contexts in which school leaders work.

There is at least one other highly significant difference: School leaders confront a different kind of problem than the problems that engineers and medical professionals normally tackle. The problems that medical personnel and engineers must resolve are largely technical. By contrast, educational leaders confront problems that are not exclusively—or even primarily—technical. Different stakeholders continue to disagree about the best way to teach reading, for instance, not merely because of the absence of technical knowledge that is applicable across different school contexts. Stakeholders also disagree because (1) they conceptualize basic concepts such as teaching and reading in fundamentally different ways and (2) these different conceptualizations have embedded within them fundamental value disagreements that cannot be resolved with empirical evidence alone. Indeed, terms such as *reading* and *teaching* must be defined—and, in the process, value choices must be made—prior to framing and conducting an empirical study. Consequently, "empirical" knowledge is never value-neutral (and never entirely empirical, either).

Thus, researchers in the field of educational administration have failed— and almost certainly will continue to fail—in their attempts to create the sort of professional knowledge base found in fields such as medicine and engineering. They have not failed because our field's researchers are necessarily less intelligent or less skilled than researchers in fields such as medicine and engineering. Rather, they have failed primarily because there is a mismatch between our field and the fields we have looked to for models of professionalism and professional knowledge.

This book takes a decidedly different tack. It articulates what is, for the educational administration field at least, an out-of-the-box approach to the conceptualization and development of professional knowledge. It also articulates innovative approaches to professional education that are consistent with—and, to some extent, logically follow from—the authors' innovative epistemology. The book's subtext also suggests a radically different vision of professionalism than the one that has dominated the thinking of academics in the educational administration field (and, also, many of their critics). The vision of professionalism and professional knowledge on display here, in fact, is more consistent with what happens in the legal profession than with what happens in the medical and engineering fields.

As in the field of law, the major focus here is on the individual case rather than on generalizations that cut across cases. General knowledge is not totally irrelevant in the visions of professionalism and professional knowledge articulated in this book, of course—just as general legal principles (and even, at times, social science theories) are not ignored in the legal reasoning process —but the emphasis here, and in the field of law, is on the symbiotic relationship between the general and the particular: Generalizations inform both (1) the interpretation of the particulars of a case and (2) the decisions that are made and the actions that are taken. Simultaneously, however, case particulars add nuance and depth to generalizations. Here, as in law, a case-based approach to thinking and reasoning is the way both individual and collective understanding advances. Indeed, in both this book and in the model of professionalism provided by the legal profession, professional knowledge is conceptualized less as a static product and more as a process, that is, a process of knowing how to think and reason about the particulars of a case.

I suspect the case-embedded approach to thinking and reasoning discussed here, along with the more process-oriented conception of knowledge they represent, has the potential to respond to and manage the previously discussed difficulties that have plagued other efforts to construct a knowledge base for the educational administration field. At the very least, the book challenges us to rethink our taken-for-granted assumptions about professionalism, professional education, and, most importantly, the form and function of professional knowledge. This book, in short, should get us all thinking about our field and our work in new and different ways!

Robert Donmoyer
Professor, Leadership Studies
The University of San Diego

Preface

With this book, we join the discussion of how school leadership can evolve to meet the many practical and political challenges that confront public education. The most visible pressures today come from the confluence of ambitious learning goals for students, accountability for annual gains on state tests, and changing demographics that require schools to overcome wide-ranging learning problems. Underlying these challenges are sharp differences about what conditions should exist in schools and what kinds of learning should be fostered, differences that pull school leaders in opposite directions as one group's reform becomes another's crisis.

We write out of concern that the educational leadership profession has not adapted quickly or substantively enough to help principals meet these challenges. The field has been remarkably forthright and self-critical in its own analysis of needed changes. Our thinking about how school leaders could respond to contemporary challenges has been influenced by many of our colleagues, who argue that educational leadership offers too little practical guidance to practitioners (Black & English, 1986; Hills, 1978), lacks clear grounding (Murphy, 2002a), struggles with how diverse forms of knowledge inform practice (Donmoyer, 1999, 2001), and has difficulty demonstrating the importance of professional education (Brent, 1998; Browne-Ferrigno, Barnett, & Muth, 2003; Haller, Brent, & McNamara, 1997). While calls for reform within educational leadership are widespread, we remain unconvinced that the field has found a path through the challenges it faces. We are committed to public schools as a critical institution in our democracy and to educational leadership as an essential profession supporting public schools, but we believe that further renewal is needed to forestall continuing declines in the perceived impact of school leaders, their professional status, and the confidence of policy makers in the profession as a whole.

At the same time, we have little confidence in the nonprofessional and market approaches frequently touted as school leadership reforms. While choice and voucher programs, open access to leadership positions, and greater accountability for student learning have become popular with many policy makers, little evidence suggests that these competitive market approaches can create the nearly universal proficiency that today's policies envision. Mainstream political support for these market approaches appears to us to be more a product of frustration with past efforts to change schools from the outside, rather than a result of evidence-based arguments for their effectiveness.

Our book is written with principals in mind, and we recommend a comprehensive strategy for how principals can succeed amid increasingly difficult circumstances. Of course, many others share in the school leadership challenge, including teachers, administrators, school boards, university scholars, policy makers, and a variety of additional public and private groups. Because any substantial change in the principalship requires wide discussion among these leaders, the book frames our understandings of principal leadership to provide a context for our recommendations for leadership practice.

The same circumstances that create today's challenges suggest to us that an effective principalship also may be the best hope for achieving the nation's goals for its schools. But in our view, succeeding in the face of these challenges requires a new way of thinking about principal practice and a new combination of leadership strategies. While our understandings of the principalship and the strategies we recommend are a departure from conventional views, we have drawn extensively from existing ideas about school leadership—some popular, some traditional, and others apparently forgotten or outside the educational administration mainstream. Taken as a whole, our synthesis provides a new and challenging way of thinking about and acting in the principalship, a way that, we believe, best reflects contemporary school realities.

Like all proposals for change, ours is grounded in a particular understanding of the real responsibilities that school leaders confront. Recommendations vary widely, depending on whether one views the core of a principal's job as supporting instruction, buffering teachers from outside pressures, fostering social connections among teachers, building linkages with families, shaping a school culture, or all of these together. We make this grounding in practice explicit. Our book begins with a set of proposals for how principals' work can be understood. We then build on this view of practice to offer recommendations for principal leadership and suggest how professional knowledge can support that leadership.

As with any view of principal practice, our recommendations also imply a particular perspective on what knowledge school leaders need in order to fulfill their responsibilities. To support our suggestions for practice, we recommend a way for the profession to define and structure important knowledge, and we offer suggestions on how that knowledge might be transmitted to new practitioners in principal preparation programs.

Our aims, then, are threefold: (1) to help school leaders think differently about their work, (2) to provide practical leadership strategies for the responsibilities that we see as most important in the principalship, and (3) to help the academic arm of the profession improve the ways it supports principals, with a particular focus on professional knowledge, how it is organized, and how it is used to prepare new principals.

Our starting point is the responsibility of principals to create conditions in their schools that are valued by the community and that result in high levels of student learning. We call these conditions "accomplishments" and our approach to leadership "accomplishment-minded practice" in order to emphasize important complexities in how these school conditions develop and whether they are valued. While we use the term "accomplishment" in a very specific way, as described in Chapter 3, the commonsense meaning is a reasonable starting point. Simply put, accomplishments are the positive results, or conditions, that schools and their leaders strive to create in order to support student learning and reach other school goals.

For principals to create and sustain a set of important school accomplishments, we suggest that they operate in four leadership domains: (1) as active participants in developing the goals toward which school conditions are directed, (2) as responsible agents in determining which school conditions are important and which should receive emphasis at any given time, (3) in day-to-day actions to establish and maintain important school conditions, and (4) as stewards for the many social connections and networks through which school work is done.

These four domains center the book on leadership practice, and we consciously return to associated themes throughout the book. We first introduce accomplishment-minded practice as a way of thinking about the principalship, describing a way of understanding why each of the four leadership domains is important for school success. We then return to the same four topics to explore practical implications and leadership strategies. Finally, we ask how professional knowledge can be organized and shared to support principals who are engaged in accomplishment-minded leadership. Figure P.1 illustrates this outline, showing the four leadership domains as the center of the book's structure.

After an introductory chapter that describes the need for a new way of thinking about principals' work, Part I develops our ideas of accomplishment-minded practice as an alternative way of framing school leadership. Chapter 2 describes a way of viewing school goals and the principal's role in shaping those goals. Chapter 3 explores the school conditions through which these goals are achieved. Here we develop the concept of an "accomplishment" as a way of framing those conditions that stimulates simultaneous consideration of ends and means in school leadership. Chapter 4 describes our thinking about the daily work through which principals strive toward desired school conditions. Chapter 5 completes this part of the book by describing the social capital that schools need in order to address all other areas.

Part II is written specifically for practicing principals. Here, our goal is to offer practical ways of approaching common responsibilities that

FIGURE P.1. Organization of the Book Around Four Domains of School Leadership

PART I:	PART II:	PART III:
Understanding School Leadership as Accomplishment-Minded Practice	The Practice of Accomplishment-Minded Leadership	Knowledge for School Leadership

Defining School Goals for Student Learning and School Conditions (Chapter 2)	Leadership for Sustainable Goals (Chapter 6)	Organizing Knowledge to Support Accomplishments (Chapter 10)
Accomplishments for School Goals (Chapter 3)	Leadership for Strategic Focus (Chapter 7)	Sharing Craft Knowledge Through Practice Narratives (Chapter 11)
Pragmatic Practice for School Accomplishments (Chapter 4)	Leadership for Effective Action (Chapter 8)	
Social Capital for School Accomplishments (Chapter 5)	Leadership for Social Capital (Chapter 9)	Developing Individual Knowledge for School Leadership (Chapter 12)

principals face as they work to develop desired school conditions and expected student learning. Part II is organized to reflect the same four themes as Part I. Each of the elements of accomplishment-minded practice that we introduce in Part II also frames an important area of leadership responsibility. We describe these as leadership domains and offer suggestions for leadership for sustainable purposes in Chapter 6, leadership for strategic focus in Chapter 7, leadership for effective action in Chapter 8, and leadership for social capital in Chapter 9.

In Part III, our focus shifts from the work of principals to the knowledge that is needed to support that work and make it effective. While useful for principals, this part also is written for our colleagues in universities and professional associations who are responsible for knowledge development and transmission. In Chapters 10 and 11, we suggest ways that an accomplishment perspective could help frame the scope and structure of knowledge that is important for the practice of school leadership. Our recommendations incorporate knowledge from many sources and intellectual traditions, including the craft expertise developed on the job by practitioners. Chapter 12 turns to the knowledge that individual principals bring to their positions and addresses what the accomplishment perspective might contribute to principal preparation programs.

By recommending a new way of thinking about the practice of school leadership and new approaches to organizing knowledge to support practice, we hope to stimulate conversations among a broad and diverse audience. Part I is intended for a broad audience with interest in how principals' work is understood. For readers who wish to skim quickly through this information and move directly to other parts of the book, we have provided summaries at the end of the chapters in Part I. Part II is written for prospective and practicing principals and focuses on the practical implementation of accomplishment-minded practice. Part III is intended for the university arm of the profession and addresses ways to support practice through organization and transmission of knowledge. Our hope is that the book will be useful for all these groups as a basis for new discussions of how the principalship can address today's challenges.

ACKNOWLEDGMENTS

The ideas presented in this book developed over many years and were influenced and supported by many colleagues in the university and school districts. The Framework for School Leadership Accomplishments originated in work with the New Iowa Schools Development Corporation, with much helpful feedback and guidance from Gerald Ott and Peter Holly. Further development occurred in conjunction with a long-term collaboration with the Adams Five Star School District to refocus school improvement planning on student learning. Judy Margrath-Huge, Cindy Harrison, and Joellen Killion provided important guidance as the Framework was adapted for their district. Development of the Framework also was supported by several colleagues in doctoral laboratories and the Colorado Principal Center at the University of Colorado at Denver, including James Bailey, Ritu Chopra, Sue Giullian, Dan Jesse, May Lowry, and Randy Sinisi.

We gained invaluable experience in applying several ideas from the book to district-based leadership development programs through a grant from the U. S. Department of Education's School Leadership Program (Grant Number S363A020159). The experienced principals who led this project—Anne O'Rourke, Karen Ballek, Steve Cohen, and Jackie Provenzano—helped translate the book's proposals into practical support for principals and district administrators, raising critical questions of applicability that sharpened many of our recommendations.

The book is also a result of continued development and revision of a principal education program over several years at the University of Colorado at Denver. Many students and school district partners shaped the program's development over this time. We particularly want to acknowledge the long-term insightful support of Tricia Browne-Ferrigno, Nancy Cebula, Mack Clark, Barbara Conroy, Sharon Ford, Pat Grippe, Holly Hultgren, Dick

Koeppe, Cherie Lyons, Mike Martin, Bill Munsell, Rick O'Connell, Bob Rehm, Ken Reiter, Bobbi Siegfried, Roy Siegfried, Julie Smith, Ray Smith, Dudley Soloman, Ed Steinbrecker, Cindy Stevenson, Marge Tepper, Dick Weber, Debbie Welch, Dick Werpy, and the late Gordon Brooks. During the 4 years of conversations that led to the book, we were joined at different times by Priscilla Huston, L. A. Napier, and David Benson. Their support and insights helped frame many of the issues in the early stages of our work together. Our thinking was also influenced and shaped by many colleagues who read and gave critical comments on earlier drafts of the book: Richard Clark, Robert Donmoyer, Virginia Doolittle, Jean Hills, Laraine Hong, Cindy Harrison, Betty Malen, and three anonymous reviewers for Teachers College Press.

These many colleagues influenced and shaped our thinking in numerous ways. Inevitably, the authors assume full responsibility for the content of the book, including any omissions and errors.

PRINCIPAL ACCOMPLISHMENTS

How School Leaders Succeed

Chapter 1

Challenges for the Principalship

Principals may have the most complex job in education. Entrusted with children's learning and safety, and responsible for stewardship of a historical symbol of community hopes for the future, principals operate at the nexus of public policy, family values, community aspirations, and emerging knowledge. The job always has been difficult and dynamic, responding to the evolving needs of students, the changing economy, and the nation's priorities. But the challenges now facing school leaders are so significant and have such high stakes that they threaten the survival of the principalship as we know it.

HIGH EXPECTATIONS AND DIFFICULT CONDITIONS

The difficult conditions confronting society today combine with ambitious policy goals for education, challenging both individual principals and the school leadership profession to make dramatic and thoughtful changes. Once responsible primarily for internal school operations, principals now are accountable to the community, school district, state, and even federal government for improving student learning and closing achievement gaps between diverse ethnic and socioeconomic student groups.

The United States set a goal for its public schools in the No Child Left Behind Act of 2001 (NCLB) that all children will be proficient in all core subjects. While similar goals have been advocated in the educational community as matters of equity and social justice (Scheurich & Skrla, 2003), their adoption in national and state policy represents a dramatic shift in expectations for what schools can and should accomplish. Despite inevitable adjustments as policy makers wrestle with the difficult problems of implementation, schools and their leaders face daunting new challenges to demonstrate that this dream of universal proficiency is possible in all communities.

Ambitious goals for universal achievement complicate an already difficult context of schooling that has become increasingly trying for teachers
and principals (Luegg, Bulkley, Firestone, & Garner, 2001; Public Agenda
Foundation, 2001). For example:

- Schools serve a growing population of children whose characteristics—
  poverty, lack of medical insurance, single-parent homes, disabilities,
  and non-English-speaking families—traditionally have been associated
  with learning problems (Hodgkinson, 2000). To help all these children reach the new standards requires principals and their schools to
  make dramatic improvements in the systems that support teaching and
  learning.
- Citizens in many states have limited the spending or taxing capacity
  of government, with significant impact on resources available to schools.
  These more general limitations, coupled with funding inequities across
  communities, mean that many schools must address new teaching and
  learning challenges with severely limited resources (Kozol, 1991). As
  a result, school principals are expected to create resources for their
  schools through active pursuit of grants, fund-raising activities, and
  business partnerships.
- The shift continues from professional to lay control in school decision making, with parents, policy makers, site councils, and other
  groups having greater voice in how schools are run, which schools
  children attend, and the priorities that guide school expenditures. The
  structures for lay control have become opportunities for various interest groups to express opposing political, religious, or philosophical views about schools (Gaddy, Hall, & Marzano, 1996; Spring,
  2002). Teacher unions, the religious right, parent groups, business and
  industry, and big-city mayors are but a few of the constituent groups
  that have joined the debate. In this context of expanding lay control,
  principals accomplish school results as much through external political engagement as through internal professional leadership.
- Schools mirror the violence in society at the same time that parents,
  because of their own work schedules, depend more and more on schools
  for child supervision and care. As parents demand safer schools, principals must allocate an increasing share of their effort and resources to
  nonacademic concerns.
- Efforts to improve schools increasingly include ideas from the market-
  place, where choice and competition are fundamental drivers of improvement (Osborne & Plastrik, 2000). School choice plans—vouchers,
  charter schools, magnet schools, and open-enrollment policies—make

principals responsible not just for educating students, but for attracting them in the first place.

- Publishers, scholars, and other "policy entrepreneurs" (Kingdon, 1995) have flooded the landscape with curriculum programs and school designs, marketing these to parents, legislators, school boards, and community leaders. As a result, principals now mediate increasingly complex community conversations about matters of teaching and learning that previously were left more to professional judgment.

Of course, principals have always had difficult jobs, facing rapid-fire, simultaneous, and messy problems in complex environments. Solutions to these problems are judged externally with concern for the institutional expectations for schools, including the qualifications of professionals hired, responsible use of public funds, public acceptance of the programs and curriculum, compliance with myriad laws and policies, and general orderliness, discipline, and safety. Principals have to deal effectively with daily challenges so that they and their schools are credible in the eyes of families, school administrators, students, educational professionals, and others in the community. Principals' decisions in these matters have uncertain consequences, differentially benefit some groups, and often require difficult ethical choices.

While difficult work is familiar, the current combination of ambitious goals for student learning and the social conditions in school communities pose pressing challenges for school leaders. Principals are expected to overcome barriers to learning, show reliable student achievement, and do both in an environment of resource constraints and political conflict about the role of schools. To succeed, principals must be comfortable in settings characterized by competition and consumer choice, serve as vigorous and successful champions of student learning, actively lead the teaching and learning process, and ensure that instruction both matches the content tested by state authorities and meets the needs of each one of a very diverse group of children.

Principals' responses to these challenges occur in full public view as state and federal policies have focused attention on schools and pressed for operational changes (Mazzoni, 1995; Wirt & Kirst, 1997). As research continues to demonstrate that principals can influence school quality (Leithwood & Montgomery, 1982; Witziers, Boskers, & Kruger, 2003), principals increasingly are held accountable for leading schools to high levels of learning.

In addition, every principal is held accountable for what business frequently calls "short-term numbers"—immediate gains on assessments of student learning. Even before NCLB, most states had adopted content standards with tests of student performance and systems for publicly reporting results. These tests have created a climate of immediate accountability for results and have shifted the focus of attention from school districts to individual schools and their leaders. For example, newspapers now report test results at the school level, and individual schools can be placed on probation or labeled as failing.

While principals can take pride in their initial adjustments to new policy goals and their efforts to accommodate changing social conditions, the profession has only begun to address these challenges. Indeed, many schools have achieved remarkable success, but positive examples serve to highlight just how far many other schools have to go.

Individual principals and the profession as a whole face an increasing sense of urgency in their efforts to change. Because Americans are an impatient people, we are—and should be—unwilling to postpone the promise of schooling as a path toward full citizenship, economic opportunity, and personal enrichment. As this impatience increasingly translates into public policies, tolerance is waning for historical disparities between a few successful schools and others where children do not progress as expected. Schools that do not succeed face administrative sanctions and negative media coverage; even more quickly, their principals typically face personal employment consequences. Whatever one might think of the appropriateness of these consequences, they do demonstrate the critical role of the principal in the nation's effort to achieve ambitious goals for student learning under demanding social conditions.

ENDURING LEADERSHIP PARADOXES

The combination of ambitious goals for student learning and changing social conditions is certainly challenging enough by itself. But below the surface of these difficult daily realities lie additional threats to the profession that affect how the visible challenges are perceived and the kinds of responses that are likely to succeed.

These deeper challenges have their roots in the natural tensions of democratic life and the competing goals that these tensions create for schools. As a society, we value both excellence and equity, both individual freedom and public responsibility, both rewards for individual effort and equity across social groups. We expect schools to prepare all students for civic participation but also to serve as a means for individuals to get ahead, to prepare individuals to succeed in a competitive economy but also to foster habits of democratic life, to be responsive to local priorities for what children should learn but also to reflect national agendas for education.

While these conflicting beliefs pose "value-laden choices that can never be resolved" (Ogawa, Crowson, & Goldring, 1999, p. 279), we depend on schools and other public institutions to help adjudicate the conflicts among these beliefs. Unlike the problem of reaching high academic standards in spite of challenging social conditions, conflicting beliefs about what schools should emphasize are not problems that can be solved. Instead, they present enduring paradoxes that continually must be managed and balanced to provide some satisfaction to competing expectations.

Mechanisms That Balance Competing Goals

Gutmann's (2001) conclusion about these competing goals poses a stark reality for schools: "It is impossible to educate children to maximize both their freedom and their civic virtue" (p. 217). Cuban (1992) responds that instead of focusing entirely on one side or the other, schools "negotiate the unappealing choices . . . by tying opposites together in some fashion to cope with differences in values. Moreover, these good-enough bargains among values that we strike have to be renegotiated again and again" (p. 7).

The mechanisms that tie these opposites together are the educational policies, school structures, and widely shared practices that help to balance competing interests in sustainable ways. While such structures are not unique to education—indeed, Cameron (1986) argues that they are a critical part of all effective organizations—they seem particularly important in schools because the ongoing value conflicts affect what schools are expected to accomplish. How schools accommodate such competing values is puzzling if one expects schools to be structured more simply to accomplish defined goals.

For example, separate and fairly autonomous classrooms are the norm in schools, but often are criticized as hindering instructional improvement efforts. Within this structure, teachers work in relative isolation from one another, and each teacher's classroom is largely her or his own domain (Lortie, 1975). Such a structure serves a balancing function among competing values associated with teacher, community, and administrative control over what children experience in school. The ability to close the classroom door has given teachers autonomy over some aspects of schooling: the day-to-day details of instruction and the curriculum that actually is taught. At the same time, decisions about the school experience beyond the classroom—the formal curriculum, school rules, events, and so on—are open to broader public involvement.

This example highlights two important aspects of school mechanisms for balancing competing goals. First, schools are susceptible to constant criticism from advocates for a primary focus on any single goal. Proponents of the positive benefits of teacher collaboration on instruction argue for opening classroom doors (Little, 1982, 1990). External advocacy groups that want more family or religious control over the content of instruction (Gaddy, Hall, & Marzano, 1996) and advocates of greater administrative accountability for teaching and learning (Elmore, 2000) make similar arguments. Second, these balancing mechanisms have staying power. They tend to persist despite ongoing criticism and become "regularities" (Goodlad, 1975) or "deep structures" (Tye, 2000) that seem to spread across schools and endure, often without an obvious rationale.

Many possibilities come to mind when considering how school structures and policies tie together opposite goals. For example, the comprehensive high school, which has been challenged by many reformers as too large to be effective (Vander Ark, 2003), balances several competing interests by supporting common socialization experiences while also allowing different curriculum goals for different students. Similarly, the 9-month school year, criticized as an anachronism from a former agricultural era, balances our competing goals for academic progress and time for family activities and recreational pursuits. And the grade-level organization of schools serves as a compromise between goals for socialization with same-age peers and individual academic progress.

Need for New Balancing Mechanisms

Balancing competing demands has always been part of public education in the United States. What is new today is the failure of existing balancing mechanisms to contain the associated conflicts successfully. Strong differences in views about schools continue, despite public support for the high academic expectations expressed in content standards and state tests (Rose & Gallup, 2005). But these changes, together with polarized public debate about what is important about schools, have destabilized conventional structures for balancing competing demands.

For example, both private philanthropists and the federal government have invested heavily in development of smaller alternatives to large comprehensive high schools, with the rationale that smaller schools can foster stronger personal relationships, more coherent goals, and greater achievement (e.g., see the federal Small Learning Communities Program [U.S. Department of Education, 2000]). But as these structural changes are implemented, strategies also will be needed to accommodate the conflicts that comprehensive schools helped to manage, including differences in priorities about socialization and academic progress, different views about the importance of preparation for work and college admission, and differences about how much the curriculum should respond to individual student interests. Consequently, as schools become smaller, they depend more on sensitive leadership from principals and teachers to understand conflicts as they arise in the community and to make responsive adaptations in the school.

Similarly, the traditional autonomy of individual teachers in their own classrooms increasingly is being replaced through school-wide and even district-wide alignment of instructional programs and greater authority of school administrators. As this occurs, the need to balance the many competing interests that want to influence what happens in classrooms will not disappear. Schools will continue to be bombarded with materials from advocacy groups that want their points of view integrated into instruction, from family members who want to ensure that teaching is consistent with their religious beliefs, and from businesses that want students to learn practical work skills. As the school structures that buffered individual teachers from these pressures gradually are removed, alternative ways will be needed to balance these many interests.

The Principal as the New Balancing Agent

In the 20 years since publication of the famous "Nation at Risk" report, the nation has invested millions of dollars in new testing programs, smaller schools, charter schools, voucher programs, multigrade schools, and new school designs. In the end, each intervention has fallen far short of the legitimate expectations for schools in our society. If we simply could replace the old balancing structures with new ones, we already might see signs of new ways of balancing these competing needs, rather than increasingly shrill debates between proponents of each side of the various debates. A different type of balancing mechanism is needed, and this is where the principal returns to center stage.

Consider the balancing mechanisms that surround us in our daily lives. To accommodate both our desire for stable, comfortable seating and the forces of gravity, we design chairs and stools with at least three legs. The same is true for most familiar transportation equipment designed to balance the competing pressures of gravity and functionality. The comparison is interesting because of recent innovations. Scientists and engineers have now figured out how to put many tiny gyroscopes on a single electronic platform. Their operation allows for continuous adjustments, so that upright balance can be maintained without familiar stabilizing structures, that is, without the third leg or wheel. The result is the popular "Segway® Human Transporter" personal mobility device that appears to defy gravity as it stands and moves upright on two wheels. What is different about this new technology is that it relies on continuous small corrections in real time to achieve the needed balance between function and gravity.

These new devices illustrate the logic behind our suggestions for new balancing mechanisms for schools. The greatest hope for achieving new balances is not new structures and policies, but rather the small, real-time adjustments that school leaders can make continuously in their own schools as they come to understand and respond to the political and social dynamics of their communities.

We say this for two reasons. First, much of the information about emerging needs is available only at the school level, where families, teachers, and administrators deal with the daily realities of schooling. Whatever structures and programs might be required by policy makers or recommended by professional leaders, implementation ultimately occurs in the context of particular social and resource constraints in individual communities (Lipsky, 1980). Because these constraints differ from one community to another and are constantly evolving, the adaptations that make policies successful depend on understanding and responding to local circumstances.

Second, because school structures and policies often reflect compromises among competing values, many groups are left dissatisfied by whatever decision is reached. Inevitably, some will work to undermine the prior decision and establish different goals and structures. If left unaddressed, the concerns of these disaffected can grow and, as they attract additional supporters, develop sufficient support to overturn the original approach. As this occurs, the result is often wide swings in school goals and organizational mechanisms as, for example, in the recent shifts back and forth between centralization and decentralization of decision making in school districts. The early stages of these efforts to overturn school goals and structures are often invisible to distant policy makers but recognizable locally, where relatively minor adjustments, if made in a timely way, might prevent escalation of these debates. Such incremental changes are far less disruptive to the teaching and learning process than are the large pendulum swings that often result from policy shifts, and diminishing these swings takes on increasing importance as the stakes continue to rise for every student's successful learning.

This reasoning places principals at the center of the school's adaptation to community values. For example, a principal who is alert to the early development of differences among various families in the relative importance they place on academic and social development in middle grades could make gradual adjustments in current programs and create a new balance of priorities before the issue becomes an open political conflict. Such principal leadership is essential to maintain sustainable balances among the many competing expectations for schools. While both policy makers and professional leaders are important in achieving needed balances, small and continuous adjustments by individual school leaders are essential to any effort to achieve the nation's ambitious goals for its public schools.

IMPLICATIONS FOR RENEWAL IN THE PRINCIPALSHIP

School leaders face a daunting two-part challenge. On the one hand, they are expected to lead schools in ways that achieve ambitious goals for student learning despite difficult social conditions. As expected outcomes have become more ambitious and social conditions more complex, simply intensifying previous leadership approaches seems unlikely to result in expected learning. On the other hand, principals are increasingly responsible for finding sustainable local balances among the competing values that underlie school goals. Faced with a swirl of competing goals and values, principals typically cannot take sides, despite intense pressure from various interest groups to make the school conform to their particular priorities.

To succeed, principals must be creative instrumental leaders who help their school communities achieve goals for student learning, whatever the particular local mix of assets and challenges. They also must be flexible, adaptive leaders who invent ways to help their schools respond to constantly evolving local values.

The complexities of this dual challenge frame the questions and suggestions that we explore in this book. We do not attempt to simplify the principal's role by taking sides in the many debates about whether schools are instrumental or adaptive organizations, open or closed systems, or professional or public workplaces, or whether principals should function as leaders or managers, bridges to or buffers of external groups, or transactional or transformational leaders. In each case, our answer is "Both!" Success, we believe, lies not in oversimplifying the principalship through such dichotomies, but rather in finding better ways of addressing the true complexities of the position.

Responsiveness to Local Situations

Our starting point is to recognize that, as principals are called on to achieve ambitious goals while balancing shifting local priorities and social conditions, success depends increasingly on careful attention and creative responses to particular school situations. Although using judgment to apply knowledge in unique circumstances is a normal part of professional practice (Shulman, 1998), successful school leadership increasingly requires heightened attention to the possibilities, constraints, perspectives, and operational details in each individual school community. Such attention has been studied widely as an aspect of "mindfulness" in both individuals (Langer, 1989; Langer & Moldoveanu, 2000) and organizations (Weick & Roberts, 1993; Weick, Sutcliffe, & Obstfeld, 1999). Mindful attention involves viewing the present situation with an openness to new information, an effort to draw new distinctions, an awareness of different perspectives, and the potential to act in different ways.

Our book reflects a two-part strategy for helping principals manage the complexity of their positions while being more mindful of their local school situations. The first is a concern with mental models through which those local situations are viewed, and the second relates to the need for multiple modes of operation to support differential responses as circumstances change.

Mental Models. Mindful attention depends on the mental models and assumptions through which a principal views the school situation. Because principals are constantly surrounded by so many issues, expectations, and demands for time, it is simply impossible even to notice everything, much less give everything heightened attention. Mental models, either implicit or explicit beliefs about how schools work and what makes leadership effective, serve as filters for a principal's attention (Senge, 1990). For example, a middle school leader who believes her primary responsibility is to support students' social development might perceive as less critical information, signs that some students are falling behind academically, while she instead attends to interpersonal and behavioral situations in the school. Similarly, thinking of good schools as well-tuned machines designed to achieve certain learning outcomes leads to heightened awareness of procedures and techniques and how well they are followed. Or viewing schools as professional communities that depend on adult sharing and learning leads to a quite different focus on the relationships among teachers and their shared norms.

Such differences highlight the importance of mental models. The way that school leaders think about schools and their own leadership role matters, because their thinking focuses attention on some aspects of the school while other aspects recede into the background. The most useful mental models help principals take a systemic view of the complex and changing circumstances in their schools (Senge, 1990). In addition, mental models become most helpful when they are articulated clearly, rather than being only implicit beliefs. This makes it easier to evaluate alternatives and view situations from different vantage points and through different lenses (Langer & Moldoveanu, 2000).

Multiple Modes of Operation. School leadership also requires multiple modes of operation to respond to the uncertainty and complexity in local situations. What's important for a principal to be mindful of can change quickly. A crisis situation, for example, requires heightened attention to specific issues associated with the particular situation and its possible consequences, quite different from the broad scanning that is normally important in day-to-day problem finding and solving (Immegart & Boyd, 1979). For example, in their reviews of organizations that operate with high uncertainty and public expectations for high reliability, Weick and his colleagues (Weick, 1987; Weick & Sutcliffe, 2001) suggest that effective organizations switch from one mode of operation—typically following rather standardized procedures—to another, more decentralized structure when problems are identified. When these different modes of operation are supported by an organization's cultural assumptions and patterns of communication, rapid changes from one mode to another are possible. Such changes help an organization handle complexity by attending to different things and using different response modes when circumstances shift.

Accomplishment-Minded Leadership

Successful principals combine multiple modes of operation, or leadership domains, with flexible mental models that help direct attention in each mode. We call this conception of school leadership "accomplishment-minded practice," because school accomplishments serve as both the focus of attention and the point of intersection of the various leadership modes.

As we elaborate in Chapter 3, accomplishments are the school conditions through which school leaders strive to achieve student learning goals and respond to community values about schooling. By attending to these accomplishments, principals focus their attention on aspects of the school over which they have some influence and through which they can achieve school goals. One school accomplishment, for example, relates to the kind of goals that are set for student learning, another to the climate experienced by students in the school, and a third to the support that teachers and other staff experience. Accomplishment-minded practice is a way of making sense of the many problems, actions, and issues that arise daily in schools.

These school conditions, or accomplishments, are multidimensional. Simply listing them raises questions: What makes one set of goals or one type of climate better than another? How would a school leader know if existing conditions needed preservation or change? How would a principal go about improving one of these conditions? Questions like these underscore the complexity of school leadership and point to the various leadership domains in which successful principals operate.

In our view, being mindful of accomplishments requires principals to operate simultaneously in four leadership modes, or domains. First, principals work with their school communities to develop understandings about school goals and the implication of these goals for what is important about the various school accomplishments. Second, they decide which school conditions, or accomplishments, require particular attention at any given time in their school and use structures, priorities, and personal engagement to bring about needed changes. Third, they guide the solution of countless day-to-day problems in ways that foster the conditions they want to sustain in their schools. And fourth, principals work to build and sustain the social capital that is necessary for the school's communities to reach collective decisions and take collective action related to the school's accomplishments.

Leadership approaches similar to each of these four domains are familiar in both professional literature and practical experience. This is not surprising, since each deals with a fundamental leadership responsibility. What does seem surprising is the propensity of practitioners and theoreticians alike to single out one or two of these domains as primary, or to suggest that selection among them is a matter of leadership style and personal preference.

Our understanding of the complexities of school leadership points to a different conclusion—that all four leadership domains are essential components of the principalship. Successful leadership requires simultaneous use of all four, with each supported by mental models that guide the principal's thinking and by modes of operation that are understood by others in the school. Each provides a dimension on which principals balance and adapt to competing interests while also working to achieve student learning results. Like a tapestry or braid, the leadership that results from simultaneous and interactive attention to all four areas is stronger and more durable than continued development of one strand while others are ignored.

Accomplishment-minded leadership, then, depends on attention to the many facets and perspectives of a school's accomplishments and is manifested as a braid of four modes of operation, four domains in which school leaders work simultaneously to steward the conditions in their schools. Fortunately, the profession has rich literature and deep experience on which such understandings can be built. But new syntheses of that information are needed to guide individual principals and the profession as a whole through what likely will continue as very challenging times.

Understanding School Leadership as Accomplishment-Minded Practice

Part I describes a way of thinking about school leadership that responds to contemporary pressures and expectations for schools. These understandings about the principalship reflect a belief that principals are central both to attaining ambitious goals for student learning and to finding balances that accommodate enduring paradoxes and conflicts within our society about schooling.

The center of our understanding of the principalship involves mindfulness of the school's accomplishments, those important school conditions that support student learning and respond to community values about what school should be like. As noted in Chapter 1, these accomplishments focus attention on aspects of the school over which principals have some control and through which they work toward school goals.

Working toward these accomplishments involves simultaneous leadership in the four different domains introduced on the following pages. The four chapters in Part I describe our understandings about why principal leadership is important in each of these domains and what that leadership entails. Building on these discussions, we propose mental models that can help focus the principal's attention on local circumstances.

First, school leaders are responsible for articulating and shaping school goals that incorporate political and professional priorities while also being responsive to local values and expectations. As we discuss in Chapter 2, the conversations through which these goals are shaped engage principals with public policies, professional recommendations, and an ongoing dialog with the school's internal and external constituencies. The importance of this domain is familiar to principals: Unless goals are clear, collective effort is difficult to sustain within the school's staff and families; unless goals are responsive to local needs, the school is at risk of dramatic shifts in direction during any school board election or leadership transition; and unless goals are aligned with priorities of professional groups and policy makers, it can be extremely difficult to recruit staff and attract resources. The challenge, of course, is that clarity, responsiveness, and alignment are often at odds with one another, and workable balances require constant attention and adjustment. The mental models and strategies we propose offer ways of sorting out the natural conflicts among various expectations for schools, and ways of understanding how decisions among these competing priorities are reached in schools that also function as public institutions.

Second, principals steward the school conditions through which goals are realized. These conditions, such as the instruction provided to students, the climate that students experience, and the pattern of resource allocation, affect whether the school achieves its goals for student learning and whether the school's conditions reflect local priorities and professional values. The importance of leadership in this domain is highlighted in many strategic perspectives on the principalship, and Chapter 3 explores related ways of thinking about school leadership. Effective leadership involves diagnosing each school, determining what is needed to sustain what is working well and to improve what is not (Portin, Schneider, DeArmond, & Gundlach, 2003). Such diagnosis requires being able to translate broad community values and school goals into specific criteria for determining whether any particular school condition is weak or strong. The mental models and strategies that we recommend in this leadership domain follow from our use of the construct of an "accomplishment," which we develop in Chapter 3. This construct allows us to highlight several important features of the school conditions that principals work to sustain—that these conditions are both means and ends, involve both moral and technical reasoning, and can be achieved through many different strategies.

Third, principals work to solve a rush of day-to-day and moment-to-moment problems that are a natural part of keeping school—improving instruction, mediating communications among teachers and with families, supporting teachers in enforcing school rules, obtaining needed services from the district, keeping operations in compliance with myriad regulations, and many others. As we reason in Chapter 4, leadership for these gritty details is important because such leadership is the means through which the principal makes progress toward more lofty goals and strategic priorities. The mental models highlighted in this leadership domain emphasize pragmatic thinking. Current knowledge provides many possibilities but few prescriptions for how to act in the principalship. As a result, each principal constantly must find approaches that work within the particular school's social and resource constraints and with the students who are being taught. Of course, this requires good judgment. It also requires constant adaptation, responding quickly with another approach when something isn't working.

Fourth, principals foster the social capital in the school's communities that enables collective decision making and collaborative work. Social capital is important because practically everything a school does depends on relationships and communication—between teachers and students, teachers and families, the principal and district staff, and so on. Chapter 5 builds on earlier suggestions for strengthening social capital and professional community by fostering dense relationships among individuals and groups, making norms and expectations clear, building trust that norms will be followed, and providing leadership that enhances networks, norms, and trust (Halverson, 2003; Smylie & Hart, 1999).

We chose the term "accomplishment-minded practice" for this part of the book because attention to the positive conditions (accomplishments) that are created in a school requires the principal to attend simultaneously to all four of these leadership domains. Accomplishment-minded leadership is concerned at once with both means and ends—what makes school conditions good and how to achieve the desired states. It also requires simultaneous attention to strategic choices among accomplishments to match immediate local needs and more general investments in the capacity of the community to reach collective decisions and take collaborative action.

The term "accomplishment-minded practice" also emphasizes those elements to which a principal pays attention. While all leadership requires mindfulness of the environment, schools are exceedingly complex organizations and choices must be made constantly about what to attend to. Being mindful of accomplishments focuses attention on the most important conditions through which the school supports student learning and responds to other community values. The model of school accomplishments that we propose in Chapter 3 helps focus the attention of school leaders as they observe and interact with a school's staff, students, and community.

The four chapters in Part I elaborate these understandings of school leadership and set the stage for more specific suggestions for leadership strategies in Part II. Readers who wish to skip quickly to these more practical suggestions may find the summaries of Chapters 2–5 helpful as an orientation to those recommendations.

Chapter 2

Defining Goals for Student Learning and School Conditions

An understanding of the principalship begins with society's goals for its schools, because principals succeed only when their schools achieve those goals. In addition, these goals are evolving constantly, and decisions about goals are made through a dynamic interaction of formal political decisions, professional values, and informal local pressures. As we show in this chapter, the principal's job is profoundly affected by school goals and the way they are reached. First, school goals are complex and interwoven with the means to achieve them, so principals cannot simply maximize results in any single area. Second, because school goals are set partially through local conversations and pressures, stewardship for school goals is an important part of every principal's job.

TWO FUNDAMENTAL GOALS

Since colonial times, public schools in America have faced many competing expectations about what students should learn in school, focusing variously on religious transmission, development of public morality, preparation for work, fostering civic engagement, and support for individual development (Campbell, Cunningham, Nystrand, & Usdan, 1990; Cremin, 1970; Tyack, 1974). Over time, these conflicts about what learning is important have been complicated by the addition of many other school responsibilities—providing reliable day care, universal health screening, programs for alcohol and drug abuse, pregnancy prevention, and so forth.

Two broad goals for schools shape much of this debate. First, whatever disagreements exist about exactly what is most important for students to learn, student learning is fundamental to school goals. Second, as public institutions in a democracy, schools are expected to have characteristics and conditions that reflect public priorities and democratic goals. Consequently, the conditions in the school are another aspect of school goals.

Student Learning That Meets Standards

Today, student-learning outcomes have taken precedence over other school goals as the nation seeks to adapt to rapidly changing economic circumstances associated with globalization. With the belief that education is essential to economic progress, state and federal governments have promoted standards for student learning as the way to define what students should know and be able to do as they progress through school grades. Elected officials increasingly have relied on these standards as a foundation for aligning various educational policies (Smith & O'Day, 1991), so that standards now serve as strategies to:

- *Reduce ambiguity and local discretion about what schools are expected to teach*. With clear content standards for each subject and grade level, teachers, schools, and districts have far less discretion to decide which subjects are emphasized, what topics are covered, and when.
- *Evaluate whether students are learning what is expected*. Common standards for student learning led to the development of state assessments of whether students actually reached expected standards. One result has been a shift in responsibility for determining how well students are doing. Once the province of professionals within the school or district (and communicated to families through grades), assessment of learning now is widely seen as a state responsibility as well, with results of annual tests providing authoritative evidence of how well students are doing.
- *Hold schools accountable for student learning*. These same tests of student learning have become central in state policies to hold schools accountable for aggregate student learning and to provide a common framework for reporting school results to the community. These reports increasingly have shifted the point of accountability from the school district to the individual school, further strengthening the link between student learning and principal responsibility (Elmore, 2000).
- *Make learning more efficient*. Standards also have focused schools on issues of efficiency in how learning gains are achieved, with an emphasis on the ability to "lead and manage schools that can consistently produce steady gains in student performance without substantial increases in school budgets" (Tucker & Codding, 2002, p. 25).

State test results also have led to evolving policies about how successful student learning might be framed. At one time, schools could demonstrate successful learning by pointing to the achievements of a few students at the top of a class. The advent of standards and tests changed this, fixing success instead in terms of the overall, or average, level of learning. More recently, with the implementation of the No Child Left Behind Act (NCLB) of 2001, successful learning also involves high reliability (Bellamy, Crawford, Huber-Marshall, & Coulter, 2005)—a demonstration that every child and every demographic group is making adequate progress each year. The shift to a focus on results is supported by a tapestry of state and federal policies (Quality Counts at Ten, 2006), broad public support (Rose & Gallup, 2005), and visible professional advocacy (Elmore, 2000). Student learning is now solidly in the foreground of school goals.

School Conditions That Respond to Community Values

While many federal and state policy makers have focused attention on student learning as *the* outcome of schools, theirs are not the only voices to which principals must attend. Family and community members, elected school boards, and local school professionals also are involved in defining school goals, and their concerns add many other expectations to the mix—safely getting to and from school, daily schedules that accommodate parent and student work, educational materials that match family values, contact with peers of whom families approve, winning sports teams, and so on.

In short, families and communities care about the nature of their schools. We all want schools that match our values because children do a lot of their growing up there. They make friends, develop interests, and build habits; test identities; form aspirations; and develop character as they interact with other students and with teachers at school. To succeed, principals must be stewards of their schools as institutions that their communities trust, and this means attending to the conditions in the school as well as its results.

Defining school conditions that reflect community values is not a simple process. Most communities hold many different views about what school should be, so schools are challenged to balance many different interests as they define desired conditions. A school cannot possibly meet all of the demands that every family might make, or avoid all of the sensitive topics that any family would rather handle at home. For example, should a school provide information about sexuality, or should that be left to the home and family? If limited resources require a choice, should a school reserve extra instruction for struggling students or focus instead on advanced courses for high-achieving students? Schools across the country have been torn by conflicts within their communities about what should be expected related to these and many other issues. Such differences are natural as schools in a democratic society fulfill their responsibility to prepare students for responsible adulthood. School leaders must be able to help communities find sustainable balances among the many competing purposes.

COMPETING PURPOSES FOR SCHOOLS

As a practical matter, conflicts about educational goals occur in three broad areas of school responsibility. In our society, we expect schools to (1) enculturate children into our democratic society, (2) develop the human capital needed in the nation's economy, and (3) provide the care and child supervision that result in healthy, adjusted, law-abiding youth. In each case, schools are expected to operate in ways that serve both *public* and *private* interests, leading to multiple competing priorities for schools. While content standards now serve partially to resolve these differences in relation to what students learn, conflicts among these expectations remain central to how broad the school's curriculum should be and what school conditions are desired.

Enculturation

Goodlad (1996) reasons that a democratic society creates expectations for citizenship that are inseparable from, and unattainable without, the enculturating influence of education.

> The mission of education comes down to two related kinds of enculturation; no other institution is so charged. The first is for political and social responsibility as a citizen. The second is for maximum individual development, for full participation in the human conversation. (p. 112)

Enculturation for public purposes leads to goals such as equal access to schooling, tolerance of differences, nondiscrimination, and equal treatment, since a democracy ultimately depends on the collective decisions of all its citizens (Labaree, 1997). Public enculturation goals are also evident in arguments for freedom of inquiry and freedom from indoctrination, so that students can become conscious of, critically appraise, and transform existing social and political institutions (Freire, 1970).

Private interests associated with enculturation exert different pressures on schools. Understandably, many parents want schools to help transmit their particular religious beliefs, cultural practices, languages, and family values, or at least not to conflict with the family's own enculturation efforts. Even in the early development of public schools in the United States, conflicts between the desire for specific, sectarian religious instruction and a more general morality in the public school curriculum were so intense that separate religious school systems were created (Tyack & Hansot, 1982).

Economic Competitiveness

The second broad purpose of schooling emphasizes economic success. For example, the widely cited call for school reform, *A Nation at Risk* (National Commission on Excellence in Education, 1983), viewed education as instrumental to national economic competitiveness: "Knowledge, learning, information, and skilled intelligence are the new raw materials of international commerce. . . . Learning is the indispensable investment required for success in the 'information age' we are entering" (p. 7). Public economic interests include universal access to education and a focus on high achievement for all students, in order to develop the human capital needed in a community or nation (Commission on the Skills of the American Workforce, 1990), and development of skills directly related to the workplace, so that students are prepared for economic life (Secretary's Commission on Achieving Necessary Skills, 1991).

Private interests in economic competitiveness emphasize the desires of individual students and their families to secure competitive advantage in the labor market through students' performance in school. Schools are one of the most important opportunities for individuals to get ahead, resulting in pressure for special programs and distinctive credentials and opportunities for those who try hard and achieve more. These credentials often mean greater public investment in a student's further learning as well as more adult opportunities: More is spent on the education of students who achieve the most, through funding of special high school programs and higher subsidies for the more competitive public universities (Labaree, 2000).

Child Care and Supervision

The school's responsibility for child care and the associated concern with group adjustment frame the third broad set of school purposes. Schools are expected to act in the best interests of children, creating safe and caring environments where children get along with one another, learn to resolve conflicts appropriately, follow school rules, and develop traits and skills associated with community living.

Advocacy for public purposes emphasizes caring (Beck, 1993; Furman, 1998; Noddings, 1999) and student belonging (Osterman, 2000; Solomon, Watson, & Battistich, 2001). Other public purposes include promotion of community safety and low juvenile crime rates. In addition, because schools provide supervision for the majority of children in most communities, they also have served as an important context for implementing public policies in such diverse areas as child health, racial integration, child abuse, teenage pregnancy, nutrition, drug and alcohol use, and good driving.

Private interests in child supervision are also important. Families often want schools to adapt to their children's unique individual interests, helping families shape the peer groups with whom their children associate, perhaps through selective access to particular programs or activities. Many rely on convenient school schedules that allow family members to work and keep other commitments during the day.

> One function of schools . . . is their role as caretakers of children and young people during the workday. . . . This expectation of child custody has effectively prevented any serious rethinking of the traditional 9-month school year in most parts of the country. . . . The situation can get even more dramatic when changes in the school *week* or *day* are proposed. (Tye, 2000, pp. 28–29, emphasis in the original)

Balancing School Goals

Content standards have served partially to adjudicate the conflicts among these competing purposes with common standards for student learning. But the adjudication is only partial, because local decisions still affect the emphasis given to subjects that are not included on state tests and the approaches that are used to support learning to reach those standards.

Conflicts among the various purposes are particularly evident in local community expectations for the school conditions that principals are expected to foster and steward. Different patterns of emphasis on the public and private purposes can lead to very different expectations for school conditions. For example, when competitiveness and individual credentials are highly valued (private purposes associated with economic development), a school climate might emphasize achievement over belonging, and special programs for advanced students over remediation for those having difficulty. A very different set of school conditions might be expected in a community that gives precedence to the enculturation of a large number of new immigrants into civic responsibilities in the United States.

Like other important institutions in our democracy, schools succeed when they find a balance among these many competing interests associated with individual liberty and the common good. And, while one might hope for clarity and stability in school goals, the opposite is more common. Tensions among the various school purposes lead to changes over time and across communities as school leaders and elected officials strive to meet the expectations of a sufficient range of community interests in order to sustain the political and financial support on which schools depend. To succeed as central institutions in a democracy, public schools continually must find and shape sustainable balances among these competing purposes.

WHO DECIDES AMONG COMPETING PRIORITIES?

Conflicting views of the proper goals for a profession are not unique to education. What is different in education is the way that balance is achieved and the resulting complexities for school leaders' work. In many professions, individual practice is mostly a matter of skillful work to achieve goals that are established elsewhere, either by the profession as a whole or by elected officials. Education is different. As we outline below, the process of establishing school goals is, at least in part, an ongoing part of the responsibility of every principal.

Like other professionals, educational leaders are well qualified to give balanced consideration to the many competing goals in their work. But unlike other professions, most educators work within a public institution that gives both formal and informal authority to others. While the education professions have a very important voice in decisions about goals and priorities, these choices are shared with the formal political milieu in which schools work and the more informal and immediate context of local expectations and pressures from families and community members.

Professional Reasoning and School Goals

In many professions, the conflicts associated with defining goals are resolved through some process of deliberation and consensus building within the profession itself. For example, while the conception of health underlying the accepted definition of medical problems reflects the same kind of value-laden choices as do the competing purposes of education, resolution of these varying views is accomplished largely within the medical profession. Similarly, accounting standards and goals traditionally have been set by accountants working together; and the prevailing conception of justice evolves from collective action of the legal profession. Of course, challenges to these accepted definitions abound. But in most professions these challenges occur primarily at the margins of the field and only gradually develop sufficient professional support to influence the goals toward which most practitioners work.

When a profession is able to make a collective decision about the goals of its practice, it is at least possible to reach a working consensus on relative weight to be given to competing values, and to develop one broadly accepted definition of the goal toward which professional efforts are directed. And once professional agreement is reached about goals, individual practice can proceed largely as a matter of solving technical problems (albeit complex and ambiguous ones) in order to reach agreed-upon goals. Such agreements are not achieved so easily in public education.

The lack of professional control over school goals is not for want of relevant knowledge. A rich professional discussion of school goals draws on moral, legal, historical, and philosophical argument (Goodlad & McMannon, 1997; S. Goodlad, 2001; Ravitch & Viteritti, 2001). Several compelling proposals for the goals of educational leadership have emerged from this discussion, including arguments for grounding the profession in concepts of effective education (Cambron-McCabe, 1999), commitment to social justice (Larson & Murtadha, 2002), explicit efforts to serve a more diverse population of children (Banks, 1993; Lindsey, Robbins, & Terrell, 1999), promotion of inclusive schools (Riehl, 2000), and development of democratic community in schools (Furman & Starratt, 2002).

These professional perspectives on the goals of schools find expression in the content of preparation programs for new school leaders (McCarthy, 1999b), professional standards for program accreditation (National Policy Board for Educational Administration, 2002), and professional codes of ethics that are intended to guide individual practice (Shapiro & Stefkovich, 2001). In addition, professional discussion of school goals can influence the formal political processes for establishing school goals, as described below. Because of the entangled nature of educational "politics," the professions of educational leadership or public school teaching cannot exert control over goals as strongly as do other professions.

Formal Political Decisions and School Goals

Constitutional guarantees give legislators and locally elected school boards considerable say about educational purposes. As the public's representatives in formal democratic processes, these individuals have authority and responsibility to adjudicate competing expectations and to establish goals for public schools. State statutes, for example, often define the content of the curriculum to be taught or tested, establish requirements for special programs, determine which special services will be funded, and define which school outcomes will be reported to the public. Elected school boards typically establish even more specific goals for schools through the adoption of particular tests, instructional programs, schedules, and so on.

Formal political authority over school goals is expressed most obviously in requirements, incentives, budget allocations, and mandated assessments.

A considerable literature on "principal–agent" relationships in public admin-istration suggests that, even when professional values and goals are differ-ent from those espoused by political leaders, policy makers can have broad influence over professional work (Braun & Guston, 2003; Forrester, 2002). And while the influence between professionals and policy makers can be reciprocal, political conversations about school goals are ultimately public, not internal to the profession. Even when school leaders are consulted on policy matters, the resulting decisions are seldom exactly what is advised on the basis of professional reasoning and analysis. deLeon's (1988) pragmatic critique is all too often true: "Politics will dominate analysis. Period" (p. 106).

Local Expectations and School Goals

Formal political decisions establish broad parameters for school goals, but considerable discretion remains for individual communities to establish unique goals for their schools: "Statutes are often vague, ambiguous, incom-plete, and contradictory, and court interpretations are slow in coming" (Frederickson, 1991, p. 403). The informal democracy of parent, commu-nity, student, and teacher expectations shapes decisions about which school purposes will receive funding, staff, and space in the schedule, and who will benefit from the programs that are supported. Real school goals can emerge cumulatively from these practical decisions as much as they do from the more formal processes of visioning and strategic planning (Fullan, 1993).

THE PRINCIPAL'S ROLE IN SHAPING SCHOOL GOALS

Shared responsibility for defining school goals has a profound impact on the responsibilities of individual principals. Principals cannot succeed by simply accepting the goals that are established either by professional asso-ciations or through the political process. Instead, the goals established through these groups provide a foundation upon which local goals must be fostered, defined, clarified, and tested within the local school community—its students, families, staff, and other community members.

School leaders can have considerable influence in local decision making about school goals, although they do not determine the outcome entirely. Principals are often in a position to articulate priorities, frame issues, and expand involvement so that more diverse groups participate in discussions of issues (Rallis, 1990; Riehl, 2000). Working together within the constraints of statutes and case law, education professionals and community members sway the educational goals for their schools, and these influences and their outcomes change over time. For both groups, this local discretion provides an opportunity to apply reasoned extensions of legal and ethical principles (Bull & McCarthy, 1995), but it also opens the door to a wide variety of other interests.

This shared development of school goals has a very significant impact on a principal's scope of responsibility. Unlike many other professionals, principals cannot frame their responsibilities primarily as the technical work needed to achieve goals that are defined elsewhere—either by politicians or by professional societies. Instead, principals succeed only by leading conversations about priorities and goals in each local school community to structure local agreements. Without local agreements about the kinds of student learning and school conditions that are valued, school leaders can be whiplashed by competing priorities that threaten school progress toward even broadly accepted goals that are defined in content standards.

SCHOOL GOALS AND
ACCOMPLISHMENT-MINDED PRACTICE

What is unique about school goals that helps to define accomplishment-minded practice? Three features deserve note. First, this view of goals differs from what many practicing principals say: that these goals are beyond their control, set outside the school by state legislatures, school boards, and district administrators. Certainly, such groups have asserted more authority in recent years; but if sustainable goals are to be reached, the principal and the school community must be full participants in this conversation.

Second, some academics pressure professionals to view school goals consistently with a favorite theory, which often reduces or ignores the complexities of the enterprise. The accomplishment-minded view of goals notes that schools are instrumental organizations designed to reach certain outcomes, as well as adaptive organizations that succeed by adjusting to their environments. Schools combine instrumental and adaptive elements into more complex structures (Gharahedaghi & Ackoff, 1994; Likert, 1967), in order to produce results demanded by overseers and to create conditions that communities expect. Similarly, while some might want to take sides in debates about whether schools should function as professional or public organizations, this view of school goals suggests that schools must function both ways. That is, goals cannot be fully determined by either professional priorities or public policy makers. The practical challenges of school leadership involve work toward goals that are defined in more complex ways.

Finally, policy makers exert pressure to separate student-learning outcomes from the school conditions through which these outcomes are achieved (Osborne & Plastrik, 2000). This is possible in many areas of public policy.

When one builds a road or prison, the result—the structure—is independent of the method. But schools and learning are more like health or physical fitness, where reaching an outcome of health is inextricably linked to the lifestyle that produces it—as both modern diet books and Aristotle have observed (cf. Holt, 1993). Leading a school toward sustainable purposes requires a way of thinking that considers means and ends simultaneously, recognizing the recursive influence that each has on the other.

We elaborate this discussion of leadership for sustainable purposes in Chapter 6, with a practical discussion of the what, why, and how of principal leadership in this domain.

SUMMARY

Principals succeed only when they act in ways that provide *both* effective support for student learning and vigilant stewardship for school conditions that respond to and support community values. Although learning outcomes are in the foreground, school leadership is both instrumental—designed to improve student-learning results—and adaptive—designed to adjust continually to evolving values in the community.

These goals for student learning and school conditions are continually evolving. An ongoing interplay of public and private interests associated with enculturation, preparation for economic competitiveness, and caring for children compete for the school's time, attention, and resources. School goals are revised continually as new balances are forged among these competing priorities.

What makes the definition of school goals such an important part of every principal's job is the way that it influences how balances among these various interests are achieved. While elected officials have authority to define goals and policies, and while the education professions influence those goals through their codes of ethics and standards of practice, informal local priorities and pressures shape much of what happens in schools. By leading local conversations about school goals, principals can influence the nature of those goals, the breadth of support for them, and the level of commitment to their achievement.

Chapter 3

Accomplishments for School Goals

Discussions of school goals often seem abstract because lofty ideals about schools often contrast sharply with daily realities. While the principalship well may be about promoting student learning and stewarding school conditions, the lived experience of most principals suggests something different: a seemingly endless chain of disjointed daily problems. One minute a principal discusses appropriate behavior with a child, the next she listens to a parent complaint, which is interrupted by a call from the district about a late report and an urgent note from the school secretary that a child's boa constrictor has gotten loose in the building and cannot be found.

LINKING LOFTY GOALS TO DAILY WORK

Success in the principalship requires a coherent way to connect the press of these daily problems with public expectations for student learning and school conditions. The connections are seldom obvious. If a principal's only guide for action is a statement of learning goals and desired school conditions, he or she could have real difficulty deciding whether to attend to the student, the parent, the administrator, or the snake. Nor would broadly framed school goals make it clear what an adequate solution would be to any one of these problems after the principal selected it for attention.

All principals use some mental models to connect their daily work to long-range school goals. These mental models come in many forms. They are often implicit beliefs nurtured during a career in schools. "My job is to protect teachers from outside pressures so they can do their jobs." "Getting more parent involvement is the most important thing I can do to increase learning." Mental models also can be complex. For example, Knapp and McLaughlin's (2003) model offers a way for principals to pursue student

28

learning through a comprehensive set of strategies that support professional and organizational learning.

In essence, these mental models serve as applied mid-range theories or theories of action that provide logical and practical links between action and outcomes (Merton, 1967; Senge, 1990). Such theories provide a lens for making sense out of day-to-day complexity and evaluating what a school needs. The lens brings some aspects of the school into sharper focus—those that are believed to relate most closely to the principal's role in improving student-learning outcomes—while obscuring other school features. This helps principals do two things. First, it guides decisions about which problems are important in the press of daily work; in effect, it guides principals in finding the right problems (Getzels, 1979, 1985; Immegart & Boyd, 1979). A principal whose theory of action rests on the belief that a safe and orderly climate within the school is critical to student learning likely would pay attention to different problems than a principal who believes that student learning is most likely when parents and teachers work together.

Second, a theory of action about principals' work helps school leaders decide what might be an acceptable solution to a selected problem (Robinson, 1993). In one school, the principal might consider parents' feelings that their children were safe as the paramount consideration in solving the lost boa constrictor problem; in another school, the solution might be framed in terms of students' opportunities to learn about snake characteristics and habitats.

Because schools are complex, a comprehensive theory supporting principal action involves a way of separating leadership work into meaningful units, as well as an understanding of how these units interact to support student learning. Whatever the unit of analysis, the result is simply a taxonomy until the elements are linked together in a model that demonstrates their combined and interactive influence. Then a theory about how the principal's work supports student learning emerges. Our challenge is to develop such a theory grounded in goals for student learning and school conditions, while also reflecting the complexities of daily leadership practice.

ACCOMPLISHMENTS AS COMPONENTS
OF A THEORY OF ACTION

The view of school goals described in Chapter 2 challenges school leaders to achieve student-learning results that meet or exceed publicly defined goals, and to nurture school conditions that respond to evolving community values about what experiences children should have in schools. Both goals are supported by developing and fostering particular conditions within a school.

Some school conditions are important because research has shown that they contribute to student learning. A school climate that communicates high academic expectations (Sammons, 1999), instruction that connects with students' prior learning (Stevenson & Stigler, 1992), and school schedules that maximize learning time (Scheerens & Bosker, 1997) all appear to be related to learning outcomes. Other school conditions are important because they reflect local priorities. A school climate can emphasize academic achievement while also being either competitive or inclusive in its activities and either tolerant or rigid in its rules of conduct. Different communities prefer different school conditions, as long as expected levels of student learning also are achieved.

In order for such school conditions to serve as components of a theory of action for school leadership, decisions are needed about which conditions are most important for a principal to address, what makes each of these "good" (i.e., what makes them effective in supporting student learning and also responsive to community values), and how improvements in those conditions can be promoted. In other words, a way of thinking about school conditions is needed that accommodates both general research results and local values, and that allows principals to consider school goals and leadership actions conjointly.

Framing Important School Conditions as Accomplishments

We chose the construct of an "accomplishment" to describe these school conditions for two reasons. First, it offers a fresh look at principal practice. Each of the existing units of analysis (e.g., problems, domains, correlates of effective schools) has developed various, sometimes competing meanings through prior use. Our hope is that a different construct might help transcend set viewpoints associated with these earlier taxonomies. Second, prior use of the accomplishment construct has several features that seem to match the school conditions that connect complex school goals with rapid-paced, improvisational daily practice. We describe these features briefly in the sections that follow and elaborate each as additional aspects of accomplishment-minded leadership are described in later chapters. Table 3.1 anticipates this discussion by distinguishing organizational goals, action strategies, success criteria, and required constituent engagement with illustrations across several different organizations.

What Are Accomplishments? The term comes from literature on performance improvement in organizations (Stolovitch & Keeps, 1992). In a conceptualization that is still widely used in the field, Gilbert (1978) proposed that organizational performance be viewed in terms of the accomplishments,

TABLE 3.1. Illustration of Key Concepts in an Accomplishment Perspective

Organization	Goal	Sample Accomplishment	Action Strategies	Sample Success Criteria	Initial Impacts
Restaurant	Profit for restaurant	Meals prepared	Prepare food from scratch; use prepackaged entrees	Taste of meals; novelty of menu; consistency	Customers choosing the restaurant
School	Student learning	Instruction provided	Use textbooks or literature-based approach	Assignments match student ability; students able to succeed with effort	Students spending effort on assignments
Legislature	Benefits for constituents	Bills passed	Negotiation and parliamentary maneuvers; deals with colleagues	Clarity of legislation; consistency with constituents' priorities	Constituents contacting legislators to support a bill

or intermediate states, of the organization as it pursues its goals, or end states. For example, accomplishments like "products manufactured" and "sales closed" contribute to the goal of profit in business, just as accomplishments like "instruction provided" and "student climate sustained" contribute to the goal of student learning in schools.

In the popular use of the word, *accomplishment* usually means something that is achieved, often designating an end point of activity toward a goal. We use the term in a more specific way: *Accomplishments are the positive conditions that schools and their leaders strive to achieve in their effort to foster student learning and address community expectations.*

Each accomplishment defines a state of affairs that results from one of the school's major processes and which, in turn, contributes to student learning. These conditions constantly evolve in response to new issues, actions of the school's staff and students, and the principal's leadership. Work toward each accomplishment is ongoing, and the results of that work, the conditions that exist in the school, can be seen at a point in time. For example, one accomplishment in the model we propose is "school operations supported." Such support is a condition that is achieved through a continuing series of activities associated with budget allocations, class and resource scheduling, staff assignments, and solution of related daily problems.

Accomplishments are not the same as an organization's goals or expected outcomes. Outcome goals—like profit for a restaurant or student learning in schools—are reached as the organization realizes accomplishments such as *meals prepared* or *ingredients purchased* in a restaurant, and *learning goals defined* or *instruction provided* in schools. The accomplishments are not the goals themselves—student learning, for example, is the result of the realization of many accomplishments—but rather components of a theory of action about what it takes for the goals to be achieved.

Success Criteria. Accomplishments become meaningful as they are elaborated by what we call *success criteria* that define the desired features of what is accomplished. Getting meals prepared results in profit for a restaurant only when those meals meet standards of quality that are expected by customers (and health inspectors!). The same is true in schools. For example, one way or another, every school creates some kind of climate for its students. But that accomplishment can contribute to—or detract from—the school's student-learning goals, depending on the features of the resulting climate. For instance, does the school's climate support mutual respect? Does it encourage academic effort? Does it honor diversity? Does it enforce school rules fairly and consistently?

The importance of success criteria is emphasized by the tendency that all of us have to add modifiers to the noun–verb construction that defines accomplishments. When we say that we want an engaging, safe, participatory, and welcoming climate with academic emphasis and strong personal relationships between students and teachers, we actually are specifying success criteria for the accomplishment *student climate sustained.*

Success criteria can reflect the profession's research, reasoned argument, critical inquiry, and legal principles as well as constraints and local expectations that affect how a school is perceived and supported. One way to conceptualize the success criteria for school accomplishments is like Simon's (1981) discussion of the linkages between purpose, physical science, and design. Bridge engineers, he says, are bound by the laws of science as they try to solve the problem of getting traffic across a ravine. Engineers must consider their design in terms of its goal—to carry pedestrian traffic, to carry a large volume of heavy truck traffic, and so forth. The forces of gravity, the tensile strength of metal, and the harmonics of materials are necessary considerations for any bridge. However, much is a matter of choice among what Simon calls *functional equivalents*—different ways of accomplishing the same thing. These choices, he says, are a matter of aesthetics.

The success criteria for school accomplishments include a similar mixture of technical information, compliance requirements, local preferences, aesthetic choices, and professional priorities. Research and theory in the social sciences helps define the features of school accomplishments that are most associated with student learning, while other success criteria come from ethical and critical reasoning within the profession and the expectations that come with each community's priorities and values.

Flexible Action Strategies. Accomplishments are different from action strategies. A legislature, for instance, may use several different strategies to get bills passed, just as a school often uses many different approaches to provide instruction. The accomplishment perspective defines desired school conditions by specifying important accomplishments and their success criteria, but leaves open exactly which strategies might be used to achieve those conditions. (This feature of the accomplishment perspective is important because it underlies a pragmatic and eclectic view of principal practice. We address this topic in more detail in Chapter 4.)

Constituent Engagement. Accomplishments do not produce organizational outcomes in mechanistic ways. Reaching an accomplishment, even doing so with high quality, does not guarantee that an organization will attain its goals. For example, even excellent meals do not guarantee that customers will choose a restaurant. Organizations depend on what we call *constituent engagement* to connect their accomplishments with their goals. Constituent engagement is the effort of various participants that the organization hopes to influence, but does not control. School personnel hope that their climate, learning, goals, and instruction will influence student effort, leading to student learning, but ultimately students control their own attention and effort. Similarly, businesses depend on customers to purchase their products, and, while they may invest heavily in advertisement to influence these decisions, the choice to buy belongs solely to the customer.

Educators and families generally agree that a principal's primary responsibility is motivating students and teachers to do their best work (Markow & Scheer, 2003). In the vocabulary of accomplishments, the efforts of these various groups become constituent engagement. Thus, accomplishments are important conditions that are created as an organization and its leaders do their work. Accomplishments are not the action strategies used, but the results achieved through those strategies. Accomplishments become meaningful as success criteria are defined to describe features that are valued and that contribute to the organization's goals. Finally, multiple accomplishments over time contribute to an organization's ultimate goals (e.g., student learning in schools) only when they influence the choices of various constituents.

THE FRAMEWORK FOR SCHOOL LEADERSHIP ACCOMPLISHMENTS

For any organization, Gilbert (1978) argues an accomplishment model can be defined that represents the critical things that must get done in order to reach organizational goals. This set of accomplishments provides a conceptual model of the work of the organization and details the results that obtain from each of its major processes (Brethower, 1997). The Framework for School Leadership Accomplishments (FSLA) is our effort to define such a set of accomplishments and organize them as a theory of action that connects the daily work of principals with the school's goals for student learning (Bellamy, 1999; Bellamy, Muth, Murphy, & Fulmer, 2006).

An accomplishment framework begins with the organization's expected outcomes and for schools student learning serves as the center of such an analysis. Illustrated in Figure 3.1, the FSLA identifies nine accomplishments through which schools influence student learning. The accomplishments are separated into three clusters to show an expected path of influence on learning and to emphasize how the school's accomplishments depend on the engagement of various members of the school community in order to have the desired effect on student learning.

Nearest the center of the figure are the school conditions (accomplishments) that create the school's environment for learning. These accomplishments—learning goals, instruction, student climate, and related services —support student learning by supporting *student motivation to engage with school work*. The second tier of accomplishments in the figure represents the environment for teaching. It includes the accomplishments through which the school and its leaders foster and focus the *efforts of teachers and other staff*: resources, school operations, staff support, and renewal. The third segment of the figure supports both the learning and teaching environments *by motivating family members* to support student effort at home and to get involved in the school.

FIGURE 3.1. The Framework for School Leadership Accomplishments

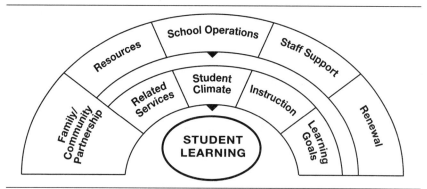

Note: Adapted from Bellamy (1999), Bellamy et al. (2006), and Ballek et al. (2005). Copyright © G. T. Bellamy. Adapted with permission.

We constructed Figure 3.1 as only half of a circle in order to symbolize the many influences on student learning and constituent engagement over which the school exerts little or no influence. For example, the economic status of the community and the attractiveness of television and recreational opportunities that compete with studying are important influences on student learning, but they are largely outside a school's control. The space at the top symbolizes the institutional, governmental, and community influences that affect and are affected by a principal's leadership. Table 3.2 (based on Bellamy et al., 2006) defines each accomplishment in the FSLA and identifies some of the success criteria that might apply in any given community.

The FSLA as a Theory of Action for School Leadership

Any theory of action for principal work highlights some aspects of a school's functioning while obscuring others. Consequently, the use of an accomplishment model to support a principal's theory of action must be evaluated in part by asking what this way of thinking encourages principals to attend to. Here we describe four ways that an accomplishment perspective shapes the development of theories of action for school leadership:

(1) Viewing school conditions as accomplishments helps principals attend to both school goals—student learning and the school character —that were described in Chapter 2.
(2) Framing school leadership responsibilities in terms of accomplishments leads to a focus on the entire school, not just the principal.
(3) Accomplishments encourage a pragmatic and eclectic theory of action, rather than commitment to a particular leadership style or program model.
(4) An accomplishment model provides the foundation for locally developed theories of action that respond to a unique school's circumstances.

Attending to Both Ends and Means. The accomplishments defined in the FSLA are both ends and means of schooling. On the one hand, these accomplishments are the means through which schools support student learning. On the other, they are the conditions that define the nature and character of the local school, itself a school goal with important consequences for students, families, and the entire community.

Using accomplishments as the building blocks for a theory of action brings both student-learning goals and community values to the foreground in considering leadership strategies. By focusing on school conditions (accomplishments and their success criteria) that support these goals and values,

TABLE 3.2. Accomplishment Definitions and Initial Success Criteria in the FSLA

Accomplishment	Definition	Success Criteria
Learning Goals Defined	The knowledge and skills that students are expected to demonstrate at various grade levels and at graduation.	Learning goals are • ambitious • comprehensive in relation to state tests • clear and well understood • aligned within and across subjects • applied to all classes and students • adapted to individual abilities
Instruction Provided	The tasks or assignments expected of students, together with the social and physical context supporting task completion.	Instruction is • organized to maximize learning time • challenging, so that all students can succeed with effort • adapted to learning needs of individual students • feedback-rich, so that students know how well they are doing • contextualized, so that it is connected to students' prior learning
Student Climate Sustained	The sum of the school's implicit messages to students about what is important as these are perceived and understood by individual students.	Students believe that the school • emphasizes academic learning • is safe and orderly • promotes strong, healthy relationships with peers and adults
Related Services Provided	The supports provided to students that help them benefit from instruction.	Related services are: • focused on and responsive to learning problems • provided, based on thorough assessments

Accomplishment	Definition	Success Criteria
Family and Community Partnerships Sustained	All of the influences exerted by the school to help parents and other community members help children succeed in school.	The family–community partnership ensures that • information to parents is accessible, frequent, and specific • opportunities to participate are frequent and varied • parents perceive respect for their culture, language, and beliefs • community connections support rapid support for students needing extra help
Resources Mobilized	The school's external communications about needs, plans, programs, and resources.	Efforts to secure resources are • creative in identifying opportunities • comprehensive in relation to the school's needs • aligned with school goals
School Operations Organized and Supported	The school's allocation of physical, human, fiscal, and information resources to various aspects of the school's work.	The school's support for operations • focuses resources (time, expertise, facilities) on learning priorities • defines clear expectations for everyone
Staff Supported	The implicit and explicit messages that teachers receive from the principal and school about what is expected, together with the social and administrative support that they receive to meet those expectations.	Professionals in the building feel that they are • known well and respected • evaluated fairly • helped to do their jobs well • given opportunities to continue learning • given opportunities to work together
School Renewal Supported	The processes and structures that a school has in place to provide itself feedback on its effectiveness, set goals for improvement, support implementation of new procedures, and evaluate results.	The school's system for school renewal ensures that • feedback is available for frequent monitoring of the school's programs • processes for decision making are clear and well understood • goals are supported by a working majority of staff and community

an accomplishment perspective provides a way of thinking about leadership that combines ends and means. Defining success criteria for accomplishments requires ongoing consideration of ends—the school community's goals and values—and leading in ways that achieve those success criteria requires simultaneous attention to finding locally appropriate means such as the leadership strategies, programs, and resource allocations that support school work.

Leadership from the Entire School. None of the accomplishments in the FSLA can be realized by a principal alone. The accomplishment perspective emphasizes that leadership success depends on what the entire school community does, rather than just the individual activities of the principal. If effective leadership is about the conditions that are achieved through the work of the entire staff, then how leadership roles are shared among staff, and exactly who does which tasks, are less important than the results of the school's collective effort. Consequently, the accomplishment view shifts the focus away from individual leadership styles and strategies toward the development of organizational conditions that support student learning. The importance of the entire school community is highlighted in the accomplishment perspective by the understanding that school accomplishments only influence student learning when they also motivate the engagement of students, teachers, and family members.

A Pragmatic and Eclectic Approach. As we elaborate in Chapter 4, using accomplishments as the unit of analysis for a theory of action emphasizes a pragmatic and eclectic approach to school leadership. By specifying accomplishments and success criteria, but allowing action strategies to vary as needed, the accomplishment perspective respects the uniqueness of schools and encourages school leaders to draw information from many sources and research traditions. Using results to decide whether what gets done in schools is important reflects a long-standing tradition of pragmatism and inquiry (Dewey, 1929). This approach also is consistent with modern critiques of the theoretical foundations of education and social science, which caution against simplistic implementation of practices that appear to have worked elsewhere (Donmoyer, 1996a).

Consequently, using accomplishments as the unit of analysis means that a theory of action for the principalship is less likely to emphasize particular strategies or approaches that may be faddish or time-honored, but ineffective in new settings (Sarason, 1972). Rather, the focus is on what school conditions need to be created and the development of a repertoire of approaches to reach those accomplishments under differing conditions.

Flexible, Locally Developed Theories of Action. An accomplishment model like the FSLA helps principals adopt a flexible and adaptive theory of action about how their daily problem solving can be linked to student learning and school stewardship. As principals consider their schools in relation to a set of accomplishments, different strengths and weaknesses become apparent in different schools. For example, while several schools might share a concern about low test scores in literacy among low-income children, one principal might find weaknesses in the school's curriculum, another in the quality of instruction, and another in a schedule that gives insufficient time to the subject. Each of these interpretations leads to a different theory of action that links the daily work of the principal to student-learning goals. Consequently, *using accomplishments as units of analysis leads away from prescribing any single theory of action for school leadership and toward a more responsive, on-site development of theories of action that match local circumstances.*

We call the process of developing and using a locally responsive theory of action *leadership for strategic focus* and elaborate its implications in Chapter 7. In this leadership domain, principals create structures that ensure attention to all important school accomplishments. Within this theory of action, an intermediate purpose—realizing accomplishments with high levels of quality—guides a principal's daily problem solving. While it is directed ultimately at improving student learning, the more immediate focus of a principal's daily work is improving the school's conditions for teaching and learning.

In addition, principals working within an accomplishment framework diagnose the needs of their schools to identify those accomplishments that have room for improvement and that are most likely to influence student-learning outcomes and community satisfaction with the school. By selecting a few accomplishments each year for particular attention, a principal defines a local theory of school improvement. This theory then is enacted as school priorities are incorporated into school structures and assignments, and is used as the basis for selecting and solving daily problems.

SUMMARY

The conditions that principals foster in their schools connect the daily barrage of problems with a community's goals for what students should learn and what the school should be like. We call the most important of these conditions "accomplishments" to emphasize the results that are achieved through leaders' actions and to show that ends and means are always considered simultaneously as principals work to establish and sustain desired conditions in their schools.

A set of these accomplishments—the FSLA—serves as a mental model for understanding major responsibilities of school leadership and organizing those responsibilities around student learning. The FSLA serves as a flexible theory of action as principals use the accomplishments it identifies to diagnose their schools' strengths and weaknesses and establish priorities for attention and action.

Chapter 4

Pragmatic Practice for School Accomplishments

Principals confront wide-ranging differences as they strive to reach school accomplishments in ways that help all children meet learning standards and respond to local values about the process of schooling. Schools are people-intensive and relationship-intensive places that operate in frequently surprising ways. Differences in how students learn often require adaptations in curricula and instructional approaches. Differences in staff interests and school cultures affect how new programs are implemented. Differences in expectations across communities affect whether programs are accepted or challenged.

As principals attempt to sustain reliable results in the face of such differences, standardized procedures have obvious shortcomings. What works with one child or in one school might not work in another; even if it did work, it might not be accepted by the school's families and community. In order to navigate the natural differences that occur over time and across communities, principals need a *deep repertoire of strategies for each school accomplishment and a way of obtaining feedback that supports continuing adjustments in the strategies used.*

THE UNCERTAIN CIRCUMSTANCES OF SCHOOL LEADERSHIP

Three characteristics of schools combine to create a high level of uncertainty in principal practice and to require adaptation to local circumstances as leadership strategies are implemented: (1) schools are relationship-intensive organizations that evolve with unique characteristics; (2) the public is involved in many aspects of school leadership, participating in decisions about which procedures are appropriate in a given community; and (3) few available procedures have demonstrated the level of reliability in student learning that is

41

now expected of schools, so multiple approaches often must be used simultaneously. As we demonstrate below, these inherent uncertainties require that principals have a deep and wide repertoire of alternative strategies for each school accomplishment.

Relationship-Intensive Organizations

Schools depend for their success on the quality of personal and professional relationships. The relationships among teachers affect both teaching quality and student learning (Louis, Marks, & Kruse, 1996). Relationships between teachers and their students influence the effort that students commit to their studies (Marks, 2000). The way that teachers perceive their relationships with their principal affects working conditions and climate within the building and translates into professional success and student learning (Waters, Marzano, & McNulty, 2003). Students' relationships with one another and their peer-group memberships have significant effects on engagement and learning (Steinberg, 1996). And teachers' relationships with families can influence the support students receive for learning at home (Epstein, 2001).

Despite the many common structural features of schools, this web of relationships evolves in quite different ways in different schools, creating unique social contexts and norms of practice. Whether one prefers to view schools as socially constructed and necessarily unique organizations (Wheatley & Kellner-Rogers, 1995), or as entities that follow general laws that can be discovered through the social sciences (Getzels, Lipham, & Campbell, 1968), the practical result is similar: It is difficult to generalize procedures from one school to another with confidence that similar results will follow. Even when one adopts a more positivist interpretation of schools as organizations, differences across settings are so complex, and interaction effects so pervasive, that empirical research on structures and procedures offers only partial information with uncertain applicability to other settings (Lindbolm & Cohen, 1979).

Public Participation in Principals' Work

The community's involvement in decision making about schools is not limited to the issues of school goals discussed in Chapter 2. Families, for example, have primary responsibility for their children's learning and development (Lightfoot, 1978); thus, educators' decisions about a wide range of topics are subject to public participation and review. Whether the issue is how to structure the school's daily schedule or how much homework to assign, principals work in a context where their decisions are often the grist of neighborhood discussions. Local practice is rooted in dialog with constituents, where understanding, support, participation, and justification are critical aspects of a principal's conversations.

Although conventional theories of how to enhance professional status have emphasized autonomy in decision making (Freidson, 1970), the context of principal practice seems to require a different approach. Instead of protecting decision making about school operations for the profession itself, Bull and McCarthy (1995) suggest that school leaders have an ethical obligation to engage a school community in dialog about important decisions.

> Educational leaders have distinct procedural responsibilities for which they must be prepared. They must, on one hand, engage in public moral deliberation in the process of developing their decisions. And, on the other hand, they must expose their decisions to public moral debate and be willing to revise them according to the results of that debate. (p. 627)

This expectation for public participation adds to the uncertainties of principal practice. In addition to finding strategies that work in a particular school's social context, principals must identify approaches that are acceptable to the school's constituents. A principal needs access to many different strategies to reach any particular school accomplishment, because some strategies, no matter how effective, will not be accepted by the affected families and students.

The Expectation for High Reliability

As we noted in Chapter 2, the implementation of the No Child Left Behind Act of 2001 has challenged schools to operate as high-reliability organizations (Bellamy et al., 2005)—to avoid failure almost entirely. The challenge is laudable. Indeed, no one wants any child to fail. However, currently available curricula and instructional programs are not so reliable. Despite the present focus on research-based procedures and programs (Shavelson & Towne, 2002), few if any current programs can demonstrate the level of failsafe learning that is now expected of schools. The resulting challenge for school leaders is to construct a reliable system—in which all students reach learning standards—from unreliable parts: programs, people, and structures that succeed with some but not all students. Writing about similar challenges in other organizations, Reason (2000) suggests a "Swiss cheese" model of reliable performance.

> Systems have many defensive layers: some are engineered (alarms, physical barriers, automatic shutdowns, etc.), others rely on people (surgeons, anesthetists, pilots, control room operators, etc.), and yet others depend on procedures

and administrative controls. . . . In an ideal world, each defensive layer would be intact. In reality, however, they are more like slices of Swiss cheese, having many holes. . . . The presence of holes in any one "slice" does not normally cause a bad outcome. Usually, this can happen only when the holes in many layers momentarily line up to permit a trajectory of accident opportunity. (p. 3)

Many strategies for school leadership and instruction are much like Reason's (2000) slices of Swiss cheese. Each is sufficient to help some students, but additional "slices" are needed to support the students who have fallen through the "holes" in the school's first-level programs. The need for such backup strategies adds further uncertainty to principal practice. To prevent failure, school leaders must select initial strategies that generally are effective and accepted by community members. But this alone is insufficient. They also must construct alternatives and determine when it is necessary to shift to these backup approaches.

A DEEP REPERTOIRE OF STRATEGIES SUPPORTED BY AN ECLECTIC KNOWLEDGE BASE

Taken together, these uncertainties about what leadership strategies and instructional methods will work in any particular context require principals to have a deep repertoire of strategies to meet each school accomplishment. While a principal may well have a preference for a particular leadership style or theory, the demands of the position typically require a more pragmatic and eclectic approach. This, in turn, requires the development of a knowledge base for school accomplishments that contains many different approaches and draws from a variety of sources.

In professions where it is somewhat more reasonable to generalize from one setting or case to another, the development of technical knowledge can be viewed as a continuing search for the most effective or most economical procedures for any given problem. As research identifies more effective approaches, earlier ones can be systematically replaced in part or in whole. For example, a surgeon normally would be expected to use pretty much the same hierarchy of procedures for a gallbladder operation regardless of where the patient lived, and to adjust her or his practice as research identified better approaches.

Such research-based practices are important in educational leadership, but the complex differences among schools mean that even the technical portion of the profession's knowledge cannot provide straightforward prescriptions. And while progress sometimes may involve replacement of one procedure with a more effective one, it is more likely to involve definition of additional options to support practice. Given the varied circumstances of practice, this array of options is an asset, presenting a range of possible strategies for different situations. Craft knowledge plays an important role in developing these options; not all useful possibilities will have been tested, and no matter how well they are researched, practitioners will depend on their own and others' practical experience in implementing and adapting procedures to their own settings.

In this context, it is neither enough for principals to know one preferred way to meet each of the school's accomplishments nor realistic to expect research to identify one best way that will be effective for all schools. Evidence-based practice is useful, but the principal's situation is a bit like that of a physician treating a condition for which multiple medications have been tested and approved. The task begins with the diagnosis; then, it is necessary to consider which of the many available treatments the patient is likely to implement, which he or she can afford, what risks of side effects are tolerable, given the patient's history, and so on. Similarly, effective practice in the principalship depends on having a deep and versatile repertoire of multiple strategies to address each accomplishment.

In educational leadership, this range of needed options often leads to stark contradictions in professional knowledge, alternatives that reflect seemingly incompatible views of teaching, learning, and organizational design. Rather than a failure of the profession's knowledge, this appears to reflect a useful theoretical pluralism (Shulman, 1986). Because of differences among schools, it is important that the field's knowledge include very different approaches to many school challenges. For instance, Donmoyer (2001) notes the value of seemingly contradictory approaches to school discipline in his comparison of the recommendations of Evertson (1989) and Florio-Ruane (1989). Depending on one's circumstances, it may be more important to maintain school discipline through formal rules, rewards, and sanctions, or to use quite different procedures to foster student self-control and self-management. While every profession contains contradictory knowledge to some degree, it is particularly important in educational leadership. To succeed in organizations that differ as much as today's schools, leaders need access to knowledge bases with multiple options, even when some of these are contradictory.

THE IMPORTANCE OF FEEDBACK

The uncertainties of school leadership temper enthusiasm for any single leadership approach with a healthy dose of skepticism. No matter how effective an approach might have been elsewhere or how much it matches a principal's personal values, no guarantee exists that it will work in any particular situation. The profession's knowledge is rich with possibilities, but it provides few prescriptions that work uniformly, systematically, or consistently across settings and situations.

These uncertainties of practice raise a fundamental question about school leadership: How can a principal use knowledge of multiple strategies effectively when an insufficient foundation exists for linking any particular strategy to characteristics of a local situation? Like other professionals, principals have to exercise judgment in selecting which approaches to use in any given situation (Shulman, 1998). But the uncertainties of school practice require even more for responsible leadership. Principals also need ways to monitor systematically the results of their initial decisions, so that adjustments can be made as needed to reach school accomplishments.

In this context, the purpose of feedback is to provide information about emerging school problems on a schedule that supports timely adjustments. As the facetious slogan, "Ready, fire, aim," implies, failures sometimes are best avoided by repeated cycles of trial, feedback, correction, and re-trial, rather than by efforts to ensure correct performance on the first attempt. Leading schools is a cumulative, long-term process. Time is usually available for iterative improvements, as long as school leaders have ongoing access to information and respond in a timely manner.

Principals constantly collect and respond to feedback on their actions. Sometimes, this process is implicit or attentive to narrow concerns. It also can be systematic and strategic. For example, most school leaders attempt to monitor the social responses of those who are affected by their actions. The responses of teachers, students, and families often provide immediate— if sometimes subtle—feedback about how the principal's actions affect them and their work. Of course, this social feedback can be supplemented with various formal and informal measures of school progress and the effect of the principal's actions on school functioning. The kinds of feedback that a principal arranges to receive, affect both the immediate adjustments that are made to leadership strategies and the cumulative lessons that the principal gleans from experience.

Like many other aspects of school leadership, the principal's challenge in designing useful feedback systems is one of choosing from among too many possibilities. More possibilities need attention than one person—or even a group of leaders—can monitor effectively. Effective feedback, then, results from making strategic choices about what is most important to monitor (ultimately reflecting the principal's theory of action). For example, it is possible to gather feedback on the immediate results of a problem-solving effort; the resulting changes in school accomplishments; whether the school's accomplishments are stimulating engagement of students, families, and professional staff; and whether expected student learning is occurring.

In our discussion of the practical challenges of leading for effective action in Chapter 8, we show that these many feedback strategies are nested, so that measures at higher levels help to focus attention on a relatively small set of accomplishments and problems.

For instance, regular monitoring of the constituent engagement that leaders try to influence through the school's accomplishments can help identify areas needing special attention. Principals depend on professional effort, parent involvement, parent support, and student effort (defined in Chapter 3) as conduits that link the school's accomplishments to student learning. A means of monitoring whether such constituent engagement is on target can provide important signals to the principal about the effectiveness of her or his leadership strategies.

Such measures need not be terribly sophisticated; the best judgments of the principal and school staff, self-reports of effort, or school records of parent involvement may be sufficient—if they are systematically and regularly obtained and studied. Particularly with today's expectations that practically all students will become proficient in all core subjects, having even one parent, teacher, or student who is not engaged can be a significant issue warranting attention. While such measures do not tell a principal exactly *what* to do to stimulate greater engagement, they do signal that *something* different should be tried, giving the principal strong notice that personal leadership strategies, responsibility assignments, or other aspects of the school should be adjusted.

A principal might track student effort monthly by asking teachers to rate each student's level of engagement. Simply identifying which students seem to be consistently low or declining in their level of effort could provide enough information for the principal to organize additional support. Personal calls to families from the principal, assignments to the school counselor or social worker to make a family visit, individual meetings with students, or discussions of new strategies with the affected teacher might change a student's level of engagement before it matured into a full-fledged learning problem.

More direct measures of student learning also can be useful. While day-to-day measures of learning provide greater support for teaching than for school leadership, periodic monitoring of what students actually learn allows principals to make timely decisions about administrative support for teachers. Learning problems often develop gradually as a student falls progressively further behind. Periodic measures that call attention to each student's status on expected learning milestones can help detect problems that might be missed in the daily processes of planning and adjusting instruction. Such periodic measures have been incorporated into several approaches to instruction and school leadership (DuFour & Eaker, 1998; Slavin, Madden, Karweit, Dolan, & Wasik, 1996), and many schools and districts now arrange for formal measures at

6- or 9-week intervals. Even when formal assessments are not conducted, periodic feedback that relies on teacher referrals or student self-assessments also can be useful. Feedback about student learning on periodic cycles allows school leaders to identify students who are falling behind and make needed adjustments in schedules, programs, or resources.

For example, a principal with whom we worked wanted to sustain a literature-based reading program, but faced quite low scores in her school's performance on the state's annual literacy assessment. Despite pressure to adopt a different curriculum, the principal chose instead to create monthly feedback cycles. Teachers were asked to make assignments each month that would allow them to monitor reading progress and to bring the resulting work to a monthly meeting for analysis and discussion with grade-level peers and the principal. This monthly process of feedback, and the instructional adjustments that the feedback enabled, were followed by one of the largest year-to-year gains on the state's annual test.

Leadership for effective action involves selecting problems for attention that are most important to advance a school's accomplishments, framing solutions to those problems in ways that address school priorities, acting to solve those problems, and making adjustments as needed in order to succeed. Two essential ingredients for success in action are: (1) a deep repertoire of alternative strategies, and (2) a feedback system that signals when any particular strategy should be modified or replaced. We continue the discussion of leadership for effective action in Chapter 8 with a focus on practical strategies for leadership in this domain.

SUMMARY

Schools reach their goals by realizing accomplishments—the conditions within the school that support student learning and reflect community expectations. But there are no formulas for realizing these accomplishments. Schools differ in the way that professionals and families work together, the particular approaches needed by various students, and the kinds of approaches that families will accept. Consequently, principals need a deep repertoire of leadership strategies supported by an eclectic knowledge base. Despite advocacy for particular theories and approaches, specific leadership strategies ultimately are valuable only as they contribute to meeting the success criteria for school accomplishments in the principal's particular situation.

The day-to-day work of school leaders involves selecting problems for attention and responding to those problems. Because the results of any strategy for problem solving is uncertain, successful leadership depends on ongoing feedback and iterative adjustments. Feedback is essential to responsible practice.

Chapter 5

Social Capital for School Accomplishments

The three understandings about school leadership presented so far frame a complex picture of schools. To succeed, principals need to (1) help diverse school communities reach agreement on which goals are most important for both student learning and the school itself, (2) make strategic choices with others in the community about what school conditions need to change in order to achieve those goals, and (3) do the necessary work to create desired school conditions and support student learning. With each of these leadership responsibilities, success depends on people in the school community working together to make collaborative decisions about goals and priorities and to take collective action to reach those goals.

Our fourth understanding of school leadership addresses the social organization of the school and the social relationships among people on which the first three responsibilities depend. However a school is organized, informal connections among people can help those in a school and community exchange information, help one another, and respond more flexibly to unexpected events (Coleman, 1990; Weick & Sutcliffe, 2001). The needed social connections are well illustrated in images of schools as "professional communities" (Smylie & Hart, 1999) or "learning communities" (Senge, Cambron-McCabe, Lucas, Smith, Dutton, & Kleiner, 2000). In this view, schools function best when teachers, students, parents, and administrators work together in open and integrated social structures that help them imagine possibilities, share information, respond to challenges, and act upon their visions of what their school could be.

The complex social relationships central to such a view of school work are increasingly conceptualized and studied as "social capital" (Coleman, 1988, 1990; Putnam, 1993, 2000). The construct of social capital incorporates both what characteristics of social relationships are important and how these characteristics, when taken together, function as capital, that

49

is, a resource that improves organizational performance (Cohen & Prusak, 2000; Productivity Commission, 2003; Smylie & Hart, 1999).

Supporting the development of social capital is critical to successful school leadership, because social capital underlies the ability of a school and community to address all other school responsibilities. In essence, social capital serves as a multiplier of the school's work toward sustainable goals, strategic priorities, and effective daily action. The impact of school leadership can be greatly increased when strong and healthy social capital exists, and significantly diminished when it does not. In this chapter, we describe important components of social capital in order to frame the principal's challenge to foster and further develop that capital in each school community. Our discussion also underscores the magnitude of the challenge: Improving the state of social capital can be a daunting process, full of fits and starts, which must be done largely through face-to-face encounters (Coleman, 1990; Putnam, 1993).

SOCIAL CAPITAL AS A RESOURCE FOR SCHOOL WORK

While not new, the idea that informal social connections can enhance a community's effectiveness has become explosively popular in the 15 years following Coleman's (1988, 1990) theoretical developments and Putnam's (1993, 2000) more popular writing on how social capital affects democratic institutions. The basic idea is that some groups, organizations, and communities accomplish more because of the way that people are connected to and cooperate with one another. The advantage that these groups have is their social capital. For example, social capital is evident in school communities when

- Groups of teachers pitch in, doing far more than their share to make an event work, trusting that others will reciprocate when they need extra help themselves.
- Teachers know their students' parents and family members by name and each group is comfortable telephoning the other.
- Families and teachers share information easily and quickly about whether homework assignments are too difficult, time-consuming, or unclear.
- Teachers share information and ideas—about how to teach particular topics or handle particular students—respectfully, honestly, and with confidence that others will respond likewise to requests for help or offers of assistance.

While varying in their emphasis, definitions of social capital generally emphasize two components: The first is made up of the social structure and interpersonal relationships in the group, and the second is the way those relationships function as resources that help group members achieve their goals (Coleman, 1990; Woolcock, 1998).

The social structures and relationships that contribute to social capital generally consist of networks, norms, and trust (Putnam, 1993). *Networks* are relationships among people that facilitate the sharing of information and other supports within and across groups. *Norms* are shared understandings that guide how individuals act in particular circumstances; they establish obligations and expectations among group members. *Trust* emerges when networks and norms are effective and reflects a belief that others, even strangers, generally will behave in accordance with accepted norms.

When networks, norms, and trust exist, they function to increase cooperation and collaboration among group members (Fukuyama, 1999). Consequently, social capital—like other forms of capital—increases productivity and gives advantages to individuals and groups who have more of it. How does this happen? Social capital reduces the cost of searching for information, facilitates dissemination of knowledge, increases the availability of assistance when difficulties arise, lessens the uncertainties about whether others will keep their commitments, and reduces the need for monitoring (Productivity Commission, 2003). Such benefits normally contribute to a group's goal attainment, whatever formal organizational or civic structure might be in place.

As Coleman (1990) notes, however, social capital is not entirely fungible—depending on the nature of the social networks and their particular norms, some kinds of goals may be supported by the social capital that is generated, while others may not. For example, when norms of trust and sharing exist among school staff, but do not extend to families of students, social capital is less useful in supporting goals and activities associated with home–school collaboration than they might be for improving within-school practices.

Similarly, the social capital in a school might support collaborative work toward some school accomplishments but not others. The norms within a school community, for example, might be sufficient to support collaboration in managing student conduct but inadequate to support collaboration in instruction or school renewal. Likewise, norms within grade-level teams might be sufficient for collaboration in improving instruction, even though the cross-grade collaboration needed for serious curriculum evaluation was missing.

Consequently, social capital is most useful as a resource for school leaders when both the network structures and the particular norms are consistent with a school's goals, desired school conditions, and priority activities. *Each school needs social capital that is directly related to the success criteria*

*that the school is attempting to meet with its accomplishments, and that
supports collaborative work on the accomplishments that have greatest priority as the school seeks to achieve its goals for student learning and the
conditions of schooling.*

ELEMENTS OF A SCHOOL'S SOCIAL CAPITAL

A school's social capital is useful when strong social and civic connections exist among individuals and groups in a school community, and when
the norms that guide collective effort support a school's goals and priorities.
The more that these conditions are present, the more that a school community is able to reach collaborative decisions and take collective actions to
support student learning and create desired school conditions.

Four interrelated elements of a school's social capital are useful in principals' work. These elements include: (1) densely connected networks;
(2) the norms, obligations, and expectations that influence behavior within
and across a school's networks; (3) the degree of trust that others will act in
accordance with those norms; and (4) leadership as a manifestation of and a
contributor to social capital. Each of these elements affects all the others,
and they all contribute to a school's capacity for cooperative actions. Strengths
in one area help the others, and weaknesses in any area weaken the others.

Densely Connected Networks

Human networks involve groups of people interconnected in some way.
In a school community, for instance, networks could consist of: (1) grade-
level teams; (2) teachers, students, and family members who are members of
the same religious or social institutions; (3) teachers and community members who are active supporters of school sports; (4) professionals who have
in-depth involvement with the teachers' association; (5) mathematics teachers; or (6) members of a school leadership team. Individuals in these networks
also might be members of a civic club, softball team, national coin collec-
tors' club, and other groups. These multiple memberships mean that quite
different networks may be connected to one another by shared members.

Why Networks Are Important. One reason networks are important in
the development of social capital is the ease with which information can be
shared within networks (Coleman, 1990). Social relationships encourage
more efficient exchanges of information as groups pool their knowledge or
use particular group members to inform them on various subjects. For example, some elementary teachers may know a lot about math, while others

are expert in technology or reading instruction. When a social system ties these teachers together and encourages critical dialog, they can exchange needed information quickly and easily. As noted below, networks also can frame and enforce norms for how people interact with one another and foster trusting social relationships.

Such positive benefits are not automatic. The many individuals and groups on whom a school depends seldom act as a single entity. Instead, they bring to a school different interests, different degrees of power, different kinds of knowledge, or different beliefs and values. Natural conflicts exist between the self-interests of teachers and students, students and families, teachers and administrators, family members and school staff, and so on. Even if everyone agrees on goals for student learning, additional motivations—for convenient school schedules, desired teaching assignments, and particular school rules, to name a few—create conflicting expectations among various members of a school community. Such divisions separate individuals and groups in a school community and make it difficult to reach agreement on goals or to take collective action.

This separation is reinforced by many structural features of schools: individual teachers working in their own classrooms, grade-level teams with similar curriculum goals, teachers with seniority who share privileged class assignments, parent groups with different levels of influence over what happens to their children in school, and so forth. Further, each individual and group chooses its own level of commitment to school goals and degree of participation in the work to reach those goals. As a result, many different levels of commitment to norms and goals typically exist in a school, ranging from enthusiastic commitment to passive acceptance to vocal support for competing approaches (Hargreaves, 1986; Swidler, 1986).

Yet, school success depends on these individuals and groups working together despite their differences (Louis, Kruse, & Bryk, 1995; Marks & Louis, 1999). As noted in earlier chapters, school goals are sustainable only when they reflect a reasonable accommodation of the community's many expectations, and a principal's actions to achieve those goals typically succeed only with broad collaboration from teachers, students, and family members.

Important Network Characteristics. Network connections influence whether a school enjoys broad collaboration across its many constituencies, or confronts paralyzing conflicts among groups. First, the density of social connections, or the extent to which all group members know and interact with one another, affects the group's ability to share information and enforce norms for group members. For example, a grade-level team whose members interact several times daily is more likely to share information and to have strong expectations for one another's behavior than a group of teachers who are connected only through their attendance at a monthly professional development program.

Second, connections among the various groups in a school's community are important, because they stimulate information sharing across different networks. For instance, Coleman and Hoffer (1987) attributed the strong learning results that they observed in low-income Catholic schools to social cohesion resulting from overlapping social structures. Multiple relationships among school staff and families appeared to provide a cohesive social system that was less prevalent in typical public schools. Similar need for overlapping networks is apparent within a school's staff in order to share information across grade levels or among departments.

Third, density of relationships within groups and cross-group connections can be affected by the structures within which people work. For example, consider how difficult it would be for teachers and families to work together if a school system did not establish a standard daily schedule. If every teacher and every family had to negotiate their own arrival and departure times, practically all the available time could be spent developing and modifying students' schedules. By establishing and enforcing a standard daily schedule, a school creates an open and dependable context for teachers and families to manage this aspect of their relationship.

The impact of strong within- and between-group connections and supportive structures is apparent when one considers what school leadership might be like in two different communities. In one school serving a relatively stable small town, teachers, families, and community leaders share shopping resources, sports events, religious organizations, recreation, and civic concerns. A second school serves an urban community in which teachers and administrators commute from surrounding communities, and parents have little association with one another. Imagine the differences in strategies that a principal might use to stimulate discussions of student behavior, institute a new homework policy, or explain the implications of test results.

Norms, Obligations, and Expectations

The social capital that results from dense interconnections among people and networks in a community can support the collaborative action that is needed for many different goals. But the focus of this collective work may or may not relate to the purposes of schools or encourage activities that are related to school work. Many school leaders have experienced strong social connections among school and community members that focus on sports and school events, but have found that the collaboration engendered through these connections did not transfer easily to academic concerns. Dense relationships are necessary but not sufficient for the social capital that schools need in order to reach important accomplishments. The specific norms that emerge from these relationships also affect whether collaboration will focus on school accomplishments and goals.

Norms are the informal understandings and rules that influence how people behave in various situations. Norms reflect the obligations that members of networks feel toward one another and the expectations that they have for others' behavior. Norms can be fragile because they depend on continuing agreement about what is appropriate and the possibility of sanctions when norms are violated. But they also can be powerful in supporting collective action. For example, effective norms make streets in certain places safe to walk at night or neighborhoods safer through citizen-watch programs. Norms strengthen families by encouraging selflessness; schools are strengthened when communities have norms for excellence and reward such behavior (Coleman, 1988).

Three aspects of the norms in school communities are important in determining whether the resulting social capital will support school accomplishments: (1) whether goals are instantiated, or only espoused, (2) whether norms apply both within and across groups, and (3) the nature of the norms themselves.

Espoused versus Instantiated Norms. The important norms are those that are instantiated in the relationships and actions of members of a school community, not just those that are espoused by school leaders. For instance, school leaders frequently articulate the norms that they want to have in their schools, and professional literature provides broad support for such espoused norms as de-privitization, collaboration, and shared responsibility for student success (Bryk, Lee, & Holland, 1993; Louis et al., 1996).

Yet, quite different norms often are instantiated in the culture of a school and in the profession. Our experiences as beginning teachers are still typical. We were advised to manage our classrooms so that outside intervention would not be needed. That meant avoiding student behavior problems, parent complaints, and any admission of problems related to instruction. Respecting other teachers' privacy and autonomy was part of the bargain, and this meant providing general social support without giving advice about teaching and not interfering in others' management of their classrooms. Because norms of practice are often implicit and preserved by custom and by school structures, norms that support improvements in a school's social capital may be hard to establish.

Differences in Norms Within and Across Groups. The impact of norms on a school's social capital also is affected by whether norms apply only to interactions within various groups or whether they have a more general influence on behavior with people outside the group. For example, teenagers may feel one set of obligations in their interactions with family members but respond in quite different ways in peer-group activities or classroom interactions.

Clearly, collaboration across groups is facilitated when norms that support collaboration extend beyond close associates. Fukuyama (1999) makes the same point by comparing behavioral norms that have emerged in some religious traditions in which honesty, fairness, and integrity are expected in all interactions, with norms of other groups in which behavior within the family or clan is held to a higher standard than activities outside this small group.

Nature of the Instantiated Norms. The specific norms that are instantiated in the various networks in a school's community also determine whether the resulting social capital supports school goals. Not all norms build social capital for a particular organization. In fact, some work against social capital. For instance, norms in schools that support the privatization of teaching lead to the "egg crate" school, diminish in-depth cooperation among teachers, and encourage the view that decisions about teaching methods are strictly individual and of no concern to the school staff. Sometimes called the "closed door" phenomenon, this norm, which usually is reinforced by snubs or group sanctions, lessens the degree to which teachers in a school can have open, critical dialogs about pedagogy. It also limits the degree to which curriculum reforms can be successful, because individuals regularly reserve the right to "do their thing." Social capital results only when group norms lead to collaboration, and this requires norms such as keeping commitments, reciprocity, and reliably performing duties (Fukuyama, 1999). Norms that support collaboration may be as simple as the reciprocity emphasized by Coleman (1990) or as complex as codified standards for professional practice and systems of religious beliefs.

For social capital to be useful in schools, norms must extend beyond simple collaboration to support collective work and toward specific school accomplishments and goals. For instance, to promote instruction and learning to standards for all students in a typically diverse school, norms would need to support a high degree of sharing among teachers with different areas of expertise. Norms in the larger community would need to include a sufficiently strong commitment to universal academic proficiency to allow reallocation of resources to provide extra support for students experiencing difficulty.

We have known for some time that improving student performance requires changing how the adults in schools feel about their work and workplace (Hart & Murphy, 1990; House, 1998; Smylie & Hart, 1999). We know that adults must be energized; committed to a common set of goals; have the needed knowledge, skills, and dispositions; work in a de-privatized environment featuring mutual trust and respect, collaboration, and norms of sharing; and engage in critical and reflective dialog. They also must share a strong, collective focus on student learning, where means of renewal are integrated and valued, and leadership is supportive and knowledgeable (Bellamy, 1999; Heck & Hallenger, 1999; Senge et al., 2000; Smylie & Hart, 1999).

The norms needed for school success will vary to some degree from one school to another. Local values and priorities must be taken into account in establishing goals for student learning and school conditions. When this is done, school goals and the success criteria for school accomplishments necessarily will vary from one community to another. And as goals vary, so too may the norms that are needed to reach those goals.

Trust That Others Will Act in Accordance with Norms

Trust emerges when members of a social network are confident that others will fulfill their obligations and meet the expectations that follow from group norms. Trust results from social capital, but it also contributes to its reinforcement and further development, as individuals act collaboratively on the assumption that others will respond in kind.

Several aspects of networks and norms can increase trust. First, trust can increase as social connections within a group become more dense, because this can make sanctions for violating norms more certain (Coleman, 1990). Second, as the norms characteristic of particular networks become more clearly defined, for example, in standards for professional practice, ambiguity about expectations decreases, again fostering trust that others will act as expected. Third, the concept of networks is important in understanding the development of trust, because quite different levels of trust might exist for individuals in and outside various groups. Putnam (1993) argues that more generalized trust is important, but there are many examples of networks where trust is limited to group members such as close kin and immediate associates.

Trust that others will not violate social norms, or "defect," is important because it allows members of a school community to foresee how others are likely to respond to their actions. For example, when a teacher experiences difficulty with a particular child or curriculum unit, having some confidence in how others will respond affects whether that teacher initiates discussions about the issue with other teachers or simply allows the problem to build while trying to figure things out alone. Similarly, if such trust extends to the larger community, a teacher is more likely to discuss a learning problem with a student's family and ask for help in supporting the student.

Such initiations by teachers are not without risk. Asking for help might be viewed by others as a commitment to each child's learning, but it also could be seen as an admission of incompetence—or even as "breaking ranks" with other teachers who want to maintain the privacy of their teaching. Responding to the many issues that arise in classrooms and schools requires that teachers, family members, and principals take such risks often in order to gain new understanding of the situation. Similar risks are involved when teachers develop new strategies for responding, coordinate with others who are in contact with the same situation, or ask for assistance. The greater the ability to project how others might respond in such situations, the more likely the collaboration that characterizes successful schools. Thus, trust is an essential element of a school's social capital that mediates other benefits of a strong professional community (Bryk, Camburn, & Louis, 1999).

Principal Leadership

Principal leadership and its influence on both student learning and school conditions are the focus of this book. Here our topic is more specific: the ways in which that leadership supports and is supported by the social capital in a school and community. In turn, such leadership is critical to developing and maintaining social capital in successful schools.

Leadership can emerge throughout a school as networks, norms, and trust lead various groups to vest authority in different individuals to speak and act on their behalf. Authority that is "delegated upward" in this way can be as fragmented or as coherent as the networks within a school community. For instance, schools may depend on different individuals to provide informal leadership on different issues, and various groups within a school might look to different individuals for such leadership. When norms are broadly shared and communication across groups is strong, this distribution of leadership can be an important asset as a school works to realize accomplishments and achieve goals. When networks are fragmented and groups have competing goals, this informal delegation of leadership can be very complicated and eventually mitigate a principal's task of focusing a school on particular accomplishments and goals. This reasoning suggests that principal leadership can be facilitated and supported by densely connected networks and trustworthy norms, as long as those norms are congruent with the principal's own goals for school conditions and student learning.

At the same time, principal leadership is critical in developing and sustaining each element of social capital. Principals do this in several ways. First, norms can have diminishing influence if they are not articulated and communicated to new members of a community. Norms can dissipate even more rapidly when it becomes obvious that individuals can violate norms with impunity to maximize their individual interests. Because of their role in a school community, principals have opportunities to articulate school norms, demonstrate that those norms have meaning, and show that violating those norms has consequences.

Principals also strengthen the social capital of their school community by bridging communication gaps within and between various networks. Identifying and filling these network "holes" (Burt, 1992) provide principals with opportunities to focus collective efforts in particular directions and to stimulate more equitable participation by groups who may have different social and economic status (Stanton-Salazar, 1997). Finally, principals strengthen social connections within and across groups by the kinds of structures that they put in place and the interactions that those structures encourage and hinder (Halverson, 2003).

These leadership strategies reflect the importance of the interaction between principals and others in a school community as a fundamental element of leadership (Ogawa & Bossert, 2000). Smiley and Hart (1999) use the term "interactional principal leadership" to make a similar point, emphasizing the "role that the principal plays in developing and sustaining productive social relations among teachers" (pp. 428–429).

Just as school success is influenced by social capital in both a school and community, so too does the principal's responsibility to nurture social capital cross a school's boundary. Some advocate such leadership for social-capital development in the larger community because a school is increasingly a source of social and civic capital for the community—a resource for or engine of community development and revitalization (Driscoll & Kerchner, 1999). But there are also more immediate reasons for focusing on social capital in the larger community. Every school's success in promoting student learning is closely linked to the relationship assets that students have in their homes and community (Search Institute, 1993).

The argument for extending efforts to build social capital to a school's surrounding communities is ultimately a practical one: Defining school goals, establishing priorities for school conditions to achieve those goals, and taking action to sustain the selected conditions all require coordinated action of many members of a school's community. Teachers, family members, district staff, students, and others in the community all contribute to school accomplishments and goals.

SOCIAL CAPITAL AND THE DEMOCRATIC PURPOSES OF SCHOOLS

The effort to build social capital that bridges groups with different interests and status is far more than an exercise in bartering over school norms. As guides for action, norms about how students should be treated, what they should learn, and how teachers should work together raise issues of fundamental values and moral choices: What is fair, how do individual choices balance with the perceived common good, what constitutes efficient and accountable use of public resources, and how does one balance commitment to children with respect for family authority?

The process for making such moral choices in democratic institutions involves deliberation—the open discussion of alternatives and their implications. While such deliberation does not guarantee that the right decision will always be reached, it does allow decisions to be reached after consideration of the reasoning of many different groups (Gutmann, 2000; Reid, 1978).

There are noticeable similarities between schools that strive to build social capital and the civic structures and processes that underlie democratic society. To undertake the deliberation needed to build social capital, schools are challenged to be microcosms of the democratic processes of the larger society, just as they prepare students for participation in that society. They do this by reaching agreements about fundamental values through procedural compliance with legal frameworks, respect for underlying constitutional values, and moral deliberation about the meaning and relative importance of those guiding values (Gutmann, 2000). Consequently, by striving to build social capital, schools model many of the most important lessons that children in a democracy are expected to learn from their school experience: enculturation into the habits and dispositions that are necessary for a social and political democracy to thrive (Goodlad, 1997).

SUMMARY

Schools succeed when members of the internal and external communities collaborate to define goals and then take collective action to achieve those goals. Fostering the social connections that make this collaboration and co-ordination possible is critical to principals' success. Recently, these social connections have been conceptualized and studied as social capital, which, like other kinds of capital, serve as a resource that can shape the work and success of schools.

The social capital in an organization or community consists of (1) the density of its social networks that determine how well information flows among groups; (2) the norms, obligations, and expectations that shape the goals and behaviors of group members and the kinds of assistance they are likely to provide one another; (3) the trust and trustworthiness that follow from network characteristics and norms; and (4) the leadership that is enabled by this trust and that can further support development of networks and norms.

When social capital is high, communities are more likely to cooperate for mutual gain and civic engagement. But high social capital does not necessarily support the goals of schools, unless the norms that are instantiated in the community reinforce the importance of student learning and the need for collaboration to achieve this end. Fostering social capital for schools thus depends on both strengthening the networks and working toward norms that support the academic and social missions of schooling.

The social capital in a school and its community serves as a multiplier for school efforts related to goals, accomplishments, and daily action. High levels of social capital can greatly facilitate the principal's efforts in these other leadership responsibilities, while low social capital and social connections focused on competing norms can hinder those efforts. We return to the discussion of social capital in Chapter 9, with more practical suggestions on how principals can approach this part of their school leadership responsibilities.

PART II

The Practice of Accomplishment-Minded Leadership

The first part of this book explored four ways of understanding schools and school leadership in order to focus attention on important aspects of the principalship and to suggest mental models that can help principals plan and reflect on their work. Part II turns to more practical concerns. Returning to each of the four leadership domains discussed earlier—school goals, accomplishments, pragmatic practice, and social capital—we offer more pragmatic advice on how accomplishment-minded practice can help school leaders improve their practice.

Our idea of an "accomplishment" helps integrate a principal's work associated with all four of these leadership domains. Accomplishment-minded leaders define success criteria for all accomplishments in conjunction with a school's communities; they select for special attention accomplishments that have the greatest potential for improving student learning; and they solve the onslaught of daily problems in ways that contribute to these accomplishments and purposes. They do all this while sustaining and enhancing the social capital needed by the school's communities in order to do the work. These four issues frame distinct, but related, domains where principal leadership is needed.

- *Leadership for sustainable goals* takes place in the arena of community values. Here, a principal's challenge is to understand the competing values within a school's community, find a working balance among various school purposes, lead discussions that sharpen and develop these purposes, and translate these purposes into coherent and sustainable agreements about goals for student learning and school conditions.

- *Leadership for strategic focus* occurs in the arena of school accomplishments and concerns questions of what to emphasize in order to achieve school goals. In this domain, a principal's challenge is to ensure sufficient attention to all aspects of the school while focusing particular attention on those accomplishments that have the greatest potential for helping the school reach its goals.

- *Leadership for effective action* occurs in the arena of day-to-day problem solving. The principal's challenges are to advance the school's status on accomplishments by determining which problems should receive attention, what results are desired from their solution, and what actions most likely would produce these results.

- *Leadership for social capital* occurs in the arena of interpersonal interaction and develops the relationships and communication channels needed for collective decisions about goals and collaborative action to reach those goals.

Although each depends on the others, the four leadership domains represent distinct responsibilities that require principals to attend to different aspects of the school, work with different constituencies, operate in different time frames, and use knowledge for different purposes. As Table II.1 illustrates, school accomplishments are pivotal in each domain.

As the table suggests, leadership for sustainable purposes lays the foundation for accomplishment-minded practice by developing success criteria for school accomplishments that reflect both required learning outcomes and community values about what schools should be like. By exercising leadership for strategic focus, the principal arranges for all accomplishments to be addressed while ensuring special attention to accomplishments that have potential for improvement. Leadership for effective action involves selecting and solving daily problems in ways that protect and enhance a school's status on its accomplishments. Leadership for social capital supports the other three domains by nurturing the relationships, norms, and trust needed for collective decisions and collaborative actions.

As we return to these four aspects of school leadership, our focus is on practical guidance: What do our understandings of schools and school leadership mean for the daily work of principals?

TABLE II.1. Leadership for Accomplishments in Four Domains

Leadership Domain	Focus of Attention	Measurement and Feedback Concerns	Illustrative Leadership Strategies	Results
Leadership for Sustainable Purposes	Externally mandated outcomes; local values and purposes	How well do school results respond to local values and required outcomes?	Conversational leadership; increase participation, focus, commitment	School vision and goals that are articulated in success criteria for accomplishments
Leadership for Strategic Focus	School accomplishments	Do accomplishments match success criteria?	Assess results, set priorities, gain support for improvements	School structures to reach all accomplishments; priorities for accomplishments needing attention
Leadership for Effective Action	Daily problems	Which situations provide an opportunity to protect or enhance priority accomplishments?	Select problems, frame solution criteria, and act to reach solutions	Improved status on school accomplishments (better school conditions)
Leadership for Social Capital	Relationships among individuals and groups in the school's communities	What commitments and norms are shared by members of the school community? What is the level of trust among members?	Serve as a communication link among groups; model social norms; create conditions for collaborative work	More interconnections among teachers and with community members; broader commitment to espoused norms

Chapter 6

Leadership for Sustainable Goals

Effective principals do not simply accept the goals established by professional associations or political representatives. They also recognize how local values create additional or modifying expectations for what students should learn and how schools should operate. As noted in Chapter 2, this means that effective principals engage in an ongoing effort to understand and influence the guiding values and priorities in their schools' various communities. This chapter builds on that discussion and turns to questions about what principals actually do to provide that leadership, how leadership in this domain can support student learning, and the ways of thinking that can help principals provide such leadership.

HOW SUSTAINABLE GOALS SUPPORT STUDENT LEARNING

Leadership for sustainable goals (1) inspires commitment and moral purpose among those responsible for helping students learn, (2) provides a clear understanding of community expectations toward which school work can be directed, and (3) fosters stability in school direction by responding to the values and priorities of a broad enough community representation.

Inspiration

Student learning is the result of effort—the effort of students themselves as they study, and that of their teachers and families who structure learning environments and experiences and give feedback. To inspire and sustain this effort, principals are advised, among other things, to help all members of the school community construct coherent understandings of the school's values and goals (Fullan, 2001). Often motivated more by passion and commitment than by requirements, and more by a belief that what students are learning is important than by lists of what they should know, teachers and other school staff choose their own levels of professional effort and commitment. Consequently, school goals and purposes that connect with individual commitments can exert broad influence over the important work of forming relationships with students, communicating enthusiasm for learning, and continuing professional development. Professional effort—and the goals that inspire it—mediate much of the learning that occurs in schools (Sergiovanni, 1992).

Direction

The more clarity a principal can bring to a description of what a school is expected to achieve, the easier it is to organize the school in purposeful ways. For example, if it is clear that a community places a high value on artistic performances and sports events, a principal can establish schedules, staff assignments, and student expectations in ways that support these goals and the learning that is assessed in state tests. A somewhat different allocation of staff responsibilities and time in the school schedule would be likely in a school whose communities had overriding concerns for student safety and elimination of gang activity.

Stability

Because school goals are so important, it is tempting for a principal to move quickly to define those goals for the school. However, school goals are sustainable only when they are widely shared among the school's communities. If purposes are established that reflect only the views of the principal, the school's staff, or any other single constituency, a real possibility exists that some community members, who value different school purposes, will believe that the school is failing. And when these dissatisfactions gain sufficient traction to affect principal assignments or school board elections, the frequent result is radical and rapid changes in school goals (Lutz & Iannaccone, 1978). Sustainable goals are achieved only by understanding the full range of expectations of a school's communities and finding a dynamic working center among purposes that coalesce various communities around achievable goals.

What might such a school goal look like? Here is one possibility: *"Granite Elementary is committed to every child acquiring knowledge in core academic subjects at levels defined in content standards and state tests. In addition, we place a high value on every child having a comprehensive program that includes the arts, physical education, and science instruction in an environment that fosters friendships and inclusion for all students."* Such a statement: (1) affirms the school's commitment to student learning as defined through the formal political processes that govern schools; (2) specifies additional areas of student learning that the community values; and (3) defines school conditions that the community sees as important.

Goals that are inspiring, clearly focused, and broadly supported are not easy for principals to sustain. And the task grows more daunting as schools serve more and more diverse communities.

> Moral purpose is problematic because it must contend with reconciling the diverse interests and goals of different groups. Diversity means different races, different interest groups, different power bases, and basically different lots in life. To achieve moral purpose is to forge interaction—and even mutual purpose—across groups. (Fullan, 2001, p. 25)

These diverse community interests frame the practical challenge of school leadership for sustainable goals.

STRATEGIES FOR DEVELOPING SUSTAINABLE GOALS

Principals provide leadership for sustainable goals (LSG) through three broad strategies—understanding the values and priorities in their communities, leading conversations toward shared goals, and translating those goals into visible success criteria for the school's accomplishments. As we show in the discussion of each of these areas, LSG requires a skillful blending of the values and priorities in a school's various internal and external communities. Understanding, shaping, and translating these values into workable goals is the essence of LSG.

Understand the Community's Balance of Purposes

Listen. A principal's first task in LSG is to listen, or solicit a wide variety of inputs from all segments of the community. The requests that parents make of the school, the complaints that come to the principal's office, the testimony before the local school board, and the questions raised by the family of a prospective student visiting the school all provide important information about community values.

Of course, some parents and advocacy groups are skilled at making their interests known, while others may feel just as strongly but have less inclination to voice their concerns. So, although principals often feel that they already have more than enough dissatisfaction to deal with, LSG depends on finding opportunities to listen to all the groups affected by the school. This can involve, for example, making time for personal contacts with new families at the start of each school year; scheduling periodic meetings with education reporters, elected officials, and others whose jobs depend on a keen understanding of community values; meeting regularly with parent and community groups; and taking time for individual conversations with school staff members and key volunteers.

Synthesize. An understanding of the community's values for its schools emerges as principals continually try to synthesize the information from these many conversations. The mix of values and purposes in a community requires that a principal engage informally in a continual "sense making" of a school's community (Denzin, 1994; Louis, 1980). Notes and memories from hundreds of conversations can be mined for meanings that are then tested recursively in new conversations. The principal's next step is to put this information out to the community for member checking.

One way to conceptualize this sense making (Louis, 1980) is to imagine a principal constantly seeking a "working center" among competing school purposes. While any conceptual model oversimplifies the complex mix of school purposes, the distinctions described in Chapter 2 among six school purposes can be helpful. Public interest in *enculturation* into the nation's social and political democracy competes for attention with the private interests of some groups for enculturation into particular religious beliefs, cultural practices, and family values. Public interest in education as a means of building *economic competitiveness* for a region or state competes for space in the curriculum with private interests in individual credentials that give economic advantage to some students. And public interest in creating places for safe and *caring development* for all children competes with private expectations that school routines and schedules will be adjusted to benefit individual children and their families.

Of course, community advocacy seldom is expressed in such abstract terms. Instead, principals are confronted with requests and complaints about far more specific issues, and they must develop their own understanding of what such advocacy means for the school's purposes and priorities. Table 6.1 illustrates how such advocacy might be interpreted within the framework of the six competing educational purposes that we have described. Using this or another conceptual organizer can help a principal synthesize the many bits of information that are gleaned from observation and conversation in a school community into a more coherent understanding of local values.

An Illustration. Differences in emphasis on these various school purposes can lead to significant variation in what is expected of schools. For example, Forest Glen Elementary School and Commerce Street Elementary School are

TABLE 6.1. Six Competing Purposes for Schools

Purposes	Description	Examples of Local Expectations
Enculturation Purposes Serving Public Interests	Schools should focus on the dual challenge of preparing students for "social responsibility as a citizen" and "maximum individual development" (Goodlad, 1996, p. 112).	• advocacy for service-learning requirements • advocacy for programs that ensure that all students have supports needed to succeed • support for programs that make the school welcoming to all cultures and religions
Enculturation Purposes Serving Private Interests	Schools should help parents socialize their children into their particular religious beliefs, cultural norms, languages, and family values.	• advocacy for instruction and activities associated with a particular religion • request for the school to avoid some topics in class discussions because these should be addressed only by families themselves or a nonschool institution • requests to ban certain library books
Economic Purposes Serving Public Interests	Schools should prepare students for productive work, building economic capital for a city, state, or nation (National Commission on Excellence in Education, 1983; Secretary's Commission on Achieving Necessary Skills, 1991).	• advocacy for smooth and effective transitions across grade levels • advocacy for curricula and programs related to the local economy • pressure to ensure that all students achieve at least minimum levels on state tests
Economic Purposes Serving Private Interests	Schools should give individual students the opportunity to earn special credentials that make them more competitive at higher levels of schooling and in the workplace. (For example, see Labaree's 1997 critique of this purpose.)	• advocacy for programs that lead to differentiated qualifications and credentials • advocacy for special advanced programs that benefit only a few students • advocacy for flexible school schedules that accommodate student employment
Child Care Purposes Serving Public Interests	Schools should provide a safe and caring environment where children themselves learn to care for others (Beck, 1993; Noddings, 1999). Public interests in caring schools serve goals such as reduction of child abuse, teenage pregnancy, child mental health problems, and drug and alcohol use.	• concern for safety of the overall school facilities, grounds, and routes to school • expectations for teacher involvement in school activities and relationships with students • support for links between school and community services for individuals needing extra support
Child Care Purposes Serving Private Interests	Schools should adjust to individual family work and vacation schedules and support parents' efforts to ensure that their children develop positive peer groups.	• pressure to adapt school schedules to fit individual parents' work and commuting schedules • expectations that schools will adapt instruction and testing to parents' vacation schedules • expectation of immediate personal notification to individual parents when potential dangers exist

located near each other but serve very different communities. Forest Glen Elementary School is located in a relatively affluent suburban community and offers a variety of special programs for children who are gifted and talented. Many families are very involved in the school and concerned that their children stay well ahead of grade-level expectations. Differentiated reading and mathematics groups allow children with greater abilities to move quickly through the curriculum and to experience a variety of enrichment activities.

Teachers get particular recognition in the community for the book that their more advanced students publish each year and for special activities, such as the school play, music recitals, and art exhibits, which allow many students to demonstrate their achievements. In the district office, the focus is solidly on academic progress, with little attention to the many social services that some schools must emphasize; in fact, the district's relative wealth makes it ineligible for compensatory education funds. Many families in the community have relatively flexible schedules, so the school has little difficulty with field trips, professional development days, and special events.

The school's families typically depend on themselves and their religious institutions for instruction in ethical issues and ask not so much that the school help, but that it not contradict the personal and religious values that they are transmitting to their children. Parents are very concerned, however, that the school does everything possible to ensure the children's safety in the school and provide access to a peer group that is desired by family members.

Across town, Commerce Street Elementary School functions under the same state education laws and works toward the same state standards and tests, but its programs reflect quite different school board policies and parent expectations. Bordering an industrial area, Commerce Street serves a largely poor student body composed of many first- and second-generation immigrants. Most students live in families where all adults in the household work full time, so a dependable school schedule is critical to the families' economic survival.

The school strongly emphasizes academic skills for all students, and does reasonably well on state assessments, despite a large number of students who do not speak English at home. The school focuses particular attention on making sure that each student gets whatever additional help is needed to stay at grade level and meet the expectations of state tests. This results in several special programs, such as tutoring, after-school assistance, and special scheduling to help those who are falling behind. The school has successfully sought grant funds to support other special services, including health services from a school nurse, support from several social service agencies, and breakfast and lunch programs. A full-time school psychologist in the building helps students address behavior problems, and a family services coordinator provides outreach and support for families.

The six competing school purposes described earlier might help a principal understand and synthesize the community expectations that lead to differences like those between Commerce Street and Forest Glen. The community's expectations at Forest Glen appear to emphasize (1) private interests associated with preparation for competitive economic and social position of individual children (focusing on programs that give some children special opportunities and credentials), (2) the support of private enculturation interests (asking schools to leave controversial subjects for discussion at home), and (3) child supervision in support of private interests (expressed as heightened concern for children's safety).

Content standards and tests are a relatively small concern because of the school's generally high achievement levels. Overall, Forest Glen places considerably more emphasis on private than public purposes of schools.

Commerce Street Elementary School has a quite different balance of purposes. The emphasis in this community is on public purposes of enculturation and preparation for employment (a focus on preparation of all children, rather than on structures that create competitive advantage for some) and both public and private interests in child care. Meeting content standards takes a relatively large portion of the available school effort, and public purposes receive somewhat more emphasis than do private ones.

Understanding a community's priorities for its schools is an ongoing process. The balance among competing purposes is developing constantly as new student needs, new parent concerns, or new possibilities enter local deliberations. In this regard, Forest Glen and Commerce Street are both oversimplifications: Few communities enjoy the consensus about school goals that is implied in these examples. More typically, within a school community there are strong differences about which goals are most important and about the balance which school leaders must maintain as proponents of different perspectives become involved and exert influence.

Tensions within a community about the relative priority that should be given to school purposes naturally intensify as funding, time, professional expertise, facilities, and space in the curriculum are assigned to functions that contribute differentially to the various school purposes. And increasing partisanship in the politics of many special-interest groups creates pressure to take sides, further complicating efforts to reach consensus on school goals. Consequently, a principal's understanding of her or his community also involves assessing the capacity of the community to take collaborative action —including the capacities of strong stakeholder groups, the history of school–community involvement, and the degree of mistrust and skepticism (Chrislip & Larson, 1994).

Influence the School's Guiding Values and Goals

Successful principals are neither passive translators of community values nor independent actors who unilaterally define school goals. Leadership for sustainable goals occurs in public and depends on the principal's ongoing interactions with the school's many constituencies.

Indeed, it can be tempting for principals simply to proclaim their own values and priorities for the school or to develop priorities that reflect a consensus of the school's professional staff. Certainly, the educational literature is rich with advocacy for school leaders to pursue specific goals, such as social justice (Horn, 2001), inclusion (Riehl, 2000), democratic participation (Furman & Starratt, 2002), and cultural pluralism (Baptiste, 1999), as well as for absolute values that transcend both situations and preferences of individual leaders (Campbell, 1999; Hodgkinson, 1991).

Despite the appeal of values advocated in professional literature, a sustainable direction for schools seldom comes from school leaders alone. Schools are part of a broader community ecology and are shaped by the limits and boundaries that emerge from the dynamic balance of community values. Schools must harmonize with their environment: They cannot go beyond their environment—at least not for long (Lutz & Iannaccone, 1978; Lutz & Merz, 1992). School leaders create sustainable change only as new balances are crafted in the larger community. Doing this does not mean that a principal abdicates professional values and knowledge, but it does require skillful integration of such values and knowledge with community norms.

Leadership for sustainable purposes thus occurs in the public arena and addresses matters of public expectations and values. Providing leadership that shapes community values toward coherent school purposes—and a commitment to student learning—is difficult, but not impossible. It is difficult because core values are deeply held, generally stable, and slow to change (Argyris, Putnam, & Smith, 1985; Deal & Peterson, 1999). Views about the purpose of schooling are held firmly as well (Senge et al., 2000), and school leaders often are disinclined to engage in value discussions.

Despite the difficulties, principals are in a unique position to influence the development of community values, if they choose to lead actively in the public arena. Such leadership occurs as principals engage others in conversations that have potential for conflicting views. Conflicts between groups about what to do, conflicts between what is valued and what actually is happening, and conflicts between different values held by the same person or group all provide the context for LSG. Heifetz (1994), for example, sees public leadership in these areas of conflict as *adaptive work*, which "consists of the learning required to address conflicts in the values people hold, or to diminish the gap between the values people stand for and the reality they face" (p. 22). School leadership in this context involves actively engaging in and leading the conversations needed to resolve differences and encourage acting on commonalities.

For example, a principal might lead community conversations about reorganizing the school's schedule to provide more assistance for students who are falling behind. Most of that school's families say equity is important and that all children should meet standards, but they also want to preserve special programs for the arts and extensive community field trips that would have to be cut. Whatever the result of the conversation on this specific issue, a productive discussion of the conflicting values can help sharpen the school's goals and foster commitment to action. The principal's role in leading these conversations involves balancing different ways of moving forward: (1) sharpen the focus of shared goals for the school, (2) expand participation in the conversation, and (3) increase commitment to action on shared goals.

Sharpen the Focus. Agreement about school goals can be easy, as long as they are stated in broad and ambiguous terms. Who would argue that schools should help all children learn to their potential in a caring environment? But as goals become more sharply focused, differences emerge. Does "all" really mean all children, including those with severe cognitive disabilities or aggressive behaviors? Does "learn to their potential" mean learn to the same content standards as everyone else? Does "caring environment" mean that the school is expected to manage students' peer-group formation in ways that each parent expects?

Conversations that sharpen the focus of a community's goals for its schools typically occur in response to specific issues. What sanctions are appropriate for high-achieving high school students who violate the school's code of conduct? Does the community support eliminating a traditional senior trip to fund a remedial program for freshmen? How should the principal respond to an altercation at a sports event? These and other daily problems provide the grist for conversations about values and purposes. Principals can serve as moderators for many of these community conversations, and in doing so they become uniquely positioned to influence the meaning of events and to frame contentious issues for discussion (Rallis, 1990; Riehl, 2000). When these conversations are framed skillfully, the discussion goes beyond the particular situation to the underlying purposes that shape what the community expects from its school. By helping the community consider each specific issue and alternative actions, a principal helps strengthen and focus school goals.

Increase Participation. A danger in working toward greater focus in public conversations about school goals is the temptation to narrow participation to those who are already of like mind. But goals are sustainable only when they have broad support; even a small minority whose interests are ignored can organize successfully to change the leadership and direction of a single school or district school board.

Increasing participation is an important strategy to stimulate consideration of school practices that have become familiar but that serve to advantage some students over others. For example, the principal of an elementary school first used the school newsletter to propose a new school schedule with an extended day for students who were falling behind. The article gave a description of the proposed program, a rationale for shifting resources to this new service, and suggestions on arranging late transportation. The article included an email address and telephone number and invited comments. Many responses were received in the first 2 weeks, but most came from families who were already involved in the school and whose children would be only marginally affected by the changes. To involve others in the conversation, the principal then asked local community organizations to host small meetings for families away from the school. Quite different questions and concerns were voiced in these meetings. To accommodate these new perspectives, the principal made significant changes in the program so that the targeted children were not singled out as failing and so their transportation issues could be handled more easily in partnership with the city bus system. Greater participation in this instance required more attention to the contexts that are created for the discussion. It was necessary to address the increased complexity in how the problem was understood and what solutions were acceptable. And, as is often the case, the resulting program was the better for the input.

The accomplishment perspective provides a shared and inclusive language to support community conversations about school goals. The very definition of accomplishments in terms of what actually gets done opens discussion about both purposes (success criteria) and action strategies, and does so in ways that respect many different types of knowledge. For example, knowledge of professional terminology is not necessary for individuals to describe how they want schools to function. Because the vocabulary embedded in the Framework for School Leadership Accomplishments (FSLA) does not require knowledge of educational procedures, it may help principals to engage a broader range of staff and community voices in the process of critiquing school practices and negotiating purposes.

Strengthen Commitment. The third outcome that principals seek from conversations about goals is commitment to act on shared goals. Inside the school, this can mean teachers adopting new ways of working; outside, it can mean parents choosing to provide greater support for student effort, working to increase funding for particular programs, or volunteering to support specific needs. Discussing disagreements about what to do in specific situations can both forge resolutions of conflicting values and create commitment to action.

To lead in ways that sharpen the focus of school goals, increase participation, and strengthen commitment, leaders create contexts within which difficult conversations can occur—think tanks, community and association meetings, community listening sessions, and so on—and exert influence by framing issues, highlighting contradictions, and providing rationales for action. While a part of these conversations naturally focuses on persuasion by the leader (Soder, 2001), their success is ultimately a matter of public collaboration.

> Leaders have to build agreement about needs, create or take advantage of good timing, develop working relationships among stakeholders, and provide a balance of attention on the process of working together and the need to get results (content). Their primary task is to create a constituency for change that can reach implementable agreements on problems and issues of shared concern, not to impose a specific solution that they themselves have defined. (Chrislip & Larson, 1994, p. 73)

It would be incorrect to think that public or political leadership focuses only on the external environment (e.g., parents, business and political leaders, community agencies). As a school is part of an ecology, so, too, are its employees. Teachers and staff of a school can be at cross-purposes with each other or with the community (Blase, 1993; Malen, 1994). Leadership for sustainable goals requires that a principal build a common vision for a school, incorporating its staff in the dynamic balance among the community's values and purposes.

Of course, others in addition to the principal are involved in these community conversations. Elected school board members and district administrators also share the responsibility of finding a working balance of school purposes. At a practical level, principals in most districts participate in the development of a working balance among competing values and purposes simply because they have more day-to-day contact with parents and access to far more information than do lay leaders and district administrators (Malen, Ogawa, & Kranz, 1990).

Connect Community Commitments to School Accomplishments

Leadership for sustainable goals is a continuing process of understanding and shaping a community's values and goals for its schools. Leadership in this domain is incomplete, however, until systematic links are forged between these emerging community priorities and the school's actual functioning.

The accomplishment perspective provides one approach for creating the needed connections. As described in Chapter 3, success criteria define the desired features of each accomplishment. School accomplishments—these positive conditions that exist in schools—are valued because they contribute to achieving student-learning goals and because they help the school conform with community values about what school should be like. Consequently, success criteria for school accomplishments are constructed partly from information about what works—what kind of student climate, instruction, and so on, most likely will lead to expected levels of student learning. Success criteria also can reflect local priorities that may have nothing to do with instrumental thinking. Communities have different expectations for student behavior, for example, and these naturally translate into different success criteria that define what is an acceptable school climate. A community that places high priority on allowing high-achieving students to earn special credentials might want a climate for students that is somewhat competitive, while a different community might see a climate characterized by acceptance and belonging as more important than competitive pressures.

In Table 3.2 we listed success criteria for each accomplishment that, according to current research, appear to be related to the school's success in achieving student-learning goals. For instance, for the accomplishment, student climate sustained, learning is enhanced when students believe that the school (1) emphasizes academic learning, (2) is safe and orderly, and (3) promotes strong, healthy relationships with peers and adults (Levine & Lezotte, 1990). As a result of understanding a school's community and what it values in schools, a principal could add criteria to respond to local priorities. These additional success criteria could include expectations that students will believe that (1) the school is a place that practices democratic principles in its interaction with students, (2) communications with peers around the world are important and supported, (3) winning academic contests and earning high test scores are highly valued, or (4) adults in the school emphasize success in sports.

Principals do two important things when they translate community values into success criteria for a school's accomplishments. First, by making public their interpretation of what school conditions the community wants, principals invite discussion, refinement, and further development of community values focused on schools. Sometimes, simply writing down what appears to be the predominant view, prompts reconsideration and further development. In short, translating one's understanding of community values into success criteria for school accomplishments can itself be a strategy for leading further conversations.

Second, when community values are translated into success criteria, the principal can provide clearer guidance to the school about the goals toward which their work is directed. For example, specific statements about what kind of student climate, instruction, or school operations are expected by a school's communities create a link between goals and the practical daily work of school professionals on whom student learning depends. With success criteria in place, much of a principal's stewardship for a school's goals and vision can occur in the context of daily conversations about practical tasks that affect the desired school conditions.

In effect, the accomplishment perspective problematizes the success criteria associated with each accomplishment in each community. This requires school leaders to analyze how school practices affect different groups and work with school communities to frame success criteria that reflect this critical reflection. Whether a local school's curriculum, instruction, climate, or family–community partnership is "good enough" or "great" is always a matter for discussion. Conversations about what success criteria should apply as a school plans and evaluates its work can connect the critical reflection needed to sustain personal commitments with the practical details of daily work in schools.

SUMMARY

Through leadership for sustainable goals, principals provide a foundation for student learning by understanding and influencing a community's conversations about values, priorities, and goals for its schools. While members of the school's internal community—teachers, principal, and other staff—are participants in this conversation, only the results of a broad public conversation can determine sustainable goals for a school.

In order to frame school goals that inspire effort from teachers, students, and family members, school leaders work within the larger community to stimulate wider participation in the discussion of what's expected from schools, to sharpen the focus of resulting goals, and to stimulate commitment to action on those goals. This broader commitment validates the school, its purposes, and its accomplishments. While difficult, this work of leadership for sustainable purposes can contribute significantly to a school's focus on student learning. It can inspire the effort needed for teaching and learning, it can clarify expectations, and it can stimulate critical analysis of daily school operations.

As school purposes are analyzed and negotiated, school leaders need a deep understanding of how various students and groups benefit differentially from programs, instructional strategies, and other learning opportunities. The ability to understand the perspectives of many different religious and cultural groups and to articulate the hidden results of school practices is essential to leadership for sustainable purposes.

Chapter 7

Leadership for Strategic Focus

Principals face continuing choices about what to emphasize at any given moment in a school's evolution in order to promote student learning and sustain school conditions that a community values; and every school brings particular human and material resources, and a finite amount of time, to the challenge of reaching school goals. Deciding how to allocate those resources—which responsibilities to emphasize, which to change from previous years, which to sustain, and which to ignore—provides a critical link between a school's lofty goals and its daily realities.

In Chapter 3, we indicated how a theory of action can link daily school goals to work, and we offered the Framework for School Leadership Accomplishments (FSLA) as a guide for developing a locally responsive theory of action. This chapter continues the discussion by presenting practical ways of thinking and acting that help principals lead in the domain of strategic focus. Leadership in this domain requires principals to be mindful of a school's accomplishments—the conditions through which school goals are achieved. Are the school's actual accomplishments commensurate with success criteria? What general approach will the school take to reach the success criteria for each accomplishment? Which accomplishments require special attention during a particular school year to improve student learning?

HOW STRATEGIC FOCUS SUPPORTS
STUDENT LEARNING

Strategic focus is the allocation of time, expertise, and other resources to various aspects of a school's work to improve its learning results while responding to the community's purposes and values. Like other organizations, schools must make choices among possible areas of emphasis in order to operate purposefully and efficiently. At the same time, they must organize in ways that attend to all necessary responsibilities, whether or not changes are needed.

Leadership for strategic focus is a part of every principal's responsibilities because the same priorities—or the same theory of action—are not useful in every school. If they were, principals simply could adopt a theory of action that was developed elsewhere and count on it to work in their own schools, skipping this domain of leadership altogether. But one set of priorities does not work everywhere. "Although some general leadership functions may be important in all schools, the manner in which these functions are implemented must be adapted to the needs of students, the expectations of the community, and the institutional context" (Hallinger & McCary, 1990, pp. 90–91). Portin and colleagues (2003) frame the challenge nicely, observing that principals must be "master diagnosticians" (p. 13), able to select changes most likely to move a particular school forward, given its current operations, resources, and community context.

Leadership for strategic focus contributes to student learning because reliable learning is the result of a very complex set of school conditions—teachers who know their subjects and are motivated to establish strong relationships with students, instructional materials and procedures that build systematically on what students already know, school cultures and family support that promote student effort, and so on. Student learning is enhanced when all of these factors are addressed deliberately as parts of a complex system. At the same time, improvements in student learning depend on changes in specific parts of this system. Strategic choices about what to emphasize for further development in a school are essential if learning results are to change from one year to the next. Such emphases may require redoubling efforts in establishing directions, taking on new frames for old problems, or reconceptualizing both the problem and methods of attack.

In sum, leadership for strategic focus supports student learning by combining comprehensive and systemic attention to the many factors that support learning, with greater attention given to particular aspects of the school that are likely to show improvement. Because it is both systemic and selective, leadership for strategic focus reflects a theory of action about how schools support learning and how changes in a school can support increased learning. As noted in Chapter 3, many models of school operation and school leadership are available to support such theories of action. The following discussion reflects our choice of accomplishments as the units of analysis for such a model and our use of the FSLA to describe important school conditions that contribute to learning.

STRATEGIES FOR ACHIEVING STRATEGIC FOCUS

Leading for strategic focus involves four major responsibilities: (1) understanding school needs and opportunities, (2) defining goals for improvement,

(3) structuring the school to be both comprehensive and focused in its attention to conditions that support student learning, and (4) refining goals in response to ongoing feedback. Leadership in this domain requires mindfulness of the actual conditions in the school and how those conditions compare with local success criteria and with models of excellence.

Understand School Needs

Assessment of a school in order to establish a strategic focus has been addressed in various school-improvement-planning approaches (DuFour & Eaker, 1998; Senge et al., 2000; Taylor, Tashakkori, & Crone-Koshel, 2001) and accreditation models (New England Association of Schools and Colleges, 2001; North Central Association Commission on Accreditation and School Improvement, 2001). General advice also is widely available on how to assess any organization in the context of strategic planning (Bolman & Deal, 1991; Crandall, Eiseman, & Louis, 1986).

Assess Student Learning. The first step of this process involves assessing student learning in relation to expected outcomes. The task is to identify students, subjects, or topics that require additional attention. As the stakes for student performance on annual tests have increased, advice has proliferated on how to analyze results of formal and informal assessments, with well-developed procedures for disaggregating student performance data to identify areas that need improvement (Barnhardt, 1994; Wiggins, 1998). For example, such an analysis might show that a school's low-income students are generally behind their peers in reading and writing assessments, and that this gap widens as they move up grade levels. In mathematics, however, where the school has developed an intensive program in kindergarten and first grade, no such gap occurs until the later grades, when the arithmetic assessments rely more on understanding story problems than on computation.

Assess School Accomplishments. Recognizing such patterns in student achievement is also important in accomplishment-minded practice, but it is only the first step in understanding school needs and opportunities. For example, how should a principal respond to the student-learning data described above? What aspect of the school should a principal seek to change to address the gap in literacy between high- and low-income pupils? Multiple explanations may be offered. Perhaps the school's curriculum is not well matched to what is tested. Or the teachers need more skills in reading instruction. Perhaps the school's climate communicates to low-income children that they do not belong. Or the school schedule gives insufficient time to reading and writing, or groups children poorly for such instruction. It would be nearly impossible for a school to change the way it addresses all of these possibilities at once. Deciding which ones have the most promise for improving literacy of low-income students requires additional information about conditions in the school: the school's accomplishments.

Assessing school accomplishments essentially means understanding which school accomplishments could be changed in ways that would lead to the needed improvements in student learning. This decision involves three steps: (1) assessing school accomplishments in relation to success criteria, (2) identifying opportunity gaps, and (3) estimating the impact of closing opportunity gaps. None of these steps can be driven by formulas or simple extrapolation from data; instead, they each represent ways of thinking that rely on best-available information about the school and the professional judgment of all school leaders, not just the principal.

Assessing accomplishments in relation to success criteria involves asking how well conditions in the school match success criteria for each accomplishment. Recall that in Chapter 3, we described general success criteria for the accomplishments in the FSLA, and in Chapter 6, we described how these general criteria are supplemented by local values about what school should be like. How well performance trends meet these criteria is largely a matter of perception—how the school is viewed by its students, teachers, parents, supervisors, and others. Consequently, assessment in relation to success criteria involves efforts to understand these views. Table 7.1, adapted from Bellamy (1999), illustrates the kind of assessment items that might guide this inquiry. Each asks for agreement or disagreement about whether a particular trend or condition exists in the school. The items are designed to avoid assumptions that any particular strategy will work everywhere—we know better! Instead, by focusing on conditions, the assessments are designed to identify areas needing improvement, while leaving open what strategies will be appropriate in any particular school.

Once a principal understands how well the school is doing in relation to the success criteria, over the various accomplishments, the next step is to ask how much improvement is realistically possible for each one. A useful way to do this is to compare the school's accomplishments with the best similar schools that can be identified. These comparisons reveal *opportunity gaps*, or levels of improvement on the various accomplishments that might be achievable in the principal's school.

For example, a school serving a low-income area that is experiencing rapid demographic changes as a result of immigration might find gaps between actual school conditions and the success criteria for the school's family–community partnership. Despite the gaps, an understanding of the improvements that are realistically possible often depends on seeing an example of what is working in a similar school somewhere else. In short, opportunity

TABLE 7.1. Assessing Perceptions of School Accomplishments in the FSLA

	Parents	Teachers	Students
Learning Goals	• What children learn in this school gets them ready for the next grade, school, or workplace. • My child's learning is usually related across subjects and over time. • I agree with the school's goals for academic and social learning.	• Curriculum goals are challenging enough to prepare students well for the next educational level. • In this school, learning goals are aligned within and across subjects. • I agree with the school's goals for academic and social learning. • I have a clear understanding of the learning goals my students are expected to meet.	• What I learn in this school gets me ready for the next grade, school, or workplace. • The order in which I am expected to learn things makes sense to me. • My family and community usually agree with the school's goals for academic and social learning.
Instruction	• My son or daughter can almost always succeed with effort on assigned work. • If my child succeeds at assignments, he or she also does well on other tests at school. • Teachers recognize the unique needs of my son or daughter when teaching and making assignments. • The teachers seem to use their time well in class. • My son or daughter receives quick feedback on assignments and tests. • My child is helped to explore new ideas.	• Each student in my class is working on a challenging but achievable goal. • I make sure my classroom activities and assignments are directly related to curriculum goals and standards. • I often design separate activities according to the needs and experiences of different students. • Students almost never have to spend time waiting for instruction or materials. • I give students quick feedback on classroom activities, tests, and homework. • Students are expected to explore their interests and new ideas.	• I can almost always succeed on my assignments if I try. • If I succeed at my assignments, I also do well on other tests at school. • Teachers in my classes try different kinds of instruction to help all students learn. • We rarely waste time in class. • My teacher gives me quick feedback on assignments and tests. • My teachers let me explore my interests and new ideas. • Almost all of my assignments involve something I don't already know how to do.

TABLE 7.1 Continued

Student Climate	• My child feels that he or she belongs at this school.	• There is a sense of belonging for all students at this school.	• I feel like I belong at this school.
	• My child feels safe at school.	• Students feel safe in school.	• I feel safe at school.
	• The school and its teachers recognize students for positive achievement and good citizenship.	• The school and its teachers recognize students for positive achievement and good citizenship.	• Students in this school are recognized for positive achievement and good citizenship.
	• Adults treat my child fairly and with respect.	• Adults treat students fairly and with respect.	• Adults in school treat me fairly and with respect.
	• Teachers and administrators listen to and value my child's ideas.	• Teachers and administrators listen to and value student ideas.	• Teachers and administrators listen to and value my ideas.
	• The school has expectations for all students to work hard and learn.	• The school has expectations for all students to work hard and learn.	• The school has expectations for all students to work hard and learn.
Related Services	• When my child needs special help, the school finds a way to provide it.	• School administrators and service providers respond quickly and effectively when I ask for help with a student.	• I am able to get special help from specialists in the school when I need it.
Family and Community Partnership	• I almost always know what teachers expect of my child.	• I give all parents information on what I expect for learning, homework, and discipline.	• My parents know what teachers expect of me.
	• The school maintains regular communication with families.	• The school maintains regular communication with families.	• The school communicates regularly with my parents.
	• I am promptly notified of problems and accomplishments.	• Parents are promptly notified of their child's problems and accomplishments.	• My parents are promptly notified of problems and my accomplishments.
	• Teachers work with me to help my child succeed.	• I collaborate with parents to help students succeed.	• My teacher and parents work together to help me succeed.
	• The school schedule and activities respect differences in family lifestyles.	• The school is respectful of different family lifestyles.	• All families are welcomed throughout the school.
	• The school works with the community to get students the services they need.	• The school works with the community to get students the services they need.	• My school gets lots of community involvement in school activities.
	• The school helps the community communicate the importance of student effort and learning.	• The school helps the whole community communicate the importance of student effort and learning.	
	• The school is creative in its efforts to involve the community.	• The school is creative in its efforts to involve the community.	

TABLE 7.1 Continued

Resource Development	• Fundraising has a purpose based on the school's goals. • This school consistently looks for new partners and volunteers who add to the school's resources. • The school is good at recruiting new staff who share the school's goals and vision. • This school is creative in getting the funding and services it needs to meet its goals.	• Fundraising has a purpose based on the school's goals. • This school consistently looks for new partners and volunteers who add to the school's resources. • The school is good at recruiting new staff who share the school's goals and vision. • This school is creative in getting the funding and services it needs to meet its goals.	
Support for Operations	• My child's teachers have the knowledge and skills to do their jobs. • The schedule and calendar give adequate time for learning experiences. • In school my child has the instruction, materials, and resources that he or she needs in order to learn. • My child's teacher knows what he or she is expected to do. • The school makes creative use of time, money, and staff.	• My teaching assignments and duties utilize my knowledge and skills. • The school schedule and calendar give adequate time for learning experiences. • The school allocates its resources to give all students the instruction and materials they need in order to learn. • My work responsibilities are clearly defined. • The school makes creative use of its resources, including time, money, and staff.	• The class periods give me enough time for learning. • In school I have the instruction, materials, and resources that I need in order to learn.
Staff Support	• The parents and the school staff have similar ideas about what they want their school to be.	• Teachers, staff, and administrators in this school work as a team. • People in the school are willing to listen to the ideas and feelings of others even when they disagree. • This school celebrates its successes and progress. • The school encourages and supports continuing professional learning.	

TABLE 7.1 Continued

School Renewal	• There are established decision-making processes in this school, so it is clear by whom, when, and how decisions are made.	• There are established decision-making processes in this school, so it is clear by whom, when, and how decisions are made. • School goals and action plans reflect careful consideration of school and student-learning results. • Once school-improvement goals are set, they become an important focus for the work of faculty, administrators, and volunteers.	• This school has a clear sense of direction and purpose.

gaps become real, not just in relation to abstract success criteria, but in comparison to actual examples. Consequently, finding opportunity gaps on which most schools can act depends on concrete aspirations—examples, models, and stories of what is reasonably possible in similar circumstances.

By identifying opportunity gaps, school leaders select a few accomplishments that have realistic potential for improvement. In the third step of assessing accomplishments, school leaders ask whether making the improvements in selected accomplishments would be likely to have an impact on student learning. Of the opportunity gaps identified for a school, which ones—if closed—would have the greatest impact on student learning? For example, if school leaders believe that they are already very near the top of what could be expected on the accomplishment, "learning goals defined," they may see little payoff in a priority of continuing to invest in further improvement. At the same time, having a large opportunity gap in "student climate sustained" might point to greater potential for impact on student learning by closing that gap.

Of course, not all school accomplishments have the same impact on student learning, so the analysis is not as simple as working on the accomplishments with the greatest opportunity gaps. As many meta-analyses of educational research show, interventions in different areas of a school's functioning can have quite different levels of impact on student learning (Lipsey & Wilson, 1993; Scheerens & Bosker, 1997; Waters et al., 2003). In general, proximal variables—those more closely associated with instruction and learning—"exert more influence than distal variables on school learning" (Wang, Haertel, & Walberg, 1993, p. 271). Consequently, closing smaller opportunity gaps in accomplishments associated with learning goals, instruction, and student climate may have greater impact than closing larger opportunity gaps in other areas of the FSLA. At the same time, principals in most schools exert greater control over the distal variables, so the likelihood of making significant and lasting change may be larger in those accomplishments. Such choices depend fundamentally on analyses of the opportunity gaps in each school.

Define School Improvement Goals

Whatever assessment methods a principal uses to understand the school, the intended result is a set of goals for improvement. A considerable body of literature and advice examines the use of participatory processes in making sense of evaluation data and setting goals for improvement (Mohrman, Lawler, & Mohrman, 1992). Rather than repeating familiar information, we focus on two specific aspects of the accomplishment perspective that suggest changes in typical goal-setting processes.

The first is the way that the goals themselves are framed. Current practice varies widely. In some schools, one finds goals such as "improve reading achievement in third grade," with little more guidance than that teachers and students should try harder in this area. Other goals often are framed as programs to be adopted ("implement a particular mathematics program") or as resource requests ("hire additional paraprofessionals to support the early-morning transition from buses to the classroom"). Still others define school improvement goals with detailed action plans for an entire year.

The accomplishment perspective offers an alternative way to frame these annual priorities. Instead of focusing on student-learning outcomes, resources, or implementation of particular strategies, goal setting from this perspective involves selecting one or a few accomplishments for particular improvement. For example, a school-improvement goal might state: "Orange Middle School intends to improve the student climate, so that at least 80% of students perceive the school as both welcoming and focused on learning, an improvement of 30% over the current level. As a result of this improvement, we expect increases in student effort reported by teachers and students, and increases in learning in core subjects as measured by district-approved tests."

What is deliberately missing in such a goal statement is a list of the strategies or steps to be followed as the goal is pursued. Rather than a detailed action plan, such a goal statement serves as a challenge to the school to find effective ways to change student perceptions of the school's climate. This can provide the foundation for a collaborative action research effort over the entire year as alternative approaches are tried out, evaluated, and modified (Bellamy, Holly, & Sinisi, 1999). Consequently, specifying school goals as accomplishments supports a pragmatic approach to improvement that encourages ongoing experimentation and adaptation during the year.

The second distinctive aspect of an accomplishment perspective on school goals is simultaneous attention to the whole and the parts. Leading a school involves more than just focusing on what needs to be changed. It also involves sustaining all other aspects of the school so that they continue to operate as expected. An accomplishment model like the FSLA helps to make this point. Expected student outcomes depend on all the accomplishments in the Framework, just as all accomplishments can be important to sustaining the school conditions that a community values, and annual goals need to address each of these accomplishments. For some, the goal will be simply to sustain functioning at the current level of quality; for others, significant improvements will be targeted. Because different aspects of the school have particular importance to different constituent groups, defining comprehensive goals can facilitate communication with the school's communities. Framing goals in this way provides a more complete basis for translating those goals into reality, because it recognizes the continuing resources and attention needed for aspects of school that are not targeted for change.

To describe the result of a school's goal setting in accomplishment-minded practice, we have chosen the term "accomplishment agenda" rather than the more familiar "annual goals." Our intent is to emphasize the unique features of accomplishment-based goals and also to stimulate a new look at a process that, while critically important, has become so ritualized in many situations that it has little influence on school functioning. The analysis and goal setting are done perfunctorily and rarely revisited.

Structure the School for Comprehensiveness and Focus

Of course, implementing and sustaining strategic focus involve more than simply defining priorities. Priorities affect daily work as they are translated into the school's schedule, budget, staff design, and policies. A school's accomplishment agenda becomes meaningful as it influences the way that resources are used in the school.

The most important resource in schools is time—the time of teachers and students and the expectations associated with the allotted time. Consequently, a school's schedule is perhaps the single best indicator of its actual priorities: Which subjects, activities, and interests have priority in the assignment of teacher expertise, building resources, and student time? How much of the available time is allotted for which purposes? How does the time allocation differ across student groups or faculty members, and why do these differences occur? The schedule is supported by a pattern of teacher assignments (Which teachers are responsible for which students and subjects?), budget allocations (How much of the total budget is spent on instruction, support services, and other needs?), and facility use (Which activities have priority access to computers, library, and other shared resources?).

For example, the school schedule and supporting organizational decisions establish who is responsible for student learning in various subjects, how and when that responsibility is shared with others, whether time is available for collaboration, and how much time students spend on various subjects. The schedule reveals many underlying values in the school and community. Are teachers with the most experience and expertise, for example, assigned to students seeking to reach advanced levels of mastery or to those having difficulty with basic proficiency?

An accomplishment agenda helps reveal questions and make these structuring decisions—typically at the beginning of each school year—precisely because it is both focused and comprehensive. An accomplishment agenda identifies accomplishments that should be sustained at current levels as well as those that need additional attention. An effective allocation of resources enables both.

Structuring to achieve strategic focus also involves day-to-day choices. Once a schedule and budget are set, improving school accomplishments still requires ongoing mindfulness. Day-to-day events create threats to accomplishments that school leaders want to sustain as well as opportunities to improve accomplishments needing change. Identifying these threats and opportunities and sustaining the motivation to act on them require the attention of school leaders as well as ongoing conversations within the school community.

Sustaining strategic focus in the social context of school work depends on conversational leadership as well as effective structures. Just as principals lead community conversations to shape shared and sustainable purposes, the goals selected for attention in any given year require ongoing internal discussions in order to become a salient part of the school's collective effort.

Refine Strategic Focus in Response to Feedback

The strategic choices involved in establishing school goals always involve uncertainty—we simply do not know enough to predict whether any particular goal will be achievable or whether it will have the intended impact on student learning even if it is. Yet, unless such strategic choices are made, the goal of improving student achievement by itself is not enough to inform daily leadership. School leaders have far more than enough to do, and doing the wrong things—even doing them well—is unlikely to result in desired outcomes.

While uncertainties are a necessary element of leadership practice, continuing to live with the result of less-than-perfect initial priorities is not.

Adjustments in priorities can be made as long as timely feedback is available about whether changes in the accomplishments chosen for special attention are having their intended effects.

To understand how such feedback systems can work, we turn again to the illustration of the FSLA in Figure 3.1. Each of the 9 accomplishments influences student learning and adjusts to community values only when school constituents become engaged. This engagement is the voluntary action of school constituents—students, teachers, and family members—whose behavior the school needs to influence in order to reach its goals. When a school's accomplishments are achieved with high quality, these school constituents are more likely to choose to get engaged and make the effort needed to support teaching and learning. Consequently, periodically checking on the engagement of these groups can provide valuable feedback on whether the school's priorities and goals are having the intended effect.

For example, as Figure 3.1 suggests, the accomplishments, "learning goals defined," "instruction provided," "student climate sustained," "related services provided," and "family–community partnership sustained," are all intended to affect student learning by increasing and focusing on *student effort*. Thus, periodic measures of student effort can serve as a check on the effectiveness of a school's efforts across all of these accomplishments. Even informal measures can be helpful if they are regular and systematic. A principal might ask each teacher to rate each student at the beginning of each month on the following four-point scale:

1. No show—attendance issues
2. Shows up, but is "checked out"
3. Selectively engaged—some areas, not others
4. Consistently highly engaged

Ratings that use a simple scale like this can be used initially to create a "worry list" of students who need extra support to stay engaged. Changes in the pattern of ratings over time can help a school decide if its priorities actually are having the desired result. For example, if a school's primary goal for improving achievement is related to improving instruction, and if no change in student engagement can be discerned after a few months, it might well be time to review the reasoning that led to this goal. Perhaps other interventions are needed instead of or in addition to instructional improvement. One can imagine several strategies, including changing the school's schedule, intensifying contacts with the home, or strengthening personal relationships with teachers.

Similar informal checks are possible for other constituent engagement on which schools depend. The FSLA accomplishments that create the environment for teaching (resources mobilized, support for operations, staff support, and school renewal) all are intended to enhance staff effort and engagement. A principal might keep track of the impact of accomplishment goals in this area with a subjective rating of teachers' engagement levels:

3. Contagious enthusiasm
2. Solid citizen
1. Problem or concern

As before, changes over time in the number of teachers who the principal believes fit into each of these categories provide a quick check on whether accomplishment goals are having their intended results. Displaying changes over the course of a school year provides quick feedback about changes in these perceptions. If school goals to improve the schedule or staff support, for example, are not resulting in an increased number of teachers in the second or third category, this could signal a need to rethink the accomplishments that were selected for attention. Perhaps a focus on other accomplishments would have more impact.

SUMMARY

Principals provide leadership for strategic focus so that their schools attend to school trends that, when changed, have the most potential for improving results at any particular point in time. This requires simultaneous attention to a broad set of factors needed for successful operation and to areas needing improvement.

Broad and systemic leadership strategies to support learning gained recognition as qualitative studies of effective schools repeatedly emphasized the role of the principal in schools with particularly strong student learning (Bossert, Dwyer, Rowan, & Lee, 1982; Hallinger & McCary, 1990; Hill, 2002; Leithwood & Montgomery, 1986; Weber, 1997). In addition to supporting instruction directly, these models connect leadership to learning by emphasizing the principal's role in managing climate, developing the school's mission, creating conditions for teacher collaboration, establishing partnerships with the community, and so forth.

More focused priorities emerge as school leaders understand and respond to the particular needs and conditions of their schools. In each local situation, the principal is challenged to be a "master diagnostician" who understands what the school needs at any given time (Portin et al., 2003). Analysis techniques associated with the accomplishment perspective help sort out the complexity in school analysis by identifying several logical steps—assessing student learning, assessing accomplishments, and estimating opportunity for improvement and impact.

Next, school leaders structure their schools to accomplish both comprehensive and focused attention to the accomplishments that support student learning. The school's schedule, budget, and staff assignments combine with ongoing mindfulness of accomplishments and continuing conversations about school priorities to create structures and cultures that support the needed school focus.

Even the most sophisticated assessment and organization involve judgments, so continuing feedback provides additional means of sustaining strategic focus. By monitoring how a school's actions affect the effort and engagement of students, teachers, and family members, school leaders can generate feedback on their goals and priorities and establish opportunities for ongoing refinements in the school's strategic focus.

Chapter 8

Leadership for Effective Action

Leadership for effective action is a domain that fits easily with the experience of most principals. Daily life in the principalship is a matter of responding to fast-arising problems (Leithwood & Steinbach, 1995; Martin & Willower, 1981; Wolcott, 1978). Some of these problems have routine technical solutions, but most are the surface layers of much larger issues of community values, school goals, and improvement strategies.

In accomplishment-minded practice, solutions to these daily problems are not ends in themselves; instead, these problems and their solutions help principals realize school accomplishments. That is, problems serve as purposeful vehicles to improve the school conditions through which a school supports student learning and responds to community values.

Similar ideas are present in many views of school leadership. Hallinger and McCary (1990) speak of problem solving in the context of particular strategic priorities, while Spillane, Halverson, and Diamond (2001) see problems and their solutions as contributing to more general "leadership functions." Considerable practical advice for managers makes the same point that effective action involves more than simply removing problems: "Don't get captured by your in-box." "It's hard to remember that your purpose is to drain the swamp when you are up to your neck in alligators."

Consequently, problem solving is seldom simply about removing an unwanted disturbance in normal school operations, and the approach to a solution signals both the accomplishment area of the problem and the importance of the solution to accomplishment realization. Thus an accomplishment-minded principal approaches problems as opportunities to enact a particular improvement strategy, enhance the school's status on particular accomplishments, or engage the community in discussions of values underlying what is expected of schools. Such a principal needs not only to be a good daily problem processor, but also to approach solutions in ways that are mindful of the community's values and expectations for schools, the school's goals for learning, and the accomplishments through which school purposes can be achieved.

The leadership domain of effective action is where other aspects of leadership find their most visible expression—the problems a principal chooses to address and the way that these problems are handled. Whatever values a principal attempts to actualize in the school, and whatever goals frame the school's agenda for improvement, a principal's leadership is, in the end, expressed in what actually is done day to day. Leadership in this domain is supported and improved by skillful attention to issues of sustainable purposes and strategic focus, as described in Chapters 6 and 7. Without effective action, however, these other leadership domains, no matter how well developed, have little effect.

HOW LEADERSHIP FOR EFFECTIVE ACTION
SUPPORTS STUDENT LEARNING

By selecting and responding to daily problems, principals seek to sustain or improve the conditions in their schools. Improved school conditions—the quality of the school's accomplishments—affect the amount and focus of effort from the teacher, student, and family. This effort, in turn, can affect student learning. Improved school conditions also can increase the fit between the school's operation and the aspects of schooling that the community values, further enhancing resources and support for the school.

Our problem-oriented view of effective action in school leadership requires some clarification, because it depends on a very specific idea about what constitutes a "problem." In normal usage, problems are either questions or situations that invite solutions. When someone says, "I have a problem," we infer that he or she wants to find a different way of understanding or responding to some situation that presents difficulty. This commonsense definition of problems also rings true for much of what principals experience. Staff members stop by and ask, "Have you got 5 minutes?" Usually, these words mean that the principal will be asked to do something about a situation involving that individual, in short, to solve her or his problem.

A more inclusive definition of "problems" is needed, however, to account for the full range of daily actions through which a principal exerts day-to-day leadership. Not all situations that a principal chooses to respond to would be considered problems by others. The view of problems that underlies our discussion is therefore somewhat different from typical understandings.

Situations constantly arise and change in schools. Some students arrive on time and ready each day; others are tardy, absent, or possibly distraught. Staff members are fully engaged, preoccupied by problems at home, struggling to understand a new program, or engaged in romantic connections with each other. Some family members are engaged to the point of extreme advocacy for their children, while others are absent. The building itself has some repair needs, is in a particular state of cleanliness, and so on. These many situations constantly change as members of the larger school community interact with one another and with educational tasks.

As this panorama of situations unfolds, discrepancies emerge between how the principal perceives the current situation and what he or she believes is desirable. Others may or may not see the same discrepancies, and often they might be quite satisfied with circumstances as they are. In other cases, the principal might not see a discrepancy between a current situation and a desired state, but others in the school do, and bring their "problem" to the principal to address. In this sense, the problems that a principal addresses through day-to-day action are "created" by the way that people perceive the situations that they encounter in a school.

STRATEGIES SUPPORTING EFFECTIVE ACTION

Viewing problems as discrepancies that the principal sees between current and desired situations focuses attention on three critical parts of leadership for effective action: (1) the situations considered problems worthy of attention and action; (2) the "solutions" that address the perceived gap between the actual and desired situations; and (3) the actions that the principal uses to influence the situation toward the desired state. Each is described below.

Select Problems for Attention

Literally thousands of situations arise in a school each day. A principal has only so much time and can respond to only a tiny fraction of these situations. As a result, finding and responding to those situations that represent the school's most important problems is key to effective action (Getzels, 1979, 1985; Immegart & Boyd, 1979).

Literature on problem selection offers several suggestions for principals seeking to select the right problems.

- Continually and systematically scan the entire school environment to identify potential issues and opportunities (Argyris et al., 1985; Etzioni, 1967, 1968; Immegart & Boyd, 1979; Martinelli & Muth, 1989).
- Be aware of operational details such as the day-to-day work of teaching, learning, schedule implementation, and behavior support. Operational awareness helps identify potential problems early, while they are still manageable, and supports timely interventions (Weick & Sutcliffe, 2001).

- Use well-developed conceptual frameworks that describe how a school achieves its goals (Hills & Gibson, 1992). Without a conceptual model for organizing information about the school and its local context and a sufficient model—one that is used consciously, explicitly, and systematically—problem identification is hit or miss. The Framework for School Leadership Accomplishments (FSLA) and many other frameworks (Knapp & McLaughlin, 2003; Portin et al., 2003) can be used to help in problem finding by highlighting particular situations and circumstances that are believed to have special importance in the school's efforts to reach its goals. For example, a principal using the conceptual framework offered by Knapp and McLaughlin might be most sensitive to school conditions that enabled or prevented professional and organizational learning, since these are highlighted in their framework as critical to enhancing student learning. Alternatively, a principal using the FSLA as a guide in scanning for school problems might be more attentive to situations affecting the efforts of professionals, families, and students, as the accomplishments in this conceptual framework are intended as supports for the ongoing efforts associated with teaching and learning.
- Supplement personal observation with more systematic monitoring of key school conditions. It is simply impossible for a principal to attend to everything. Principals need measures that help them "troubleshoot," by pointing to areas where further attention might be helpful. For example, we suggested in the previous chapter that regular subjective measures of student, professional, and family effort might help a principal evaluate the school's strategic focus. The same measures help with troubleshooting. They point to areas where a principal might look more closely for situations that seem problematic and require attention.

Whatever strategies are used, a principal's problem finding is ultimately an effort to select from the many situations that arise each day, those for which a leadership intervention might have the greatest leverage for student learning and the school conditions that improve student learning and support community values.

Selecting problems for attention is much like first learning about whitewater rafting. A raft's momentum downstream is affected by many simultaneous forces—the speed and direction of the current, the location of rocks and other obstructions, the depth of the river at any given point, the location of bends and eddies, and so on. A skilled rafter notices each of these situations as they appear and allows many of them to influence the momentum of the raft without intervention. Other situations, however, require action, perhaps to avoid a hazard, change course and find swifter current, or

simply get closer to an interesting view. While novices often flail about trying to respond to every situation as it appears, experienced rafters skillfully
select those situations that require a response, simply keeping a watchful eye
on those that sustain the raft's desired speed and direction.

Schools are similar in many ways. Countless situations arise each day as
teachers, students, and staff interact with one another, as families contact
the school, and as the facility itself is operated. Most of these situations are
part of desired school operations. They give the school momentum by encouraging similar situations and interactions in the future. Other situations
reflect danger—a child falling behind, strained relationships that could affect teachers working together, or a behavior that is unsafe. Still others offer
opportunities to make improvements in what might develop through the
momentum of existing situations. In this dynamic and constantly changing
environment, selecting where to intervene is the first step in leadership for
effective action.

Frame Desired Solutions

Once a situation is selected as problematic and worthy of the principal's
attention, the next step is to decide on a desired solution. That is, what different situation would the principal like to see after intervening? Deciding
on a solution to selected problems is an opportunity to think systematically
about the changes in current situations that could foster improvements in
the school's accomplishments. For example, a principal decides to respond
personally to a situation of playground bullying. The desired solution might
be a stronger focus on rules of conduct, with a resulting intervention that
focuses on enforcement and power-oriented confrontations with the student
and, possibly, his family as well. Alternatively, the desired situation might
focus on enhanced learning opportunities for students who have difficulty
with social behavior, resulting in an intervention that focuses more on the
development of self-control strategies for the individual student.

Robinson (1996, 1998) describes the process of defining acceptable solutions as one of defining "constraint sets" for the problem. A constraint set
is the list of requirements that must be satisfied for the problem to be considered solved. For example, a principal who has to intervene in a classroom
of struggling students might develop the following constraint set for an
intervention:

- The students will spend more time on academic tasks during the school
  day.
- Curriculum adaptations will be carefully tailored to individual performance levels.

- The teacher will ask for assistance from other teachers when selected approaches are not working.
- The intervention will not negatively affect the positive working relationship between teachers at this grade level.
- The affected teacher will believe that he or she has the support needed to make adjustments.

On a different scale, the process of defining solution constraints is much like the definition of success criteria for school accomplishments discussed in Chapters 3 and 6. Success criteria for school accomplishments describe the desired features of the primary conditions (accomplishments) through which the school supports student learning and responds to community values. These success criteria reflect the values and priorities about what students should learn and how schools need to function as defined by laws, policies, and informal local advocacy. They also include information from research and theory about what kinds of school conditions actually work to achieve the desired results.

Similarly, solution constraints for daily problems reflect a mixture of values, priorities, and leadership strategies. In the accomplishment-minded approach that we recommend, solution constraints for daily problems reflect the success criteria for the accomplishments that a principal hopes to improve: If attention to a playground bully is intended to improve student climate, then the desired type of climate has much to do with how the individual problem is addressed. In a school whose success criteria for student climate emphasize order and safety, the solution constraints for the bullying problem could be quite different than in a school with success criteria for student climate centered on student self-direction.

The process of deciding what solution constraints are important gives principals the opportunity to link daily problem solving with conditions that the community expects in its schools, the school improvement goals, the success criteria for the school's accomplishments, and the principal's theory of action about how to influence school conditions and student learning.

Although often implicit, solution constraints are excellent windows on the values, goals, and strategies that are actually in use in a particular school. As Robinson (1998) suggests, the solution constraints that actually guide problem solving in a school show how the school balances competing goals such as student learning, orderly environments, schedule convenience, staff social coherence, family contacts, safe facilities, and so forth. Critical reflection on the solution constraints that appear to be in use as a school solves its problems can help to identify underlying patterns of privilege, differential treatment of different groups, and implicit norms about teachers' responsibilities in the school.

The challenge for the accomplishment-minded principal, of course, is to do this critical reflection prospectively by framing solution constraints as problems are identified. Discussions about what would constitute an acceptable solution to school problems can provide the context for engaging students, staff, and families in core issues related to the school's values, goals, and strategies.

Take Action

The third critical part of leadership for effective action is the action itself. Unless the principal does something, one reasonably can expect the momentum of the existing situation to continue the school's direction. To change this momentum, the principal must act—have a conversation, develop a policy, provide support for an activity, convene a meeting where an issue can be discussed, provide reassurance, personally clean up a messy school entrance, call a student's family member, or provide feedback on someone's performance.

Despite an enormous amount of advice on how to respond to various problems, principals have little assurance that their actions will have the intended results. The knowledge base for leading organizations is rich with possibilities but contains no prescriptions. And even when the principal's actions do produce the desired results, unexpected consequences still can arise in other areas. A principal might believe it prudent to handle a problem of student behavior in a way that promotes optimal learning and reengages the family in supporting the school, only to find that several teachers are upset at what they see as lack of support for their disciplinary efforts. And, to complicate the principal's uncertainties even more, it is impossible to know for sure if the problem selected and its solution constraints are ones that actually can improve conditions in the school.

What makes effective leadership possible with such uncertainties is continual adjustment to the school's changing conditions. With constant attention to the situation and how it is affected by actions taken, leaders often have opportunities to try one approach, see its results, modify or discard it, and try again. Sometimes failures are best avoided by repeated cycles of trial, feedback, correction, and re-trial, rather than by concentrating on having exactly the right solution to each problem on the first attempt. Leading schools is a cumulative, long-term process. Time is usually available for iterative improvements, as long as school leaders have information about the panoply of possibilities.

Two things make this pragmatic and iterative approach to effective action possible: lots of information and a substantial repertoire of possible strategies. Information comes from constant environmental scanning, mindfulness, and more formal feedback mechanisms. Continual adjustments lead to improvements when they build on information about previous results.

A deep repertoire of action strategies allows a principal to adjust as needed when a particular approach doesn't work or is not accepted for any reason. The knowledge supporting leadership for effective action is *procedural* in the sense that it offers a menu of alternative action strategies for addressing various school problems. Some of these action strategies include how a principal can act directly to solve a problem—for example, by speaking directly with a disruptive student or concerned family—while other strategies involve knowledge of organizational structure and culture that support interventions in these arenas.

A SPECIAL FOCUS ON TEACHING AND LEARNING

In the effort to connect school leadership to student learning, an obvious starting point is the principal's direct involvement in issues of teaching and learning. As a principal scans the school for potential problems that offer opportunities for improvement, it is reasonable to look carefully at the school's instructional efforts. Along with many other recent authors, Elmore (2000) firmly argues that principal leadership in today's standards-based environments should focus on improvement of instruction, rather than on the school conditions surrounding instruction.

Instruction is the aspect of the school that is most under pressure to change. With new policy requirements linked to assessment and accountability for year-by-year learning, familiar responses to situations that arise might not always be sufficient. And, when the principal attends to school conditions associated with teaching and learning, there is potential for increasing leverage for learning results. Research shows that interventions in these areas can have greater influence on student learning than more attention to other aspects of the school (Wang et al., 1993).

The importance of direct leadership for instruction is apparent in the FSLA, where learning goals and instruction are presented as key accomplishments. Their placement adjacent to student effort and learning in Figure 3.1 signifies their capacity to directly influence students, and their function as pathways through which many other school accomplishments influence student effort and learning. Consequently, while the FSLA argues for a systemic view of how a school influences teaching and learning, it also emphasizes the importance of attention to curriculum, instruction, and climate issues that most directly affect learning.

The difficulties that principals encounter as they focus on instruction are well documented. Instructional leadership is made complex by the micropolitical difficulties that principals encounter in direct supervision of instruction (Blase, 1989) and by competing responsibilities that limit available time for instructional leadership (Osborne & Wiggins, 1989).

Few schools are really organized to influence teaching. Both traditional evaluations of teaching and teachers' relations with one another reinforce teaching as individual work based on personal expertise (Little, 1988, 1990). And while the most specific recommendations for instructional leadership imply particular models of instruction (Hunter, 1976; Popham, 1987; West & Staub, 2003), research indicates that quite varied instructional approaches can produce equally high levels of learning (Clarke, Davis, Rhodes, & Delott-Baker, 1996; Jesse, Davis, & Pokorney, 2004). It is therefore not surprising that, despite long-standing advocacy for principals to assume instructional leadership roles (Bossert et al., 1982; Greenfield, 1987), studies of how school leaders actually spend their time demonstrate that few principals spend much time in direct support of teaching and learning (Murphy, 1990; Public School Forum of North Carolina, 1987).

Recommendations for *how* principals focus on instruction in this complex milieu are important, for they suggest which problems merit attention and what kinds of actions might have the greatest leverage for teaching and learning. Recommendations cover how and what to observe in classrooms (Holland, 1998), how to talk with teachers about instruction (Blase & Blase, 1999; Glickman, 1985), how to engage teachers in supporting one another's work by distributing leadership for instruction (Elmore, 2000; Gronn, 2002), and how to support teachers' continuing learning about instruction (Hoy & Hoy, 2003).

One interesting area of possible principal attention and action related to student learning is suggested by the increasing expectation that all students and student groups will make sufficient year-to-year progress on state tests. To meet this expectation, schools have to function with higher reliability, that is, become more adept at avoiding student failure (Bellamy et al., 2005). The challenge is somewhat similar to that in many organizations where the public expects fail-safe performance—for example, air traffic control, dangerous chemical manufacturing, electrical power grids—and these "high-reliability" organizations offer an interesting perspective on how school leaders might support teaching and learning as the public expects increasingly greater reliability in student test scores.

While high-reliability organizations are different from schools in many ways, Bellamy and colleagues (2005) suggest two commonalities: To avoid failures, schools and these organizations need to detect problems in the early stages, before they develop into full-fledged failures, and they need to change approaches when these problems are identified. For example, much of today's aircraft-landing process is highly automated and controlled through standard landing patterns. Yet, when detecting a potential problem, a pilot can override these procedures and take manual control of the landing. Similar response alternatives are available when unexpected events arise, for example, in hospital operating rooms and on the landing decks of military aircraft carriers. In schools, however, students gradually can fall further and further behind their peers when instruction does not fit with their past experiences, learning styles, or interests. If undetected, these problems can emerge over time as full-fledged failures.

Thus, the lesson from high-reliability organizations is twofold. First, schools need the capacity to identify learning problems early, before they become failures. Individual teachers usually know this. The school-wide issue is how teachers can make the information public when help is needed. Does the school have a culture in which early identification of learning difficulties is okay, or one in which such early identification could be considered by peers and administrators as evidence of poor performance? Second, the school needs the capacity to provide different instructional experiences to those who are identified as having difficulty. Does the school environment support continual adaptation, or is it wed to a single instructional model?

Leadership strategies to respond to these two problems are not unknown, but neither are they commonly used. For example, establishing structures in which groups of teachers review samples of work from struggling students can create a safe environment for teachers to share such information, while at the same time generating new strategies for intervention by bringing the experience of several teachers to the task (Blythe, Allen, & Powell, 1999).

SUMMARY

Leadership for effective action supports student learning by influencing the constantly changing course of events in the school. By selecting and responding to particular circumstances that seem problematic, the principal seeks to improve school conditions in ways that support professional, family, and student effort and enhance student learning.

Leading for effective action involves selecting from the thousands of situations that arise in a school each day, the ones that offer promising opportunities to protect or improve the school's accomplishments. Selecting the most important problems requires constant mindfulness of the school's operations and systematic use of conceptual frameworks that help identify significant events.

Once problems are selected for attention, the leader's task is to frame a set of solution constraints, a set of conditions that should be satisfied by a successful response to the problem. These solution constraints reflect the success criteria for the accomplishments that the principal hopes to sustain or improve through the problem solution, as well as the school goals and community values that underlie those success criteria. Finally, the principal acts to address the selected problems, with each action typically involving a series of adjustments as initial efforts are tried and their results observed.

The FSLA offers a framework for thinking broadly and systemically about the problems that can affect student learning. At the same time, instruction occupies a central place in the framework, illustrating that much of a principal's problem selection will directly address issues of teaching and learning. One way to enhance the effectiveness of any of the available instructional support strategies is for school leaders to focus on the school's ability to detect learning problems quickly and to respond with strategies different from those used when the problems emerged.

Chapter 9

Leadership for Social Capital

This chapter shows how principals can foster the development of social capital and, through that effort, increase the effectiveness of their schools and the success of their students. In Chapter 5, we reasoned that social capital—the relationships, norms, trust, and leadership that exist in a school's communities —affects whether a school can realize important accomplishments and reach goals for student learning and school conditions. Because schools and their communities contain many overlapping social networks, the relationships among members of various groups and the norms that affect how they act with one another underlie the school's ability to share information, reach collaborative agreements on school goals, come together around strategic priorities, and work collaboratively toward those priorities and goals. In this chapter, we explore how principals can provide leadership to develop the interpersonal and intergroup relationships critical to all aspects of school work and school leadership.

The social capital needed for school success is shaped by relationships inside the school as well as powerful factors that lie beyond the school's doors. Within the school, norms about the school's work as well as relationships among teachers, administrators, and students affect the extent and quality of social capital. Outside the school, the presence of overlapping community institutions that engage teachers, students, and families; the homogeneity and stability of the community; and the community's history of collaboration on other issues can all affect a school's social capital.

Because these internal and external networks are critical to the school's success, a principal's effectiveness often depends on the ability to strengthen and influence the social capital in the school's community. As important as such efforts are, they are also quite challenging, for two reasons. First, good and bad news lies in the fact that social capital is very stable, regardless of its quality, and very difficult to change quickly. Thus if a school is blessed with positive social capital among its staff, students, parents, and larger community, it is likely to stay that way. Social-capital theorists tend to say that social capital is "self-reinforcing." On the flip side, the bad news is that, if a school has a social-capital deficit, it also is in a stable state that will be difficult to improve. In low-performing schools, the stability of a school's social capital presents a dual challenge. The norms, networks, and trust needed for social capital resist change. In addition, stable social capital also helps to clarify why structural reforms have had such mixed results. For instance, structural changes such as team teaching, open school design, differentiated staffing, and integrated units have all succeeded in some schools, but gradually disappeared in many others where norms and relationships among teachers did not also change. Norms and traditions can undermine structural reforms quickly.

Second, at its center, social capital is about cooperation for mutual benefit and civic engagement (Coleman, 1988; Putnam, 1993). At first glance, some would assume that school staff would demonstrate high levels of cooperation and trust; therefore, they would have high levels of social capital. However, as others have pointed out, schools have structures and norms that discourage productive cooperation, trust, and engagement. The "egg crate" organization of the school reinforces the norm of privacy, for instance. The norm of civility, the agreement among teachers that they will not make or dispense judgments about one another publicly, discourages serious critical dialog among staff about teaching, discipline, and school organization (House, 1998; Malen, Murphy, & Hart, 1987). Bureaucratic traditions in school systems and schools make it difficult to build dense, horizontal connections and active civic participation (Putnam, 1993). And the "uncertain technology" of teaching reinforces isolation, thus reducing cooperation and encouraging privacy (Lortie, 1975). In short, under the surface many schools are places of distrust, lack of cooperation, and low civic-mindedness (cf. Putnam, 2000). We will offer some suggestions to remedy these situations, but school leaders must recognize that healthy social capital cannot be built "instantaneously or *en masse*" (Putnam & Feldstein, 2003, p. 9).

HOW SOCIAL CAPITAL SUPPORTS STUDENT LEARNING

Social capital influences student learning directly and indirectly. Direct influences occur as students see and respond to a set of norms that support school goals: a clear and coherent school focus on learning, rational consistency in the expectations between home and school, persistent oversight from community members who know the students individually, and abundant information available from school and community members who share their expertise.

Social capital indirectly influences student achievement as it supports a school's collaborative work in each of the leadership domains previously discussed. In the domain of leadership for sustainable goals, for example, natural conflicts emerge among the interests of various groups in all school communities. Social connections among groups can help ameliorate differences between the mutually supported goals for student learning and school conditions, and the ongoing competition among groups expressed through conflicting pressures constantly applied to school leaders. Insofar as student learning appears related to the coherence of messages and priorities in the school (Jesse et al., 2004), the potential exists for significant impact on learning when collaborative relationships are strong.

Collaboration across individuals and groups also is needed as a school defines a theory of action about how to reach goals—what to emphasize at any given time. Again, different interpretations of problems and varying interests lead naturally to alternative formulations of what the school should emphasize in its structures, policies, and priorities. The capacity to discuss these alternatives and reach agreement is central to the kinds of collaboration and collective action that are related to both teacher and student learning (Bossert, 1988; McLaughlin, 1993).

Social capital also influences student learning by strengthening the daily work of instruction and school operations. When social capital is strong, teachers share information, plan collaboratively, and take time to talk to colleagues about their concerns. When this happens, students benefit from the collective knowledge of the school staff, rather than depending solely on one teacher's expertise (Louis et al., 1996).

Leadership for social capital is an important aspect of every principal's job because it emerges from the particular social context of each school and community. This creates unique leadership challenges for school principals as they strive to foster communication and trust across all communities affected by the school and to influence the norms that support collaboration in all aspects of the school's work.

Finally, schools support student learning when they develop ways to influence the development of social capital in and among families. Child development and learning improve in families having strong social capital, and these outcomes are reinforced in communities with dense connections across families (Coleman, 1988; Putnam, 1993).

STRATEGIES FOR IMPROVING SOCIAL CAPITAL

Principals foster social capital through their social interactions with members of the school community and by creating conditions that foster relationships among these individuals and with the principal. Such interactions create opportunities to strengthen commitment to school goals and norms, increase connections among staff and community members, and share information across groups. Social capital is developed mostly through the principal's "face-to-face" interactions with individuals and small groups (Putnam & Feldstein, 2003). This "people work" is complex because schools operate at the intersection of many strongly held views about children and their education, teachers and their roles, and families and their prerogatives. It is complex also because no one person can lead or participate in all the important conversations. By necessity, leadership in this domain is shared among many.

Although leadership can be a social-capital asset, as we argued in Chapter 5, research on social capital shows that vertical social relations (as in bureaucratic institutions) are relatively ineffective in building social capital (Coleman, 1990). In fact, vertical structures may lead to distrust, lack of cooperation, and little civic engagement. More successful are horizontal relationships among relative equals, or social relationships with equity. This does not mean that principals must be "one of the gang," but that overall leadership must be shared and validated by the group (Smylie & Hart, 1999, p. 436).

Seven strategies form the core of a leader's work in this domain. Principals must (1) understand the school's evolving social context well enough to respond in adaptive ways, (2) steward the norms that underlie the school's collective actions, (3) strengthen connections among people in the school through frequent and purposeful conversations, (4) establish a work structure that supports dense interactions among groups, (5) stress democratic modeling in the school, (6) help families build social capital, and (7) connect constructively to the surrounding communities.

Understand Current Social Conditions

Our first recommendation for principal leadership for social capital is perhaps obvious, but nevertheless deserves note. Such leadership depends on appreciation of the current social capital in the school and its communities, because quite different leadership strategies are likely to be useful under different conditions. Early recommendations from effective schools studies recommended "vigorous selection and replacement" of teachers as an important leadership strategy (Levine & Lezotte, 1990), while recommendations for enhancing social capital include emphasis on maintaining stability in the school's staff (Evans, 1996; Smylie & Hart, 1999). As experience suggests, both approaches can be useful, depending on the current state of the school's social capital. Similarly, the social capital in a school's communities may be adequate to support collaborative work and progress in some aspects of the school's work, but not in others. Understanding these differences, then, can help the principal target leadership strategies more effectively.

Appreciate the Context for Collaboration. Chrislip (2002) frames this need for careful diagnosis as a matter of appreciating the "context for collaboration" and suggests two broad issues for consideration: the range of viewpoints on critical issues and the political dynamics among the various affected groups. A useful approach to organizing information about various viewpoints comes from the typology of school norms suggested by Firestone and Louis (1999): beliefs about students and how they should be treated, academics and their importance, and how teachers should relate to one another. The degree of agreement about these three issues, plus beliefs about broader school goals for student learning and school conditions (Chapter 2), underlie important norms for collaboration.

Chrislip's (2002) second issue relates to political dynamics. Here the focus of a principal's effort to understand a school's social capital centers on the degree of conflict among groups, the extent to which various groups are motivated to change, the extent to which "relationships among unlikely parties" (p. 34) already exist, and whether other conflicts unrelated to the school might impede agreement. In this regard, Putnam (2000) describes two types of social capital: bonding and bridging. Bonding social capital describes instances when like individuals link together (the "superglue" in networks). Bridging social capital, on the other hand, involves networks of dissimilar individuals. Putnam calls this the "WD-40" of networking. That is, bridging networks have more diversity and thus more potential for conflict and more problems with long-term mutual cooperation. They have more potential to fragment and for individual and group defections. It is harder to develop norms and effective sanctions in bridging networks like, for instance, PTAs. Nevertheless, in Putnam's view these networks are more important as they bring unlike parties together into social relations that can make important contributions to civic society.

To understand these aspects of a school's community, a principal needs to be sensitive to the emotional and political crosscurrents in the school. This, in turn, depends on emotional intelligence—empathy with others, awareness of the social conditions within a school, self-awareness, and an ability to manage one's own emotions in productive and effective ways as information is solicited (Goleman, Boyatzis, & McKee, 2002).

Take Advantage of Start-of-Year Opportunities. The beginning of each school year is a particularly important time for principals to focus on understanding the social capital on which they depend. The start of school brings new teachers, students, and parents to the community, along with the possibility of different goals and expected norms. And as experienced principals know, much can happen in the relationships among teachers over the summer as social relations are initiated or terminated, competing personal commitments emerge, or new skills are developed. Although the beginning of the year is busy in many different ways, it is a critical time for listening to staff and families and understanding how the community has changed. Many new principals appointed early enough in the year rely on individual interviews with teachers and community leaders during the summer to gain the same information.

Steward School Norms

The norms of a school community are the values and assumptions that guide how it works day-to-day toward its mission and goals. Norms constitute an important foundation in a school's social capital, because they reflect shared meanings and undergird mutual trust. For example, the norm, "we will collaborate with each other to improve our instruction," implies a view about both teacher and student learning; it also helps teachers know what to expect from one another when they describe a difficult teaching situation or ask for help.

As considerable literature on school culture indicates, the norms that guide actions and relationships in a school are often unstated, taken-for-granted ways of doing things that have emerged over many years of practical experience in a particular school and community. Regardless of what is said about collaboration, teachers and others in the school learn over time what seems to work best. In one situation, the norm might be simply being quiet about difficulties to avoid special attention and intervention in one's classroom. In another, attributing learning difficulties to student and home characteristics might be a reliable way to get emotional support from others. And in other instances, discussing instructional approaches with colleagues might have proven to be an effective strategy.

Principals improve this aspect of their schools' social capital by influencing what the norms are, how widely they are shared, and whether they are trusted. Working toward trustworthy norms is as difficult as it is important. Misunderstandings about the norms themselves, and about others' behavior in relation to norms, seem inevitable for several reasons. First, school norms always exhibit some ambiguity because the professed values may not be consistent with implicit values that have developed over time in the school. As a result, different individuals and groups may have different understandings of what is expected. Second, different groups in the school have different interests that compete with school norms and views about education that often are strongly held. Consequently, some individuals may respond in ways that reflect their own agendas, rather than the collective expectations. Further, limited time during the school day for adults to talk with one another and with families complicates the development of shared understanding. Without conversation, it is difficult to check one's interpretation of another's behavior and to understand how it might fit with school norms. Finally, norms in schools are necessarily complex because different patterns of working together may be needed in different circumstances: The more complex the norms, the greater the potential for confusion.

Articulate Desired Norms. While no prescriptions exist for overcoming these difficulties, collaborative development of a set of desired norms can be a useful starting place for principal leadership. For example, DuFour and Eaker (1998) recommend that a principal establish small work groups to frame statements for discussion, with the provision that the statements specify how the school will work toward its mission, be few in number, focus on behavior rather than beliefs, focus on actions that the school's staff will take, and be direct about what is expected. Such a statement, they suggest, might say that "we will model the life-long learning and commitment to high-quality work that we hope to develop in our students," or that we will "collaborate with one another and our students so that we can achieve our collective goals more effectively" (pp. 90–91).

As difficult as such recommended norms are to achieve, current expectations that practically every child will succeed every year on state tests may require even more challenging changes in the norms that underlie teacher collaboration. In their review of the potential lessons that might be drawn from other organizations that are expected to work with such high reliability, Bellamy and colleagues (2005) note that when problems arise, these organizations shift rapidly from one mode of operation to another. They surmise that these "fail-safe conditions" will be possible only in schools with supportive cultural assumptions that handle the paradoxes that are involved. Simultaneous beliefs in both teacher autonomy and collaboration may be needed. Normal school operations depend on teachers working somewhat separately simply because of the sheer volume of teacher–student interactions that are involved in teaching and learning. At the same time, collaboration among teachers is needed to respond quickly to any learning difficulty that arises. When a teacher sees that a child is falling behind, the opportunity to discuss possible strategies with others, engage in collective inquiry, or actually share instructional tasks can make the difference between failure and successful recovery. Examples of these more complex norms that may be needed to support highly reliable learning are provided in Table 9.1, organized around the typology suggested by Firestone and Louis (1999).

Norms that are this complex require extensive communication and may not be possible to achieve without dense social connections. They also require mutual trust among teachers, administrators, and families, because the potential for misunderstandings and unexpected responses increases as norms become more complex.

TABLE 9.1. Sample Statements of School Norms

Sample norms about teachers' work and how teachers should relate to one another	• We depend on one another to work independently and effectively in our classrooms, but we learn from one another and can improve our effectiveness with assistance from others. Consequently, we ask for and provide assistance as often as needed. • We each take full responsibility for our students' learning. At the same time, we will honor every teacher's request for help when a student is falling behind, as a service to both the student and the school community.
Sample norms about academics and their importance	• We select, design, and commit to programs that we believe will be the most effective in teaching academic skills, but we know that no program works with everyone. Consequently, we will be vigilant and shift to alternative programs as soon as they are needed for any single student to progress. • Subjects that are tested by the state were selected through legitimate political processes. We support these decisions, but we will do more for our students in order to prepare them for life, civic participation, and work.
Sample norms about students and how to deal with them	• Students are responsible for their own learning, but this does not diminish teachers' responsibility for learning outcomes. • Falling behind sometimes is inevitable; failing is not. When any student starts falling behind, we immediately do something different and continue our special efforts until the problem is solved.

Of course, development of any list of *desired* school norms is only the beginning. Defining desired norms through a collaborative process can indeed develop shared meaning, but the values that are espoused in these statements may have little relationship to the implicit norms that actually guide behavior in the school. Ongoing stewardship is necessary before such a list of values actually provides guidance for behavior and a new foundation for mutual trust.

Shape the Norms in Use. We have noted earlier that norms are usually very stable and self-reinforcing when accompanied by effective sanctions. For instance, if a new teacher enters a school where the norms about student discipline favor a tough attitude and external controls, and the teacher favors an approach using a more inner-directed discipline system, that teacher has really only three options: switch to an externally directive approach and be tough; talk tough in public, but continue with the inner-directed approach in the classroom; or leave. The normative set, and the risk of being ostracized for violating it, are frequently too strong for a teacher, particularly a new one, to oppose. In contrast, a new teacher who believed in being tough with students would face the same dilemma if he or she joined the staff of a school where the norm was inner directedness.

Responding to these dilemmas, Schein (1992) suggests an approach to ongoing stewardship for school norms, observing that norms and values often begin as hypotheses that are tested in an organization's work and gradually become accepted as they are found to work. Following this reasoning, a principal who is actively engaged in day-to-day issues of teaching and learning might suggest that the school's stated norms be tried out as various problems arise. For example, when a child is observed as having difficulty in a teacher's lesson, a principal might establish a context for discussion with other teachers and provide input, if needed, to make the exchange of information positive and supportive. Repeated experiences where the school's espoused norms actually work to solve problems, strengthen and solidify the norms as part of the school's culture. "Values develop as problems are solved. When a solution to a problem works reliably, it becomes invested with special significance. It comes to be seen as 'the way we do it'" (Evans, 1996, pp. 42–43).

A second approach follows recommendations offered by Heifetz (1994), who says that leadership involves helping a community deal with conflicts and contradictions among its values or discrepancies between its values and reality. In this context, a principal's challenge is to frame and lead conversations about whether what actually is done in the school is consistent with espoused norms and to challenge members of the school community to address the discrepancies.

Third, a principal can strengthen norms through effective use of the authority vested in the office. This might involve, for example, ensuring that the school norms are central in selection criteria for new staff, staff evaluations, selection of professional development opportunities, and so on. Particularly important opportunities arise at the beginning of each school year as new teachers, students, and parents become acquainted with the school. Norms can be strengthened by careful attention to who provides the orientation that new members receive and how the school's culture and expectations are described.

Walk the Talk. While the shared goals and norms, trust, and relationship networks that enable school work depend on widely distributed participation and leadership, principals have a unique role in shaping these components of the school's social capital. Principals who positively affect the school's social capital not only communicate clearly about school goals, but also work consistently and purposefully toward those goals. They "talk the talk" and walk it as well.

A principal's own work commitments provide one of the best opportunities to communicate what is important. High expectations for students imply hard work for adults, and the principal's own work commitments are often the most visible symbol of whether such an espoused value is really important. Consistency in such leadership is apparent in the use of the principal's own time and energy: visible presence in the school, engagement with issues of teaching and learning, and support for those who take risks to achieve goals.

Most of us strive for such consistency among our values, words, and actions in our personal and professional lives and know all too well the difficulties involved. What makes this aspect of school leadership even more challenging is the importance of coherence *as it is perceived by others in the school community*, not just by the principal.

The nature of school goals and norms makes it particularly difficult to work in ways that are perceived as consistent by others. As we noted in Chapter 2, conflict surrounds community discussions about goals for what students should learn and the nature of schools; and the mixture of goals constantly evolves as the community builds new agreements and understandings. Similarly, differences between implicit and professed norms make it difficult to foresee what will be taken for granted as communications are interpreted. Under these conditions, no matter how reasonable a principal's action might seem to some, others inevitably will misunderstand the intent and rationale for actions taken, which can undermine confidence in school norms. Consequently, an important part of a principal's communication task is to take advantage of opportunities to draw explicit linkages between her or his actions and the school's goals, theory of action, and social norms.

Strengthen Connections Through Conversation

Norms that foster collaborative relationships provide a foundation for a school's social capital. Principals build on that foundation through the daily work of listening and talking. While conversational leadership in the school is multidirectional and widely shared among members of the school community (Hart, 1995), the principal's role is central. Being present and actively participating in the normal day-to-day problem solving in a school create opportunities for frequent, spontaneous, and relevant conversations. Such conversations can serve many purposes: linking specific issues to school goals and norms, identifying gaps in information exchange, encouraging collaborative work, framing issues for productive discussion, and identifying conflicts that require attention.

Build a Shared Vocabulary. Conversations progress more quickly as a school builds a shared vocabulary for discussing goals, theories of action, norms, and strategies. In this regard, the Framework for School Leadership Accomplishments (FSLA) offers assistance. By defining school conditions that are important for both meeting student learning goals and expressing community expectations for the nature of schools, the FSLA offers a set of categories for discussing school strategies and theories of action. And because the Framework distinguishes between success criteria and action strategies for each accomplishment, it generates conversations about both aspects.

With a common language, participation in these conversations can be broadened to many others in the community. One needs no particular proficiency with professional jargon to describe what one wants from the school's climate, support for families, or school schedule.

Fill Communication Gaps. Frequent conversations also allow the principal to serve an important role in bridging across various groups in the school to ensure that information is widely shared. When groups within the school or community are not well connected (i.e., they do not share many members or have only infrequent contact with one another), gaps develop in the flow of information and assistance. When this occurs, individuals in contact with multiple groups have important advantages: They have access to the information associated with each group; they have opportunities to share that information with others; they can selectively share the information in order to emphasize certain points; and they can point to areas of agreement in order to increase interaction among groups (Burt, 1992, 2000). When the principal is sufficiently engaged with all parts of the school community, he or she stands at the crossroads of interaction among groups and has the opportunity to increase information flow and to shape the direction of the resulting collaborations.

By keeping the flow of information regular and open, the principal ensures that social relationships are not undermined by having a few individuals who are "in the know" while others feel left out. Principals personally can help groups that have less access to information because of class schedules or social-group membership and can ensure that groups with less power are heard in the school's conversations.

Establish a Supportive Work Structure

The school's work structure is a combination of organizational arrangements, work assignments, policies, and traditions. This structure maintains the conditions within which teachers work and sets expectations that affect their interactions with students and families. While many aspects of a school's work structure are established through district policy, principals typically have flexibility in how a school's work is designed. The structures and policies that a principal supports communicate what kinds of activities are valued and supported in the school. It is one thing, for example, to say that teacher collaboration is valued, but another to create policies, schedules, and assignments that encourage such collaboration (Halverson, 2003).

Create Schedules That Encourage Collaboration. An obvious starting point in establishing a work system that supports social capital is the school schedule. Spillane and Louis (2002) note that one component of the typical work structure of schools—teachers working separately in their own classrooms—mitigates the development of social networks and trust. "One factor that appears in all studies that look at professional community is time to meet and talk" (p. 99). Principals can design the school schedule to include coordinated planning time that enables teacher collaboration and mutual support. Other schedule adjustments can encourage stronger relationships between teachers and students by reducing the number of students each teacher sees in a day or by extending the time that teachers and students are together through cross-grade classrooms or looping arrangements.

Organize Responsibilities so That Collaboration Is Necessary. Additional benefits can be gained by the way that tasks and work groups are organized in the school. For example, required district reports can be organized in ways that depend on collaborative discussion. Teacher groups can be formally charged as collaborative decision-making committees and intervention assistance teams (Myers & Kline, 2001/2002). Teacher-led groups also can be established to conduct action research and support professional development (Hubbard & Power, 1993).

In each case, the principal's focus is on creating new connections among the school's various groups, fostering shared norms, and establishing contexts in which trust can be built through conversation. Structures that "give teachers opportunities to discuss practice, develop programs, and understand assessment information help to create the kind of trust within the organization that marks professional community" (Halverson, 2003, p. 10).

Stress Democratic Modeling in the School

As noted in Chapter 2, an important priority of school is preparing students to take their place in a democratic society (Goodlad, 1996; Senge et al., 2000). This means that, in addition to academic preparation, students need to develop skills and attitudes for participation in a social and political democracy.

An important way that schools contribute to this goal is by modeling democratic practices. What does this mean? While much has been written about democratic schooling (Ravitch & Viteritti, 2001; Soder, 1996), Gutmann (2000) provides a useful introduction with her conceptualization of three distinctive features of democracies: First, democracies have fair procedures for making decisions. Usually this means majority decision, but with the understanding that majorities do not always make the best or correct decisions. Second, they have mechanisms for protecting basic individual rights, that is, some form of constitutionalism. Third, they have guarantees that difficult moral decisions will be deliberated openly and constructively, with mutual respect and tolerance given all participants.

Enacting these three features of democracies in schools is not a call for anarchy—or endless dialog. But each of the three does suggest practical strategies for school leaders. First, making decisions by majority decision is not always possible in schools where elected board members and district administrators have legal responsibility for many aspects of schooling. But it is possible for principals to minimize the verticality in school bureaucracies by supporting dense horizontal relationships within the school. For example, principals block the bureaucracy of the school system from interfering with social relationships in the school when they create opportunities for everyone in the school to participate in discussions about how the school uses the flexibility that it does have.

Second, principals can ensure that school rules are defined and implemented in ways that provide fair treatment for all students, particularly those whose life circumstances remove them from the social mainstream of the school. When the school is able to guarantee that respect from peers and adults is a basic right that everyone enjoys, other democratic processes are more likely to develop as well.

Third, schools constantly deal with difficult moral decisions and are called on to act in ways that are responsive to the values and priorities of many different groups. Democratic processes are evident when these decisions are made after open discussion and when extra effort is made to bring less well-represented voices into the conversation.

Help Families Build Social Capital

Social capital first was identified in studies of families. Sociologists discovered that children in families with strong social capital were more likely to do better academically. Generally speaking, where social capital was stronger, child development and education were better. Coleman (1988), for instance, found that strong family social capital could overcome a mother's educational level as a predictor of school achievement. In fact, only poverty is a better predictor of student achievement than is social capital (Putnam, 2000). To support high achievement, then, families need high levels of cooperation around learning; students and parents need high levels of trust; and all must be highly engaged in learning.

Support Family Connections. If schools are to produce high levels of student learning, an important strategy is to help families achieve strong social capital. Schools and school leaders have several ways to offer this assistance. They can share knowledge about child development and academic achievement: Schools have knowledge that parents and family members also need. Schools can give adults the tools to be good parents and enable them to interact with their children about school work: In simple terms, this may mean doing what many schools already do—have read-ins for families and students, encourage family members to read with their children each night, or, when the school has an expert in reading for teacher staff development, hold sessions for family members where the expert shares information about reading and answers questions parents might have. With the many competing commitments that families have, it is not easy to design such activities so all families participate. But effort could not be better spent.

Help Families Connect with Others. It has been shown repeatedly that, when parents of school children are connected in dense networks, child development and student performance benefit (Coleman, 1988, 1990). Family members can interact with one another about appropriate norms and expectations, and feel more comfortable about their relationships with their own children when they know what limits are set for their children's peers. Families also are more likely to engage with the school when strong bonds have been developed among adults as well as children.

Connect Constructively to the Surrounding Community

The principal further supports social capital by attending to the school's boundaries with outside influences. Some of these influences support the school community's goals, theory of action, and norms, while others threaten the school's social capital by diverting attention to other goals or introducing excessive conflict. The principal's challenge is to create a bridge to the former influences and a buffer from the latter.

Bridge to External Resources. Bridging to external resources is important. Social capital is enhanced when external information and expertise are added to internal sharing and collaboration. For example, teachers who are working together on a particular instructional program probably will benefit from external expertise at some point in the process. Similarly, partnerships with businesses and universities, engagement of parents in collaborative work with teachers, and connections between the school and social services can all enrich a school's social community.

This may mean that school leaders, to some degree, have to become "joiners." Dense network connections are important, and belonging to local service clubs (Rotary, Lions, Kiwanis) is important for building networks. A principal also can meet with and listen to other groups active in the community, such as neighborhood improvement groups, or have face-to-face discussions with representative council members. Finally, principals should resist structuring show-and-tell sessions or walkabouts. These do significantly less for social-capital development than do more personalized actions.

Buffer from Disruptions. The effective schools research often identified successful principals as "administrative 'mavericks' who are willing to challenge or even disregard pressures or directives from the central office or other external forces perceived as interfering with the effective operation of their schools" (Levine & Lezotte, 1990, p. 17). Principals often are expected to buffer teachers from unique demands of a single family that cannot be met without disrupting the education of other children. Similarly, careful attention to the kinds of professional development resources that are brought into the school can be important, because so many different goals, theories of action, and norms are implied in different approaches to curriculum and instructional improvement. As with most aspects of the principal's work, finding the right balance between buffering and bridging is a matter of using professional judgment in a particular school context.

SUMMARY

Although social capital is quite stable and difficult to change, it also is so central to school success that a systematic effort to influence its development and direction is an essential component of a principal's role. Principals strengthen social capital and focus underlying values on school work by a combination of activities aimed at understanding and enhancing any of the social capital in a school's internal and external communities. Internally, principals foster the development of supportive norms and steward those norms through conversation, personal example, and supportive school structures. Externally, principals can help families increase social capital supporting their children's learning and foster productive connections with other community groups. Both kinds of efforts to build social capital contribute to a school environment where skills and dispositions needed for participation in democratic life are modeled for students.

KNOWLEDGE FOR SCHOOL LEADERSHIP

In earlier chapters, we discussed the demands that today's challenges create for principals, offered ways of thinking that put those demands in perspective, and suggested responsive leadership strategies. The picture of the principalship that emerges from our recommendations is challenging. As we have framed the role, school leaders must understand their communities' priorities for student learning and school conditions, see the potential in each of their students and the school itself, and engage the school's internal and external communities in effective action to reach that potential.

Part III turns to questions about the knowledge principals need to succeed in such challenging roles. The knowledge supporting school leadership is *public*, in that it is developed and shared across the school leadership profession, and *private*, inasmuch as each individual principal brings a unique set of personal understandings and abilities to the role.

The profession's public knowledge is a continuously evolving result of documenting, sharing, evaluating, and critiquing information about principal practice. Public knowledge allows principals to learn from distant colleagues and benefit from the scholarly analysis and critique of leadership approaches. The scope of this public knowledge and the way that it is structured have much to do with whether the profession can offer useful guidance to individual practitioners.

The first two chapters of Part III offer complementary views of the scope, structure, and representation of public knowledge for school leadership. Geertz (1980) provides a foundation for our recommendation to frame the profession's knowledge in two ways with his distinction between "laws-and-instances" and "cases-and-interpretations" approaches to explanation (p. 165). In the principalship, the laws-and-instances approach encompasses social science theories, legal and ethical principles, and even packaged programs that have been identified or developed as solutions to particular school situations. The cases-and-interpretations approach finds expression in accounts of the intentions, experiences, and meanings that arise for principals in the course of leadership in a particular school and community.

Just as effective school leadership involves attending to both the whole school and its parts, knowledge of both laws-and-instances and cases-and-interpretations can support professional practice (Richardson, 1996). While both knowledge traditions have wide-ranging applicability, we suggest that a laws-and-instances approach is particularly useful in organizing knowledge associated with school accomplishments, while a cases-and-interpretations approach has special utility in sharing craft knowledge associated with leading schools in integrated ways over an entire school year.

Chapter 10 explores how our concept of an accomplishment can serve as one organizing scheme for professional knowledge from the laws-and-instances traditions. In our analysis, accomplishments serve as units of analysis for the work of a school and as instances to which the field's knowledge should be applied. The more knowledge that a princi-pal can bring to the effort to realize each accomplishment, the more likely is success. Because accomplishments are both means through which schools foster student learning and ends in themselves (school conditions that respond to community values), knowledge supporting leadership toward any single accomplishment involves wide-ranging principles and theories about what is good in school accomplishments and how to achieve it. Chapter 10 builds on the construct of an accom-plishment to show how the Framework for School Leadership Accom-plishments could serve as an organizing guide for knowledge from the laws-and-instances tradition.

Knowledge from these laws-and-instances traditions has typically been associated with the advancement of professional status (Freidson, 1986) and is the focus of much federally funded research in education (Shavelson & Towne, 2002). But it is also incomplete. Practical limits on research methods makes it impossible to test how various approaches might work under the many and varied circumstances that exist in different schools (Lindblom & Cohen, 1979), so that much action necessarily is left to the judgment and craft knowledge of individual principals. Equally important, because both school goals and methods are subject to local decision making, the meaning that participants give to events as they unfold over the school year can greatly affect perceptions of school success.

Chapter 11 responds to the importance of such interpretations and turns to a more holistic and contextualized view of principals' work, asking how knowledge about this dimension of school leadership might be organized and shared. Here we develop the idea of narrative cases as a comprehensive strategy to represent knowledge that results from the experience of individual principals as they work in particular school contexts. We suggest annual cases of school leadership as a way to build and share the contextualized, narrative-based craft knowledge that accrues from these experiences. Through such sharing, it may be possible both to accelerate mutual learning among practitioners and to generate important questions for more formal research.

The personal, or individual, knowledge that principals bring to their work comes from many sources, including their own personal and emotional development, the problem-solving and communication skills that they may have developed through general education, the observation of leadership and direct leadership experiences that they may have had as teachers, and their formal preparation for the principalship. While all are important, formal preparation programs offer the most direct link between the profession's public knowledge about school leadership and the individual knowledge that new principals bring to their roles. Chapter 12 offers a view of principal preparation programs that follows from the accomplishment perspective elaborated throughout the book. In Chapter 12, we explore how the two ways of organizing knowledge that we propose in Chapters 10 and 11 might help structure curriculum content and performance assessments in principal preparation programs.

Our comments on professional preparation programs join a rich dialog about reform within the profession (Council of Chief State School Officers, 1996; English, 2003; Griffiths, Stout, & Forsyth, 1988; Murphy, 2002b; Tucker & Codding, 2002), as well as a debate in the policy community about the utility of the current structure of professional preparation and licensure that supports practice (Hess, 2003; Levine, 2005). While our goal is not a comprehensive alternative to current suggestions, our discussion of professional knowledge is germane. The way that knowledge is framed for practice, the public confidence that such knowledge is sufficient for the challenges that schools face, and the reliability with which that knowledge is imparted to new practitioners are all central to professional education for the principalship and how it should be conducted.

Chapter 10

Organizing Knowledge to Support Accomplishments

Knowledge is an essential part of all professional practice. Like other professionals, principals bring specialized knowledge to bear on local problems that have significance for both clients and the larger society. The more complex the problems, the greater the demands on both the profession's shared knowledge and the knowledge held by individual practitioners.

Why is this so? From a public perspective, knowledge in a field becomes more important as the risks associated with individual performance problems increase. In fields where the public stakes for failure are not high, individual expertise often can be developed on the job without assistance from a profession's knowledge base. For example, many of the small businesses that start each year fail or simply stumble along as owners develop needed skills on the job. These casualties of insufficient knowledge do not necessarily harm the public; in fact, the public benefits of a few successes may far outweigh any public difficulties associated with failure of new businesses.

In other areas of society, however, the need for reliable performance makes it unwise for the public to rely on each individual's trial-and-error learning. For example, we expect medical care to be provided by someone who has expertise in the accumulated knowledge of diagnosis and treatment, and public policies link entry into the profession with some mastery of this knowledge base. In medicine and many other professions, the high levels of individual expertise expected by the public depend on a general professional knowledge base that is accessible to practitioners.

How is such a knowledge base sustained? In successful professions, stewardship for the general knowledge that supports practice comes from the profession as a whole. Acting through the public academic dialog that is fostered through research and professional associations, professions define the *scope* of the knowledge that is important for practice and they *structure* that knowledge for transmission to new and current practitioners. To attend to scope and structure of the needed knowledge, most professions have developed academic arms within universities that are responsible for research, preparation of new practitioners, and transfer of emerging knowledge through a variety of training and technical assistance programs (Rogers, 1967).

School leadership is more like medicine than business. The performance of every school is important, and too much learning by trial and error is inappropriate at the expense of children's academic progress. Without a clear and well-structured knowledge base that supports the profession as a whole, it is unlikely that many principals could develop the expertise they need quickly enough or completely enough to achieve the results that the public expects from their schools. Consequently, development of and stewardship for a knowledge base to support practice have been core responsibilities of the educational leadership profession.

Stewardship for the profession's knowledge base is particularly important for school leadership today. As we argued in earlier chapters, the demands facing individual principals have become more complex, with politically defined goals for near-universal proficiency, difficult social conditions that affect learning, and strong debates about what students should learn and what schools should be like. To succeed in these circumstances, individual principals need access to knowledge that is different from what was needed under earlier expectations. This, in turn, challenges the profession as a whole to examine both the scope of its knowledge base and how that knowledge is structured. Given the magnitude of the changes that continue to affect principals, it is hardly surprising that a continuing debate within the profession questions the relevance of knowledge to practice (Hills, 1978; Silver, 1983), the adequacy of knowledge to justify state licensing requirements (Hess, 2003), the knowledge-base justification for program accreditation (English, 2003), and the conceptual coherence the field's knowledge (Donmoyer, 1999, 2001). A brief sketch of the development of knowledge for educational leadership will help bring these debates into focus and point to the contribution that our accomplishment perspective offers.

CURRENT KNOWLEDGE FOR SCHOOL LEADERSHIP

Evolving Scope of Professional Knowledge

The educational leadership profession supports principals with a rich and eclectic knowledge base, developed through several decades of research and critical inquiry. Knowledge in educational administration evolved in what Forsyth and Murphy (1999) call "university-evolved disciplines" (p. 266), specializations within educational administration that grew out of preexisting disciplines in the university. Reviews of professional knowledge often reflect the organization of knowledge into these disciplinary categories (Leith-wood & Duke, 1999), as does the structure of many university faculty positions (Forsyth & Murphy, 1999; McCarthy, 1999a).

Evolution of the profession's general knowledge reflects trends in these underlying disciplines. In educational leadership, as in other fields, a strong post-World War II emphasis on theory and research has been conceived in what has become known as the "positivist" tradition. In this tradition, theory serves to develop testable hypotheses that can be shown to be true or false. Knowledge, in this way of thinking, is objective and detached from values. Similar use of scientific methods in medicine, for example, has yielded tremendous advances, so that established and accepted procedures now exist for a variety of professional challenges. Many believe that scientific rigor in the study of teaching, learning, and school leadership will produce similar advances in educational administration. This perspective has led professionals and policy makers to emphasize public knowledge in educational administration that is derived from the social and behavioral sciences, that seeks to define methods with general applicability, and that relies on measurable aspects of performance (Shavelson & Towne, 2002).

Despite progress in the scientific study of education and continued advocacy for its importance in providing knowledge for professional practice, several limitations of this traditional research approach have led to a greatly expanded conception of important knowledge. As a practical matter, problems of expense and logistics make it impossible for social science research to deal with more than a limited range of the problems confronting principals (Lindblom & Cohen, 1979). And more fundamental concerns about the limitations of positivist research approaches have led to a growing chorus of criticism and alternative views of knowledge—neo-Marxist and critical theory, feminist theory, postpositive analysis, and policy analysis, to name a few.

Today, increasing agreement underscores that knowledge for educational leadership is shaped by the perspectives and interests of researchers, and is ideologically infused, so that it necessarily advantages some groups over others (Donmoyer, 2001; Lincoln & Guba, 1985). Various strands of scholarship have emerged to emphasize, for example, the social construction of meanings in schools (Bruffee, 1986, 1993; Scott, 2001), the political implications and uses of research (Cooper & Randall, 1999), the power relationships and social injustices associated with knowledge (Aronowitz & Giroux, 1991; Giroux, 1997), and the cognitive processes involved in professional practice (Leithwood & Steinbach, 1995).

The field's knowledge continues to progress toward "greater flexibility, experimentation, and eclecticism in terms of philosophical stances and methodologies" (Heck & Hallinger, 1999, p. 157). But methodological and conceptual progress within such different intellectual traditions also poses challenges. The field's knowledge continues to be criticized as "highly diverse and fragmented" (Goldring & Greenfield, 2002, p. 1) and failing at conceptual unity (Erickson, 1979). Donmoyer (1996b), citing Bernstein (1993), sums up the state of the field's knowledge as "paradigm proliferation," with these paradigms being largely incommensurate.

Structure of Professional Knowledge

With such ongoing debates about the *scope* of the profession's knowledge, it also has been difficult to structure that knowledge in ways that support a principal's work. Competing paradigms provide a substantial base of foundational knowledge related to school leadership, but they have made it increasingly difficult to synthesize and organize what professional knowledge offers practitioners. Silver's (1983) assessment is still current: "In educational administration, practitioners do not resort to the literature in the field because they know they will not find there current knowledge about how to solve the problems they are addressing" (p. 11).

This is not for lack of trying. Over time, attempts to organize the profession's knowledge for use by practitioners have included efforts to define procedural prescriptions out of successful practice (Gulick & Urwick, 1937), develop coherent theories that link knowledge to practice (Sergiovanni, 2001), and organize knowledge around problems of practice (Forsyth & Tallerico, 1993; Thompson, 1993). To date, none of these approaches to defining and organizing the field's knowledge, taken by itself, has seemed to work. None has enjoyed broad support within the profession's academic communities, and none has been embraced by practitioners as providing the needed link between knowledge and practice.

No doubt, many reasons account for the difficulties encountered by previous efforts to frame and organize the profession's knowledge for use by practitioners. The sheer diversity of knowledge in the profession encourages political accommodation of the various knowledge traditions within educational administration at the expense of conceptual or practical coherence. While organized professional knowledge is critical to supporting practice, any particular structure implies a point of view about whether human affairs are caused or constructed, and institutionalizes some set of power relationships in the profession and the schools it serves (Donmoyer, 1999). And as Goodlad, Soder, and Sirotnik (1990) argue, efforts to frame the profession's knowledge often have emphasized technical knowledge to the exclusion of the important moral and critical dimensions of work in schools. To support practice, a framework is needed that organizes knowledge for practice and at the same time encourages continuing debate and development about conflicting values, action strategies, roles, and relationships within schools.

USING ACCOMPLISHMENTS TO FRAME
THE PROFESSION'S KNOWLEDGE

Framing school leadership in terms of accomplishments, as we have done in the previous chapters, offers an alternative approach in the continuing challenge of defining and organizing the profession's knowledge so that it is useful to practitioners. Although our general approach is grounded in many previous efforts to organize professional knowledge, we believe that ways of thinking associated with the accomplishment perspective offer new approaches to the central questions about the scope and structure of knowledge.

Because accomplishment-minded practice requires principals to consider ends and means simultaneously and because it requires pragmatic use of a deep repertoire of alternative approaches, the accomplishment perspective makes a virtue out of the profession's fragmented and diverse knowledge. When viewed from an accomplishment perspective, an eclectic knowledge base offers more guidance in establishing success criteria and more possibilities for creative problem solutions.

Grounding in Previous Efforts

Our recommendations for defining and organizing professional knowledge around accomplishments has its conceptual roots in the recommendations of Hills (1978) and several subsequent efforts to organize knowledge around problems of practice in school leadership (Forsyth & Tallerico, 1993; Silver, 1983; Thompson, 1993).

As a result of his examination of medicine and his own experiences bridging between the life of an academic and a practitioner, Hills (1978) argued that a profession's knowledge is defined by the needs of practice: "The ultimate focus is not the pursuit of knowledge itself, but the effective attainment of practical goals where serious interests of clients are often at stake" (p. 2). Thus, while disciplinary knowledge may or may not have practical application, the knowledge supporting applied professional work is defined by its potential utility in addressing important problems. With the scope of professional knowledge defined in this way, Hills continued with recommendations for how that knowledge should be structured: "Applied professions are oriented toward the development of specialized bodies of knowledge which, while grounded in the theoretical knowledge of the disciplines, are organized around the problems of practice" (p. 5). Consequently, the knowledge base for educational leadership, or any other applied profession, is

a corpus of knowledge the elements of which have been mobilized selectively from a variety of sources, on the basis of their relevance to the clinical problems encountered by practitioners in the field. Elements are drawn not only from a variety of subdisciplines . . . but also from clinical experience. . . . Problems in the world of the (educational) administrator seldom come in the form of psychological problems, sociological problems, economic problems, or political problems. . . . It is thus the case not only that every applied science is the confluence of many disciplinary sciences, but also that most, if not every, clinical problem solution contains elements of several disciplines. (Hills, 1978, pp. 2–3, emphasis in the original)

Ensuing efforts to organize knowledge in educational leadership around problems of practice confirm that an eclectic knowledge base can indeed be organized in this way. Leadership strategies that seem incommensurate from a theoretical perspective often turn out not to be incompatible in practical application. Just as Donmoyer (2001) suggests that different research purposes can help to organize knowledge from seemingly conflicting traditions, so too can the practical problems facing principals serve to organize a diverse knowledge base.

Structuring Professional Knowledge Around Accomplishments

What has been missing in these previous efforts to organize professional knowledge around problems of practice is a systematic way to integrate moral and critical perspectives with the more technical knowledge for problem solving. As others have noted, the way that problems are selected and framed for solution involve moral as well as procedural technical knowledge (Goodlad, 1990; Robinson, 1998). Indeed, this need was recognized by Thompson (1993), who supplemented his taxonomy of problems with categories that address the moral, political, and legal issues that arise in school contexts. But moral, critical, and legal reasoning are more than add-ons. Ends and means constantly interact in principals' work, and a structure for organizing knowledge is needed that supports this simultaneous consideration.

Accomplishments do just that. They offer a way of defining the problems principals face that involve simultaneous consideration of ends (the success criteria for each accomplishment) and means (the action strategies through which the success criteria are satisfied). Because a principal's work toward each accomplishment involves both defining success criteria and acting to reach those criteria, accomplishments define a scope for professional knowledge that includes moral, legal, political, and critical reasoning, as well as technical information for problem solving.

A set of accomplishments like the Framework for School Leadership Accomplishments offers a perspective on both the scope and structure of professional knowledge for school leadership. The scope of knowledge includes what is important for individual practitioners to know in order to understand each accomplishment, define success criteria for the accomplishment, and act to realize the accomplishment in the organizational context of schools. Structuring knowledge around these same accomplishments helps principals to organize their own thinking and access new knowledge in ways that are relevant to their leadership goals.

A practical benefit of defining school leadership problems as accomplishments is that each element of an accomplishment model for schools is similar to all others in several important ways: Each defines a condition that is achieved through the principal's work; each is critically important in the school's effort to reach valued outcomes for students; each has success criteria that reflect the school purposes and priorities of the community; and each requires that the principal have a repertoire of action strategies to reach the success criteria in different circumstances. Because of these shared features, knowledge can be organized around accomplishments by asking similar questions about each accomplishment and by using all available knowledge in the effort to answer these questions.

Two central questions structure the organization of knowledge around each accomplishment: What is the nature and development of success criteria, and what repertoire of strategies, tools, and programs might help the principal and school achieve the success criteria?

What Constitutes Quality in the Accomplishment (Success Criteria)? What are the requirements for success in school accomplishments such as student climate sustained, instruction provided, or resources developed? How would someone know if a school's climate for students was of high quality or if the effort to mobilize resources was reasonable in relation to opportunities for support? By offering answers to these questions, the profession's knowledge should help principals directly define excellence in each accomplishment and confirm to what degree important quality features associated with each accomplishment are present in their schools.

The profession's knowledge should inform two aspects of the question about the success criteria for each accomplishment. The first addresses how the accomplishment contributes to valued student learning. This is largely a matter of asking what evidence exists for the claim that certain conditions in the school—the results achieved by realizing the accomplishments—enhance student learning. The question is similar to the many meta-analyses of school procedures (Lipsey & Wilson, 1993; Marzano, 2003), but with a focus on the impact of school conditions, rather than the specific procedures used to create those conditions. For example, to establish empirically supported success criteria for an accomplishment, say, student climate sustained, one would ask of the accumulated professional knowledge, what characteristics of school climates are related to student learning?

The second issue associated with defining success criteria concerns the development of success criteria that reflect the locally unique mix of values and goals in any particular school community. Different emphases on the private and public purposes of education result in different local expectations for school goals and for the accomplishment through which those goals are pursued. Success criteria translate these different expectations into concrete descriptions of the desired school conditions.

Because of these local differences, the profession's knowledge should help principals relate the conditions associated with each accomplishment to various mixes of school purposes evident in their own communities and help them lead local conversations about goals and purposes. Such knowledge includes a broad range of ethical, critical, and legal understandings that help professionals lead discussions about school goals, identify contradictions and dilemmas facing the school, and build support for more coherent school purposes.

What Strategies Are Potentially Useful in a Principal's and School's Pursuit of Excellence on Each Accomplishment (Action Repertoire)? Sometimes the strategies to be followed in pursuit of an accomplishment are prescribed by law or policy. But the knowledge base underlying most school accomplishments is far less prescriptive, offering a range of possible strategies rather than a single, required course of action. Consequently, organizing knowledge about action strategies is largely a matter of identifying various strategies, programs, approaches, and tools that may contribute to a particular accomplishment. By including a range of useful approaches to each accomplishment, the profession's knowledge can help each principal bring an extensive repertoire of action strategies to her or his school and use that information as a basis for whatever adaptation or reinvention is needed to realize accomplishments in any particular school (Emrick & Peterson, 1977).

Scope of Professional Knowledge from an Accomplishment Perspective

The two questions that organize knowledge about each school accomplishment specifically invite knowledge from multiple disciplines and traditions. To answer questions about the success criteria for each accomplishment necessarily involves consideration of the values associated with the school's underlying purposes, related legal requirements and principles, and critical understandings about how school practices benefit some groups at the expense of others. And to answer questions about the repertoire of strategies that can help principals meet the practical challenges associated with each accomplishment, it seems only reasonable to consider the experience of excellent principals as well as the results of research (Hiebert, Gilmore, & Stigler, 2002).

An accomplishment perspective thus leads to a knowledge base with broad scope that accommodates both traditional social science results and the alternatives that have become increasingly important in the educational administration literature. The professional knowledge needed to answer the two questions associated with each accomplishment comes from broad sources of: (1) ethical and critical reasoning, (2) research in the social sciences, (3) craft knowledge, and (4) legal reasoning. Of course, these and other distinctions among types of knowledge are ultimately arbitrary, with constantly shifting boundaries among what one might categorize as craft knowledge, social science, ethical reasoning, and so on (Bohman, 1991). Nevertheless, the categories are familiar and provide a useful way of describing how an eclectic knowledge base might be arrayed to support practice. Table 10.1 illustrates how the two organizing questions and information from these four

TABLE 10.1. A Structure for Knowledge Organized Around an Accomplishment

	Ethical and Critical Reasoning	Legal Reasoning	Social Science Research	Craft Knowledge
Accomplishment One—Learning Goals				
What success criteria?				
What action repertoire?				
Accomplishment Two—Instruction				
What success criteria?				
What action repertoire?				
Accomplishments Three Through Eight				
What success criteria?				
What action repertoire?				
Accomplishment Nine—School Renewal				
What success criteria?				
What action repertoire?				

sources frame a structure for organizing the profession's knowledge around school accomplishments. Bellamy and colleagues (2006) illustrate how current professional knowledge could be organized by using the categories indicated by the cells in the matrix.

Ethical and Critical Reasoning. Education's importance in today's diverse and complex world makes it a field where values intersect and conflict. Educators are called on daily to make practical decisions that involve consideration of competing values and priorities in the school and community, and they are expected to do the right and good thing as they confront competing needs (Goodlad, 1990; Oser, 1994). These decisions are supported by knowledge that helps professionals take a critical stance in relation to their work.

> To be critical is to question and question constructively; to appraise knowledge in the context of practice; to challenge existing knowledge and practice with an eye toward improvement; to situate knowledge and practice in historical, current, and future perspective; to recognize the reflexivity of human inquiry, of knowing and acting; to consider and reconsider fundamental values and human interests in knowing and acting; and to ethically ground the actions that people take that affect the lives of others. (Sirotnik, 1990, p. 314)

As a moral process, critical inquiry ultimately addresses what principals set out to do, helping to define the success criteria they establish for school accomplishments. Similarly, ethical reasoning concerns "conduct insofar as it is considered as right or wrong, good or bad" (Shapiro & Stefkovich, 2001, p. 10). To accommodate the many perspectives on what is "good" in schools, Shapiro and Stefkovich propose three frames for viewing ethical decisions: the ethics of justice, critique, and care. These frames serve to integrate knowledge from traditional ethical writing and contemporary critiques from feminist, Marxist, and critical theory perspectives. Taken together, this literature provides a rich and diverse knowledge base for principals' decisions about the success criteria that principals define for school accomplishments and for evaluating various actions associated with efforts to reach those accomplishments.

Law, Case Law, and Legal Reasoning. Laws that empower and constrain principals come from many sources: constitutions, statutes, administrative law, local school board policy decisions, and common law (Valente & Valente, 2001). The law reflects judgment—the political consensus of policy makers and the accumulated wisdom or incremental consensus over time of judges (Polanyi, 1962). School administrators are public officials whose duties and authority are assigned civilly. They are always limited by and accountable within a legal framework. But legal reasoning does more than establish boundaries for professional practice. It offers a set of principles and a model of reasoning that help school leaders analyze difficult situations and choose courses of action when, as is often the case, no clear requirement or precedent exists (Bull & McCarthy, 1995). Consequently, knowledge supporting principal practice necessarily includes an understanding of the legal frameworks that create obligations, constrain actions, and set tests for acceptable performance.

Social Science Research. Research from the social and behavioral sciences has been the traditional source of information about teaching, learning, leadership, and organization. Dewey wanted teachers to be trained in "laboratory" rather than "apprenticeship" settings because he believed that they would internalize the latest scientific knowledge (Shulman, 1998). The emphasis on rigorous theory-based research has continued through much of the history of educational administration (Griffiths, 1959; Shavelson & Towne, 2002) and resonates today in major federal education legislation, including the No Child Left Behind Act of 2001. As we observed earlier, critiques of research in the social and behavioral sciences have led to acceptance of both expanded inquiry methods and alternative knowledge traditions. Nevertheless, little doubt exists that much of the knowledge that undergirds practice will come from this source, although its use naturally will be affected by the values and intentions of both the researchers and the users.

Accumulated Public Craft Knowledge. Lindblom and Cohen (1979) observe that social problem solvers rely much more on "ordinary knowledge" than on social science research for the solution of problems. By ordinary knowledge, Lindblom and Cohen mean knowledge that derives from "common sense, casual empiricism, or thoughtful speculation and analysis" (p. 12). In this vein, Hills (1978) noted that medicine made great strides when efforts were made to codify and organize ordinary knowledge of physicians; and proposals for making ordinary knowledge public are cited frequently as important in the effort to strengthen the knowledge bases in education (Hiebert et al., 2002). Following this concern with building the profession's shared knowledge, we use the term "craft knowledge" to mean the "ordinary knowledge" described by Lindblom and Cohen (1979), with an emphasis on knowledge that is shared and public.

As a practical matter, craft knowledge includes the wisdom resulting from experience, learning from mistakes, shared misconceptions, myths, and norms. Craft knowledge may be biased, prejudicial, and wrong, but it is used by practitioners and frequently serves as the basis for action. Craft knowledge is codified in a plethora of "how to" books and articles and professional association presentations and bulletins, but the field lacks a coherent way to record, synthesize, and evaluate its craft knowledge (Silver, 1983). This hinders the systematic use of craft knowledge to frame research hypotheses and to build more formal knowledge from the wisdom of practice.

Personal Knowledge. A fifth source of knowledge is important in professional practice, but is not a part of the profession's general knowledge because it is held by individuals, rather than shared publicly in the profession. Personal or individual knowledge includes tacit knowledge used by individuals as they solve problems but which they may be unable to articulate (Polanyi, 1962). Personal knowledge also includes what political economists call "specific assets"—knowledge that is held by individuals and not shared because it gives them a competitive advantage in their work (House, 1998). We return to a discussion of personal knowledge and how it is structured in our discussion of preparation programs in Chapter 12.

REFLECTIONS ON AN ACCOMPLISHMENT FRAME FOR PROFESSIONAL KNOWLEDGE

While our effort to organize knowledge around accomplishments—and previous efforts to use problems of practice as the organizing framework (Forsyth & Tallerico, 1993; Hills, 1978)—offers important possibilities for strengthening the link between knowledge and practice, we are also mindful of the very significant challenges that any such reframing of professional knowledge entails. Organizing knowledge in this way diverges from the knowledge and experience base of much of the professoriate, challenges the field to develop new models of professional preparation, and requires a new integration of practical knowledge, typically the province of school districts, and the technical knowledge associated with university programs (Forsyth & Murphy, 1999). It is not surprising that one of the most widely cited recent efforts to organize the knowledge base for educational administration (Hoy, 1994) relied on categories that reflect underlying disciplines, rather than problems of practice, and recent reviews of the field's knowledge use similar structures (Leithwood & Duke, 1999).

Despite the difficulties, the challenges facing both individual principals and the school leadership profession invite bold recommendations. The need for professional knowledge begins with the concrete realities of principals' lives, where practical problems consume much of each day's time and energy (Achilles, Reynolds, & Achilles, 1997; Hills, 1978; Leithwood & Steinbach, 1995). Because these problems contain more troubling value conflicts and more complex technical demands, the effort to define and structure professional knowledge is increasingly important.

As an evolutionary step in the field's effort to define and organize its knowledge around the challenges that practitioners face, our accomplishment-based organizing structure has two potential advantages. First, it invites simultaneous consideration of a more eclectic knowledge base that includes consideration of moral, legal, critical, and practical aspects of the school circumstances that principals face. As a result, rather than privileging one kind of knowledge over another, the approach looks for knowledge that is useful in defining success criteria and planning action from all intellectual traditions. Rather than attempting to resolve differences among the field's many intellectual traditions, our approach to knowledge organization encourages scholars in each tradition to continue their work, while also attending to how the resulting knowledge informs practice.

Second, organizing knowledge around accomplishments can make professional knowledge more accessible to practicing principals. Because accomplishments and their success criteria can be seen as statements about principals' intentions (the conditions that they want to create in their schools), principals can find relevant knowledge, not by categorizing problem situations, but by understanding their own intentions.

As important as we believe it is to organize knowledge around the accomplishments that principals strive to realize in their work, we also recognize that knowledge for practice cannot be fully captured through the component parts of a principal's role. School leadership requires continual movement between the part and the whole, between efforts to improve specific school conditions and to promote coherence in a school's overall development. The knowledge supporting practice has a similar twofold function. While important in supporting specific aspects of school work, knowledge also supports and is created as principals work toward a more integrated and coherent whole, which always occurs in a particular place and time with specific members of the school community in unique relationships with one another.

Knowledge for this more contextualized and holistic aspect of leadership is better captured in narratives than in discrete elements. We turn our attention to this complementary aspect of knowledge scope and structure in the next chapter.

Chapter 11

Sharing Knowledge Through Practice Narratives

Although their work is supported by wide knowledge about what constitutes quality in each school accomplishment and how to achieve it, principals operate in complex and uncertain contexts with few prescriptions for how to lead effectively. Precisely because circumstances are uncertain, principals must always be learning about their practice, their schools, and themselves in order to lead effectively (Dewey, 1938; Riessman, 1993). Successful principals build an understanding of what works in their schools and communities, generating knowledge through continuous observation, trial and error, reflection, and formal evaluation of their practice.

The craft knowledge resulting from this continuous learning is specific to each individual situation. It can provide insights about schools, in general, or be narrow and limited in applicability. It can reflect prejudices of a particular principal or community, or transcend historical patterns; it can lead to effective practices, or it simply can be wrong. Yet, with all its possible limitations, craft knowledge developed by individual principals gives the profession its most concrete information about the challenges and strategies for success in this rapidly changing role. Thus, this process of continuous learning in their work by principals precipitates the need to "uncover" (Wiggins & McTighe, 2005) how such craft knowledge might be captured, organized, and systematically shared to support the entire profession. Practice narratives offer one promising approach to fostering and sharing this craft knowledge.

Although craft, or narrative, knowledge acquired on the job may be trusted by practitioners, it lacks broad credibility (Barth, 2001): Quite simply, narrative knowledge—that knowledge developed personally through individual cases and other self-reflections (Bullough & Pinnegar, 2001)— is not collected consistently or rigorously, or codified systematically. All of this is perfectly understandable. Narrative knowledge is typical in practice settings, but its codification is at best of marginal concern to practitioners and only recently of general concern to researchers (Boje, 2001; Clandinin & Connelly, 2000).

A primary use of research on practice has been the development of cases for teaching (Ashbaugh & Kasten, 1991; Kowalski, 2001; Snowden & Gorton, 1998). Developed more systematically, cases also can be used to codify craft experience across a wide range of situations and events, generating many research possibilities while also improving personal and professional understanding (Conle, 2003).

This chapter explores one approach to organizing practitioner craft knowledge in professional cases. The discussion reflects the inherent respect for craft knowledge held by practitioners, the importance of systematizing the collection and sharing of craft knowledge, and the need to develop and use craft knowledge for improving practice and preparation. We conceptualize leadership during each school year as a constant process of weaving together the four leadership domains described earlier: leadership for sustainable purposes, leadership for strategic focus, leadership for effective action, and leadership for social capital. The result is an *annual case of school leadership* that supports and documents continuous learning and that can be combined with other cases to provide perspectives across multiple schools and across several years, improving knowledge *of*, *in*, and *for* practice (Jenlink, 2001). The chapter also describes a rationale for how such cases can be structured, with examples from early implementation of the method with practicing principals in high-poverty schools.

PROFESSIONAL CASES FOR BUILDING CRAFT KNOWLEDGE

Practitioner craft knowledge is important because it expresses the consequences of actions related to specific situations of practice in "detailed, concrete, and specific" ways (Hiebert et al., 2002, p. 6). When organized in personal narratives, such knowledge can reveal the complexities of practice in schools in a manner distinctly different from formal research methods (Gudmundsdottir, 2001). Even so, practitioner knowledge is hard to collect, accumulate, and exchange, because contexts are idiosyncratic and sharing such knowledge beyond immediate colleagues is problematic. Thus, practitioner craft knowledge too often remains tacit (Polanyi, 1962) or strengthens practice only in small communities. For this knowledge to accumulate and strengthen the profession, ways are needed for documenting, stockpiling, and communicating practitioner knowledge of educational leadership.

Although case documentation serves many professions as the foundation for the organization and communication of practitioner craft knowledge, it has been much less used in principals' practice (Silver, 1983).

Benefits of Professional Cases

Professional cases serve many purposes. First, as analyses of professional practice and its outcomes, they extend the profession's knowledge base through the explicit inclusion and recognition of practitioner knowledge as a source of information essential to effective practice. Second, professional cases generate questions and hypotheses, connecting practitioner knowledge with formal research, analogous to the way that medical cases constitute the accumulated "professional text" of treatment prescriptions. Third, professional cases support transitions in responsibility and could undergird smooth leadership succession in schools. For example, because case notes in law are standardized, attorneys quickly can become familiar with the background of a case when responsibility for a case changes. Fourth, case notes could facilitate communication among constituencies in schools, in the way that case notes in city planning help regulators, residents, and others see what is planned and its potential impact. Finally, professional cases can become a basis for professional development and learning. Although professional cases as outlined here are different from teaching cases, which generally are distillations of events for convenient review, professional case development and sharing can show how decision processes work in schools.

Requirements for Useful Professional Cases

As Hiebert and colleagues (2002) suggest, the way that professional cases are constructed has much to do with their likely utility. To serve the many purposes just outlined, annual cases of school leadership should: (1) focus on a meaningful and important unit of principals' work; (2) be in a form that is public, sharable, and structured to support analyses across cases; and (3) provide a context in which principals can share their understandings about existing school purposes, priorities, and problems.

A Meaningful Unit of Principals' Work. While much has been written about how principals select and respond to the ongoing problems that arise in school leadership, equally important is how a principal frames the context in which these problems are addressed. To succeed in daily problem solving, principals also need to encourage and lead the development of a mission for a school (Fullan, 2001) and make strategic choices about school priorities that respond to the school's unique needs and circumstances (Portin et al., 2003). At its best, then, problem solving advances the larger functions framed in the mission and priorities of a school (Spillane et al., 2001). A meaningful unit of principals' work thus should include these broader leadership functions that define the context of the school's work as well as the daily process of problem solving.

An *annual cycle of school leadership* appears to meet this requirement. It includes a cross-section of most of the activities associated with leading a school and is bounded by the natural break between school years. Like most organizational leaders, principals have to plan and act with longer time horizons than leaders with more focused responsibilities, so it should not be surprising that the unit of work for principals is considerably larger than that recommended for teachers (Hiebert et al., 2002). One principal describes the annual cycle this way:

> At the beginning of the year, I'm spending time orienting new staff and checking in with them and making more frequent observations. November and December are such frustrating months with too many interruptions; I don't feel like that's a very strong time in terms of instruction. January through March is a time when you're really going to get a lot of teaching and learning so I try to minimize interruptions. There's a lot of tension around the WASL time. After Spring Break, after the testing has ended, there's a kind of collective sigh and people are actually enjoying themselves. (Mather & Hopkins, 2005, p. 15)

A Case Format That Is Public, Sharable, Storable, and Analyzable. Craft knowledge benefits the entire profession when it can be shared widely, analyzed across contexts, and critiqued by others. This is done in some professions with highly standardized formats for written case notes. We offer similar recommendations for annual cases of school leadership. Current literature on school leadership includes several journals for sharing craft knowledge among practitioners, including the popular *Educational Leadership* and *Phi Delta Kappan*. A structured annual case process could supplement this information and support more detailed analyses across practitioner reports. A consistent outline for the annual case could help in both storing and analyzing cases (see below).

A Context for Sharing Understandings and Working Theories. To be most helpful, annual cases of school leadership should include descriptive accounts of major activities during the year and reports of the principal's understanding of how the school's purposes, priorities, and problems relate to one another and to the field's formal knowledge. Structured opportunities for sharing such reflections can ensure that cases of school leadership examine the linkages between practical problems and the profession's ethical, critical, legal, and scientific knowledge.

THE ANNUAL CASE OF SCHOOL LEADERSHIP

Responding to the criteria proposed by Hiebert and colleagues (2002), we have proposed elsewhere an "annual case of school leadership" as a way of representing principals' craft knowledge (Muth, Bellamy, Fulmer, & Murphy, 2004). Essentially, the annual case is a first-person account of the considerations, actions, results, and reflections associated with school leadership over the course of a school year. The annual case focuses attention and reflection on the four leadership domains described in Part II—leadership for sustainable purposes, strategic focus, effective action, and social capital—and invites discussion of how each evolves over the year and how they interact with one another. Figure 11.1 illustrates this design by showing each of the domains as one strand in a braid of leadership that is constructed over the school year. Each of the leadership domains presents unique tasks and challenges at different times during the year. While these naturally vary from one school to another, an illustrative set is provided in Table 11.1.

Because the yearly calendar for most schools provides natural beginning, ending, and reassessment periods, an annual cycle makes sense as a meaningful unit of principals' work. While each school year builds on prior years and sets the foundation for the next one, each also can serve as the basis for a substantive case history of a school's leadership and renewal.

Preparing an annual case, then, involves developing an account of leadership strategies and activities over the course of the year. Using a consistent outline for annual cases facilitates collection of related information, preparation of the case, sharing across schools, and analysis of multiple cases for more general

FIGURE 11.1. The Annual Cycle of School Leadership as a Braid of Four Leadership Domains

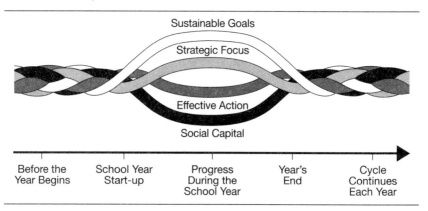

Table 11.1. Sample Concerns Associated with Each Leadership Domain as the School Year Progresses

	Sustainable Goals	Strategic Focus	Effective Action	Social Capacity
Before the School Year Begins	Understand competing priorities in the community	Select improvement goals for the greatest impact	Structure the school for success	Understand how school norms might have changed with new people
School Year Start-up	Communicate about values and goals and understand priorities of new people	Communicate about goals for strategic change	Organize quickly to get a fast start to instruction	Communicate norms to new school members and understand their priorities
During the Year	Engage staff and community in discussions of school issues and priorities	Increase involvement, focus, and commitment to action on school priorities	Attend to and solve problems with the greatest potential to impact goals and results	Bridge communication across groups; model the school's values
Year's End and Summer	Test constituents' satisfaction with school and its results	Review student learning results and extent of organizational improvement	Review leadership strategies; set personal learning goals	Assess gap between espoused and real norms

learning. The outline with which we are working in initial case development is shown in Table 11.2. As noted in the table, each case begins with a description of the school context, then progresses through the four stages that we have identified as critical leadership opportunities during each school year—the summer before the year begins, the start-up period, during the school year, and at year's end. Each case concludes with the principal's reflections on the year.

Following are descriptions of each of these case components, together with illustrations from initial use of the method. The cases illustrated were developed through a series of interviews with participating principals over one school year, which were transcribed and edited by both the interviewer and principal.

The School Context

To be useful beyond its immediate locale, each annual case requires a rich description of the context for leadership during the year. This information should include local demographics, the nature of the communities that the

TABLE 11.2. An Annual Case Outline

Name of School: _____ Annual Case Year: _____

Name of Principal: _____

Names and Positions of Participants in Case:

_____

_____

Part 1. The School Context

    A. School Profile

    B. Principal Background

Part 2. Before the Year Begins

Part 3. School-Year Start-Up

    A. Analysis of Student Learning Data

    B. Analysis of Data on School Functioning

    C. School Improvement Plan and Principal's Agenda

    D. Strategic Changes to Implement the Agenda

Part 4. During the School Year

    A. Representative Problems Addressed in Pursuit of School Goals

    B. Conversations to Advance the Purposes and Agenda

Part 5. End of the Year

    A. Results

    B. Reflection

Appendices of Supporting Artifacts

school serves, and significant trends or events that would help a reader understand the community's involvement in and expectations for its schools. Descriptive information, such as the school's size and nature of the school facility, provides useful background information for interpretation of an annual case. Another important part of the context for a school year is the experience that the principal brings to the school.

Guiding Questions. In addition to the "location" information at the top of the template (see Table 11.1), the case section on the school context seeks details about the school and about the principal's background. Whether the case is being constructed by the principal, a team of doctoral students, or a team of aspiring principals in a preparation program (see below), some basic information is required to facilitate comparisons across cases. Prompts that help a principal describe the context within which he or she works include, for example:

- Describe your school (e.g., its size, history, nature of the facility)
- Describe the communities your school serves (e.g., demographics, recent changes, current public issues)
- Describe your background and connection with the school (e.g., previous work history, experience in the school, knowledge of the community)

Sample Annual Case Excerpts. Even a brief description of school and community demographics can help a reader understand and interpret the annual case, as this selection illustrates.

> Eva Baca Elementary is a small school located in the closely-knit Eastwood Heights neighborhood in Pueblo, Colorado. This community has experienced growth after remaining stable for several years. A new housing development, targeting families who qualify for moderate to low-income housing, brought new families to the community. . . . Of the 280 Eva Baca students in preschool through fifth grade, 80% are Hispanic, 14% are Caucasian, with few Asian, Native American, or Black students represented in the school. . . . 86% qualify for free or reduced lunch. During the 2002–2003 school year, the student attendance rate at the school was 94.4%; the student stability and mobility rates were 69.97% and 30.03% respectively (reflecting) . . . a growing population of students from migrant families who live in a housing complex in the neighborhood. (Andrews & Ballek, 2005, pp. 2–3)

A second selection illustrates how a summary of the principal's experience and her or his connection with the particular school and community can be critical in understanding an annual case.

This is the second school where I've been a principal, and my eighteenth year as a principal. I was principal at Eastwood Elementary . . . for six years. After leaving Eastwood, I came back to Goodnight where I had taught for seven years. . . . My oldest son went to school here, and so it was a feeling of coming home. Not only had I taught here, I lived in the community, attended church in the community, and my boys were very involved in sports activities in the community. It made me very visible in the community. I believe it allowed parents to see me as a parent, as well as the principal, and as an advocate for our children. Another strong piece was that I have a Master's degree in special education and I have a special-needs son who has severe learning disabilities. I think this allowed people to see me as a real parent dealing with real issues. It's now been thirteen years, and it has been a great experience. (West & Ballek, 2005, p. 3)

Before the Year Begins

Most principals begin planning for each school year long before the previous year ends, working to understand how school goals and priorities need to be adjusted, searching data from the previous year for areas needing improvement, determining whether new structures are needed for the school to work more effectively, and looking for new or replacement staff who will contribute to the school's skill base and desired norms. This part of the annual case invites principals to use the four leadership domains as a guide for planning and as a framework for sharing the critical elements of the planning process with others.

Guiding Questions. Table 11.3 provides sample questions to prompt reflection and conversations in the four leadership domains as a principal plans for the next year. Responses to these questions provide data for a case, and if these or similar questions are asked across cases, then comparative analyses become ever more possible. Of course, any such list of questions is incomplete and should be supplemented with queries specific to the school's priorities, the problems at hand, and the nature of the school community.

Sample Annual Case Excerpts. Planning in many schools begins with the priorities and requirements of the district, where community and district requirements for school-improvement priorities have been established.

When I was hired as principal, the need for a clear focus on academic achievement was articulated by the superintendent, the school board, and the local newspaper. "High achievement was defined as every school achieving, whether it was low socio-economic, high minority, high mobility, or Title I." (Owen & Ballek, 2005, pp. 5–6)

TABLE 11.3. Questions to Guide Development of Case Component "Before the School Year Begins"

Leadership Domains	Guiding Questions
Leadership for Sustainable Goals	• What do you believe are the school district's priorities? • What special factors in the evaluation of principals reflect the district's priorities? • Put yourself in the shoes of parents in your school. What is most important to you? What issues might prompt you to call the principal? • Put yourself in the shoes of students in your school. What are your expectations or requests that you have of your school? • What are the major points of conflict among community groups? • What messages does the teacher union give about school priorities?
Leadership for Strategic Focus	• What components or topics must be addressed in your school plans? • What were the results of the school's efforts to achieve prior years' goals? • How well did various student groups do on state tests of learning? • In which subjects and grade levels did students do well? • What aspects of the school, if changed, might result in the greatest learning gains? • What particular content standards appear to give students difficulty on tests? • What new structures or policies might refocus the school on priority goals?
Leadership for Effective Action	• What district policies constrain how students are taught? • What district requirements address concerns about discipline? • Describe the process you use as you put together your school plan.
Leadership for Social Capital	• How much stability/change is expected in the school's staff, students, and parents for the coming year? • What best describes the norms for how teachers work together? For how teachers and parents communicate? • How much agreement existed last year about these norms? • With which community groups has the principal spent the most time and to what ends?

Whatever the district priorities, it is also critical for principals to know the concerns and priorities of families, school staff, and other community groups, and this requires constant listening.

> All the families want their kids to be safe. . . . [Some don't] want their kids to be here if they [are] not learning. . . . The staff's universal response is that they want to feel supported . . . to feel recognized . . . their goal is . . . that [each] child is reading at grade level, . . . feels good about himself, . . . likes coming to school, and is successful. (Mather & Hopkins, 2005, p. 10)

Such musings might become the first draft of possible goals for the year, goals to be articulated more fully, shared widely, and condensed to the precious few accomplishments that reasonably can be pursued over the course of the next year. In another school, Barbara Camerlo, the principal, clarifies the planning process for her school.

> As part of our annual planning process, we formally analyze student data each spring. We primarily use the CSAP, *Terra Nova*, and quarterly assessment data for this annual planning. We determine areas of strength, weakness, and any progress we have made toward previous goals. (Camerlo & Ballek, 2005, p. 8)

Finally, an important part of the planning process for each school year involves being alert to the climate within the building and how that might be changing.

> During my first few years here, the staff had concerns about safety. They wanted to have a safe school and wanted to be assured that I would address discipline and safety issues. When asked about student achievement several teachers said, "Nobody even knows who we are, except for our low achievement." That has changed significantly. The staff has worked very hard to improve achievement. . . . Teachers now have higher expectations of themselves, and of me, to meet our students' needs. (Baca-Anderson & Ballek, 2005, p. 6)

School-Year Start-Up

The first weeks of each school year are busy and important. Students are getting to know new teachers and classmates, teachers are organizing their classrooms and working together to make the school schedule function, and principals find time in a whirlwind of activity to welcome students and families and orient new staff. Principals also seek to set the tone for the year, get instruction started quickly, and implement organizational changes associated with new school priorities. Much happens in a short time that can be important to a principal's leadership for the entire year and is thus important to include in an annual case.

Guiding Questions. Questions that can prompt planning and reflection related to the start of the school year focus on how the school's students, staff, and families have changed since the previous year, what changes in procedures are needed to reach new goals, and how the principal can strengthen support for school goals, priorities, and norms. Table 11.4 provides questions that can provide a useful starting point for these reflections.

TABLE 11.4. Questions to Guide Development of Case Component "School Year Start-Up"

Leadership Domains	Guiding Questions
Leadership for Sustainable Goals	• Do new families in the school bring different priorities and expectations? • What changes in district priorities and goals need to be communicated? • Have events occurred during the summer that focused public attention on safety or any other specific issue?
Leadership for Strategic Focus	• Is there general agreement among staff on school goals and priorities? • What perspectives do new staff members bring regarding school priorities? • Who are key community or district partners for implementing changes required to meet annual goals? • What community actions suggest constraints on the school's plans?
Leadership for Effective Action	• What organizational changes are needed to respond to school goals? • What barriers exist to rapid implementation of the school schedule? • Whose assignments need adjustment from last year? • What meeting and reporting processes will foster improved collaboration among teachers? • What opportunities exist to increase student-learning time? • Should space in the building be assigned differently from before?
Leadership for Social Capital	• Have relationships among teachers and with family members changed over the summer? • Do new staff members agree with norms that underlie school operations and teachers' expectations for each other? • What personal or professional conflicts might disrupt collegial support within the school? • How can the school help families connect with one another?

Sample Annual Case Excerpts. With limited time at the start of the year, principals naturally select what needs primary emphasis. In some situations, this may be how to implement new organizational arrangements, while in others the focus might be on school-wide planning for instruction or developing norms of collaboration. In the first excerpt, the principal is building both individual capital (mining and using data) and grade-level capital (collaboration and planning) as well as developing effective action strategies.

> At the beginning of the school year, teachers are responsible for creating a class profile based on student data. When they analyze their current students' data, they can see which students are performing on level (coded green), slightly below level (coded yellow), below level (coded red), or at the advanced level (coded purple). Then after teachers organize their students' information, they develop their instructional plans for the year. They create a tier map to explain what they will do with students in the green level, yellow level, red level, or purple level. To facilitate teacher use of data, I use site money to schedule one retreat each semester, to give teachers time to monitor student progress data. I bring in three subs to free up one grade level team for an entire day. During the fall retreat the teachers analyze student data and develop their instructional plans. During the spring retreat, teachers take all the information they've compiled and develop their strategic plans for reading, writing, and math for the following year. (Garcia & Ballek, 2005, p. 15)

In this case, school start-up is about regeneration or rejuvenation, building perhaps on the summer hiatus.

> In August when staff returns I do some kind of an activity about how each person is going to contribute to the new year. For example, last year everybody made a chain link with a personal goal or contribution and how the links are connected. It's still hanging on the wall around some photos of all of us. We also review what our basic charges are, our School Improvement Plan goals we've agreed on. What happens in the very beginning is to set up a tone of excitement and positive feelings about the year starting—what we've accomplished and what we're going to continue to do. Another thing is to identify some real targets where we haven't been as bright as we'd like to be and really make this year count in those particular areas. There's a natural degree of stress with new students and new families, particularly next year with that new community joining us. (Mather & Hopkins, 2005, p. 27)

During the School Year

The school year incorporates most of the calendar year, leaving much ground to be covered, from how well the school is doing in addressing the accomplishments chosen for the year to unanticipated problems that arise.

Mid-course corrections are made, strategies that appeared sound are bolstered when they do less well than imagined, and entirely new tactics may be engaged to address unexpected issues. The annual case format samples these many events by asking principals to describe a few representative or important problems that are addressed during the year.

Guiding Questions. Questions for this component of the annual case (see Table 11.5) prompt reflections on problems that the principal selected as particularly important or representative of work during the school year. As with other case components, the questions are intended to support the process of school leadership as well as its documentation through the case process.

Sample Annual Case Excerpts. Schools with strong social capital often develop commitments to particular ways of teaching or particular interactions

TABLE 11.5. Questions about Selected Problems Addressed by the Principal During the School Year

Leadership Domains	Guiding Questions
Leadership for Sustainable Goals	• Why was the selected problem important in relation to school goals and community values? • Did your conversations about the problem lead to new understandings of the community or new commitments from community members?
Leadership for Strategic Focus	• Why was the selected problem important in relation to the school's annual plan and priorities? • Was this seen as a problem by others, or did you need to build agreement that it was important to address?
Leadership for Effective Action	• What was your "ideal solution" to the problem? • How did you decide that this solution would be the best solution? • What did you do to address the problem? • What did you learn from conversations with staff about strategies for addressing the problem? • What results were achieved? • Should space in the building be assigned differently from before?
Leadership for Social Capital	• Did the process of addressing this problem strengthen or weaken collaboration among teachers and between the school and families? • How did the process of addressing this problem affect the school's norms and expectations?

with the community. When new staff members join the school, these commitments can be quite different from their own prior experience and may even be inconsistent with their own views of good teaching. Principals then have to balance support for each teacher's prerogatives with the coherence of the school's approach.

> We had a person come to our school who was not a good match and who knew it and was unhappy. When you have a negative staff member, that's a significant problem because it can taint other people's behavior over time. Even if they realize that person is not moving us in the right direction, it still has an influence. The person's major issue was that we were working too hard and trying to do too much, reminding teachers that they did not have to do this past their contracted hours. . . . I met with the person directly, both when the person requested it and when I requested it. At one point I said, "This is not working and you know it and I know it. So we've got to figure out a way to get beyond here." [I dealt with it by] addressing it directly, noting it, talking with peers when they would. I guess it's just calling it when you see it, not letting down [on] what you believe, and trying to work through it with the person. You just take a stand and say "this is what our school's about." Maybe that is a message to everybody else, too. As all people do, the person had some excellent qualities and could make some contributions if they had wanted. We never stopped talking. I didn't want to lose the person totally, but we also both acknowledged where we stood. (Mather & Hopkins, 2005, p. 18)

Other problems serve as reminders of how intensely personal relationships in schools can become and the stresses that creates for school leaders.

> We had a case of suspected student-to-student sexual abuse [that] rocked me to my core. . . . Both parents didn't want to pursue the legal route. . . . I wanted to make sure I had correctly followed district policy. The parents had the option of taking the child to the Child Advocacy Center where they notify the police if they believe something happened. It took three days of my time to investigate, meet with the parents, and complete all the necessary documentation. The emotional drain was quite intense. I could see myself as both the mother of one student, and the mother of the other student. My husband even came to check on me at school because he was concerned about the emotional toll that issue was having on me. These are the kinds of issues that you are never quite prepared to handle, no matter how many years of experience you have as a principal. (West & Ballek, 2005, pp. 20–21)

Year's End

Even though the school year ends, schools never actually "close." School personnel are always working on the year to come, whether in actuality or simply rehearsing by thinking about what to do and not to do and what might be done better. This is when results are examined, people take stock, and plans are made for the coming year.

Guiding Questions. While the year's end may provide a breather, it also is the time to consider results and lay out plans for the future. The year's successes, big and small, require review as do plans and actions that produced less-than-preferred outcomes. Guiding questions are presented in Table 11.6.

Sample Annual Case Excerpts. End-of-year assessments can be exhilarating and humbling. Were the most optimistic expectations realized? Did what was hoped for actually occur? Taking everything into account, what was learned? First, a reflection on self.

> It became clear to me that I not only have to get initiatives moving, but I have to maintain them. After getting the teachers to a certain level of empowerment, I have to keep the ball afloat. I've still got to keep them motivated—that was a different phase I learned last year. A big part to me is being able to focus on getting better at what we are already doing, being able to go deeper and deeper and bringing staff along with it. (Rahim & Hopkins, 2005, p. 32)

Second, a reflection on parent involvement and what was learned from efforts to get more parents involved.

> It was important for us to focus on parent involvement. We knew that we needed our parents working with us to improve student achievement. Over time, we have learned a few things. First, we need to plan engaging programs with a specific theme. Next, the kids need to attend and bring their parents. Then, we need to have activities for the kids, and a rotation of hands-on activities for parents, not lectures. I think we're beginning to get a handle on ways to increase our parent involvement. We are thrilled about going from only five to ten parents to two hundred or more attending these events, and we will make some of our activities annual events. We are encouraged to see that our parents are more willing to partner with us. (Camerlo & Ballek, 2005, p. 26)

Third, a bout with math led to an understanding of the importance of focus.

> I feel the learning gains targeted in our school goals were met, except for the math. There are a couple of reasons why that happened. It was just a crazy year for math last year. We started out with Developing Mathematical Ideas or DMI. We already had the Addison Wesley [textbook series] and we were doing the Technical Education Research Center or TERC and then the district came up with the DMI. It threw everything up in the air and the teachers really didn't know how to focus on math—they were trying to do a little bit of all of them. Also we didn't have a good math assessment to go along so we couldn't measure

TABLE 11.6. Questions to Guide Development of Case Component "Year's End"

Leadership Domains	Guiding Questions
Leadership for Sustainable Goals	• Where did your school make progress? • How well do school results match community priorities? • Did results during the year measure up to your own values? • How has your understanding of community priorities changed during the year? • What makes you a good fit with the needs of this school and community?
Leadership for Strategic Focus	• What lessons are apparent from an analysis of student achievement data? • Were particular students, grade levels, subjects, or standards problematic? • What changed about the school's capacity to reach its goals during the year? • What transitions need to be managed over the summer to ensure a smooth start to the next school year?
Leadership for Effective Action	• What continuing problems will be important to address next year? • If you were to be promoted, so that you served as the supervisor of this school's principal next year, what advice would you give him or her? • In retrospect, what is one event that you wish you had handled differently? • What results were achieved? • Should space in the building be assigned differently from before?
Leadership for Social Capital	• What changes occurred during the year in the social connections among teachers and with families? • What changes occurred in the norms that actually seemed to guide professional and student behavior in the school? • Are there structural changes that might foster additional collaboration? • What differences exist between the principal's view of the school and that held by teachers, students, and families?

it. Plus we have the six math strands and we had no assessment to go along with that. Each program has its own assessment. . . . Math just fell apart. . . . We have got to have more coherence. (Rahim & Hopkins, 2005, pp. 32–33)

Supporting Artifacts

Many of the same materials and notes that principals use in their daily work can assist in case development if they are collected systematically over the year. Much like maintaining a file of receipts that may be useful for income-tax filing, the case process is facilitated as principals file various artifacts for later examination. Some simply will be used to prompt reflection, and others may be significant enough in the year's story to be included in the case itself.

Important information about the school's context and the priorities of school and community constituents can emerge at any time. News stories of changes in the community, special events that focus community attention on safety, or major changes in community employment can all signal the emergence of different expectations for schools. Informal notes from ongoing conversations with community members, newspaper clippings, minutes of various community meetings, and occasional surveys all can provide useful information about community expectations for school goals.

As plans are set for the school year, important artifacts naturally include data on student achievement, results of other school and community assessments, district requirements and plans, and results related to prior school goals. At the start of the year, school schedules, staff assignments, and professional development records can stimulate reflection about whether the school's facilities, time, opportunities for collaboration, and outreach to the community all were aligned with priority goals.

To support reflection on representative problems selected for discussion in the annual case, principals might draw on wide-ranging artifacts: data that led to identification of the problem, notes from conversations about whether the problem is important to the school, records of meetings in which strategies for addressing the problem were discussed, results of action research to address the problem, and reflections about whether the result had the intended effects.

Artifacts at the end of the year are particularly important. Typically, student achievement data and other information included in accountability reports will be included in the case, while reflections in the case itself might be expected to answer questions that are implied in these reports.

The Rest of the Story

Narrative cases of school leadership provide an interesting choice. When the principal and school are identified, cases can include school report cards and other artifacts that strengthen a reader's understanding of the school context. Publicly available data about school performance, demographics, and staffing allow users to conduct further analyses. Such cases also can serve local purposes, including orienting new staff to a school, enriching communications between principal and superintendent, or stimulating conversation among members of a leadership team.

But full identification has limitations. Schools succeed in part because trusting relationships develop among various members of the school community, and the simple act of reporting about such relationships can change how they function in the future. In addition, strong legal protections exist to support confidentiality of much information about students and staff and about how critical issues affecting both are handled. Much that is important in school leadership cannot be reported in an annual case when the identity of the school and principal are known. For example, the story behind personnel issues, accounts of conflicts with the union or district, or even the "residue" of previous leadership normally will be omitted because description could harm both the principal and others. It is these lost tidbits of information that vitiate the utility of cases that are not anonymous.

While local colleagues know immediately to ask about the rest of the story, case readers elsewhere can only surmise what else might be animating the events described in the case. Consequently, it may be useful to supplement the annual case process we have described with another approach that supports development of cases that are sufficiently anonymous to include richer descriptions of the more sensitive interpersonal challenges of school leadership.

USING ANNUAL CASES

As has been suggested, annual cases can be used in multiple ways, providing a school's staff with an annual look back to help them systematically evaluate the year's goals, trends, and outcomes as well as plan for the coming year. Cases that follow a common framework can be used for several other purposes. First, professional development for practicing principals and preservice preparation for aspirants are obvious applications. Second, such cases can provide researchers in the field a ready supply of authentic settings that are complex, contextual, and complete when compared with most cases currently used in teaching (Ashbaugh & Kasten, 1991; Snowden & Gorton, 1998). Third, cross-case analyses can inform practice-based theories about school leadership, offering examples of how various approaches have fared in different circumstances. Fourth, as the number of cases grows, they can significantly expand the field's practice-based knowledge. Each of these uses will be enhanced dramatically by a common framework and common procedures.

Case Teams

Principals are busy people. Their work lives are frenetic, and their focus on the success for children and youth almost single-minded. Adding another task to an already full plate simply may be too much. Consequently, it is unlikely that a substantial collection of annual cases will emerge if principals are expected to prepare written cases on their own. Each of the cases we have developed so far has involved contracting with an experienced school administrator who uses a structured protocol to interview participating principals over the course of a school year and who takes responsibility for initial editing of transcripts into a draft annual case.

It is possible that embedding the annual case process in expectations for school improvement and continuous reflective practice could help the annual case process become a natural part of principal work. To facilitate this cultural change, case teams, comprising faculty, doctoral students, and aspiring principals, could work with practicing principals to implement the annual case process over time. A typical team would include a case manager, with students expected to work closely with the principal. Since a case would be developed over the course of a year, the results could become part of the principal candidates' portfolios. As a result of their management experiences, perhaps across several cases, doctoral students could develop dissertation topics that address program requirements, in turn adding cross-case data about effective practice to the field.

A case team could begin by meeting with a principal to work through the necessary design, implementation, and assessment processes, ensuring that the focus of the case is on the improvement of student learning. The team could conduct and transcribe interviews with the principal over the course of the school year, obtain data about a school's successes and challenges, and assist the principal in crafting plans that address current and future problems. Successive drafts could be critiqued regularly during case team visits, perhaps facilitating the emergence of an annual accomplishment agenda.

Chapter 12

Developing Individual Knowledge for School Leadership

The previous two chapters discussed knowledge for the principalship by asking how the field as a whole might organize and further develop the knowledge that helps practitioners succeed. This shared knowledge in the profession is important, but successful school leadership ultimately depends on the knowledge that individual principals bring to their jobs. Here we turn to questions about what this individual knowledge includes and how principal preparation programs might foster its development.

Our aim in this discussion is narrowly focused on curriculum issues in principal preparation. As we inquire about the specific knowledge that new principals need in order to fulfill their responsibilities, we address two interrelated questions: (1) What knowledge is important for individual practitioners to develop in preparation programs and how should that knowledge be structured, and (2) what strategies make it more likely that candidates will use their knowledge to succeed as they confront novel school situations? In each case, we explore how the accomplishment perspective we have developed can contribute to the conceptual challenges facing principal preparation.

We also suggest ways that the Framework for School Leadership Accomplishments (FSLA) and the annual cases of school leadership might help in the development of practical performance tasks that support learning and assessment in those programs. Principal education programs—like most of education—increasingly are focused on what students actually learn, rather than what is covered in the curriculum, and this has led to growing interest in performance tasks that allow students to demonstrate their knowledge (Barnett & Muth, 2003).

When well constructed, performance tasks require integration and application of learning (Wiggins & McTighe, 1998), allow for assessment of individual learning (Linn & Baker, 1996), and provide early feedback and support as students solve problems in context (Fredericksen, Glaser, Lesgold, & Shafto, 1990; Lajoie, 2003). Performance tasks increasingly serve as the link between broad curriculum goals and students' actual learning. Performance tasks also can allow students to participate in the generation of knowledge for local use as they engage with current problems in specific schools (Fulmer, 1994).

Here, we describe the potential of the FSLA and the annual case of school leadership to supplement the growing array of performance tasks in preparation programs. In doing so, we intentionally maintain both approaches to developing and representing professional knowledge described in the previous two chapters. Performance tasks linked to the FSLA draw more on the field's research and theoretical knowledge, while those linked to the annual case emphasize development and use of more contextualized narrative knowledge.

INDIVIDUAL KNOWLEDGE

To meet leadership challenges in schools, principals draw on their prior professional experience and skills, formal education, and a broad range of tacit knowledge about how schools work, how to work with people, how to interact effectively with students, and so on (Polanyi, 1962). Like other professionals, principals use wide-ranging and eclectic sources in their search for knowledge that "works." While principals make use of social science research, they also draw on legal and ethical reasoning (Haller & Strike, 1986) and depend on "ordinary" or craft knowledge that is culled from experience and shared among practitioners (Lindblom & Cohen, 1979). Individual principals integrate information from these many sources into a more or less unified structure of what Lindblom and Cohen call "usable knowledge" that helps them navigate a difficult and complex job.

An important perspective on enhancing this individual knowledge comes from wide-ranging studies of how experts differ from novices in their approach to problems in their fields. Experts structure their knowledge around fundamental principles or major ideas in their fields (Chase & Simon, 1973; Chi, Feltovich, & Glaser, 1981). This, in turn, helps them notice patterns of meaningful information in the problems they observe (Egan & Schwartz, 1979; Lesgold, Rubinson, Feltovich, Glaser, Klopfer, & Wang, 1988) and to frame the solutions and opportunities in their situations more effectively (Chi, Glaser, & Rees, 1982). For example, anyone who has watched a televised sports event with a former player or coach immediately recognizes the difference in what is seen as plays develop. Experts see more than novices, understand better the implications of what they see, and offer more creative and successful solutions to those problems. "All experts have reasonable technical knowledge. What distinguishes them is what they can do with this knowledge" (Sternberg, 2003, p. 5). The goal, then, for principal preparation programs, is to find ways to move a candidate's individual knowledge and knowledge structures from novice to expert levels.

DEVELOPING AND STRUCTURING
INDIVIDUAL KNOWLEDGE

Formal principal preparation programs are only one part of an individual's development of the knowledge and expertise needed for school leadership. Knowledge for the principalship also comes from personal efforts to develop skills associated with personal and social awareness, communications, and relationship building (Bunker, Kram, & Ting, 2002; Goleman, 1998). Important, too, are the many opportunities that most individuals have for learning on the job through mentoring, coaching, special job assignments, evaluation, and feedback (Chappelow, 1998; Day, 2001; Sosik & Lee, 2002).

With such learning as a foundation, formal professional preparation programs can, among other things, help prospective principals formalize and fill gaps in their knowledge, structure and integrate that knowledge into a coherent whole, and develop skills for application in varied and changing circumstances (Conger & Benjamin, 1999). Consequently, the effectiveness of the curriculum relies on attention to the knowledge to be learned in a preparation program—its content—as well as to the way that knowledge is structured.

Important Knowledge for Principals

The selection of knowledge areas that are considered critical for effective practice is fundamental to all professional preparation. Over time, the content of principal preparation programs has evolved from a cluster of practical and technical managerial skills (Newlon, 1934), to a set of theories and principles based on positivist research in the social sciences (Silver, 1982), to a more eclectic definition of knowledge from several epistemological traditions (Griffiths, 1991; Thompson, 1993). These changes reflect ongoing debates about how to make the content of principal education programs more relevant to problems of practice (Silver, 1978), more inclusive of different perspectives on knowledge and leadership (Goldring & Greenfield, 2002), more grounded in reliable knowledge (Culbertson, 1964), more coherent internally within programs (Murphy, 1992), and more consistent with particular professional and democratic values (Murphy, 2002b).

In recent years, efforts to strengthen content in principal preparation programs have focused on the development of standards that specify the knowledge, skills, and dispositions that preparation programs are expected to help principal candidates develop (National Policy Board for Educational Administration, 2002). These standards serve to link the profession's evolving knowledge directly with the content of preparation programs and the requirements for professional licenses. As such, standards play an important role in both professional and public efforts to ensure that individual practitioners have the knowledge they need. Despite their importance, standards also present difficult choices: Too narrowly defined, such standards can debase professional knowledge and de-skill future practitioners (English, 2003). Too broadly defined, standards are not very useful measures of the competence of new professionals. Further, if standards do not include commitments to children's welfare, they miss the essential moral character of school work (Goodlad et al., 1990). By including these commitments, however, standards can open preparation programs to accusations of political bias in candidate selection and assessment (Leo, 2005; Wilson, 2005).

As such choices stimulate continued discussion and evolution of content standards for principal preparation, our accomplishment perspective suggests additional ways to frame central issues and build on the progress that has been made with broad adoption of content standards. First, accomplishments offer a different way of posing the question about what content is most important to include in standards and preparation programs. Rather than privileging particular academic disciplines or particular leadership approaches as professional and policy groups consider standards, the accomplishment perspective selects knowledge as important when it contributes to critical school accomplishments. That is, the justification for including knowledge in a principal education curriculum is its contribution, and its usefulness, in helping principals frame success criteria for and realize school accomplishments. As noted earlier, such contribution is of two kinds: Knowledge helps define success criteria for accomplishments in varied contexts, and knowledge provides action strategies for how those success criteria can be reached. This leads to a very eclectic knowledge base for principal preparation, in that information from ethical and critical reasoning, legal reasoning, social science research, and craft knowledge all can contribute to defining success criteria and action strategies.

Second, while accomplishments provide a rationale for an inclusive definition of knowledge for preparation programs, accomplishments also highlight the uncertainty of that knowledge as a guide for practice. Leadership within an accomplishment framework is well supported by knowledge of both educational goals and leadership strategies to reach those goals. But while it is replete with resources to support practice, the profession's knowledge is not prescriptive. Professional knowledge about both goals and methods is refined and adapted through each principal's collaboration with others in the school community. Because not all communities will accept any given set of success criteria for school accomplishments, and because the same procedures will not work in all settings, the accomplishment mind-set argues against standards with too much specificity about particular methods of instruction and leadership or too many prescriptions about the priorities that underlie success criteria.

In the accomplishment view, this lack of prescriptiveness in the field's knowledge is not an argument against standards for preparation and licensure, as Hess (2003) has suggested. While little specific procedural knowledge may be mandatory for every new principal, every principal must know enough to realize important school accomplishments. Thus, as standards evolve, it may be helpful to ensure that each candidate has *sufficient* knowledge and skills to realize school accomplishments, without defending any particular strategy or viewpoint as absolutely *necessary*. Such an approach could allow for the flexibility in program approaches advocated by English (2003), without compromising the professional quality that standards help ensure.

Third, because accomplishments are school conditions that are influenced by everyone in the school community, the accomplishment perspective shifts the focus of attention from what the principal does alone to what the whole school gets done. Again, this serves to broaden the scope of knowledge needed in principal preparation, because the principal's actual role and knowledge needs vary depending on the capabilities of others in the school and community. Principal preparation programs cannot assume that others in the school will have all the expertise needed to lead instruction, coordinate with families, or analyze student-learning data. As with leaders in other settings, principals help their schools realize accomplishments sometimes by doing the work directly; sometimes by selecting, mentoring, and inspiring others who do it; and sometimes by creating the fiscal, social, and structural conditions that support the work. Knowledge related to all of these roles is important.

Helping Principal Candidates Structure Their Developing Knowledge

Developing expertise for the principalship, like much other learning, involves helping candidates build new cognitive structures to reflect the major ideas and underlying principles in the field and how these are interrelated (Bransford, Brown, & Cocking, 2001). In this regard, principal education programs face challenges similar to many other professional programs because candidates enter formal education with large stores of informal knowledge and, often, strong biases built up over years of working in schools. This existing knowledge affects how the candidate interprets and organizes learning from formal preparation programs and can interfere with the development of new cognitive structures.

Fortunately, evidence indicates that, through education, an individual's structuring of personal knowledge can become more like that of a teacher (Shavelson, 1972). This suggests that systematic use of a scheme for organizing the curriculum in a preparation program can help candidates develop more useful knowledge structures, whatever learning resulted from their prior experience.

While several organizing schemes are possible, Hills's (1978) recommendations for general professional knowledge seem to be a useful starting point. He argues that knowledge for professional practice is most usable when it is organized around the major responsibilities, or problems, for which the individual practitioner is responsible. In our formulation of accomplishment-minded practice, these major responsibilities are the school's accomplishments—the conditions that support student learning while also responding to community values. Consequently, the same structure that we recommended in Chapter 10 for organizing knowledge for the school leadership profession seems useful as a framework for helping individual principal candidates structure their own knowledge.

Like the formal professional knowledge base, each principal's individual knowledge would be structured to answer two questions about each school accomplishment in the FSLA: (1) What informs the definition of success criteria for each accomplishment, and (2) what strategies or approaches are useful elements of a repertoire of possible leadership actions associated with meeting each accomplishment's success criteria? And similar to the profession's shared knowledge, each principal candidate's knowledge structure needs to include information associated with philosophy and values, legal requirements, social science research results, and public craft knowledge within the profession.

An individual's knowledge structure also includes the candidate's own personal knowledge and experience. Consequently, an explicit effort to help candidates structure their knowledge around the FSLA could help principal candidates establish stronger links between their prior, often tacit, knowledge about school leadership and the knowledge, skills, and dispositions that are included in the formal curriculum.

Performance Tasks That Support the Development of Structured Knowledge

In essence, we argue that what is important to learn in principal preparation relates to principals' responsibilities for realizing school accomplishments. Realizing accomplishments, as noted earlier, includes both framing responsive success criteria and taking action to achieve those criteria in varied circumstances. Similarly, we argue that if individuals are helped to structure their emerging knowledge around the accomplishments in the FSLA, they will be better able to access, apply, and continue to develop that knowledge in practice. The FSLA offers several possibilities for constructing performance tasks that could help principal candidates achieve such learning. Three that have shown some promise in our work are a structured leadership resume, a personal knowledge-base assignment, and an organized reading log.

Leadership Resume. Simply asking candidates to organize their resumes to highlight leadership experiences associated with each of the FSLA's nine accomplishments may foster an awareness of the breadth of the school leadership role and stimulate reflection on areas of strength and weakness (Ballek, O'Rourke, Provenzano, & Bellamy, 2005). Such a leadership resume also can serve as a bridge between leadership development in a school or district, where most leadership experiences occur, and the formal principal education program, where these experiences should be elaborated through an internship and grounded in professional knowledge.

A principal candidate's previous leadership activities might have included chairing a school-improvement team, heading a team to work on the student handbook, or leading a group of fourth- and fifth-grade teachers to create performance assessments for the science curriculum. A leadership resume simply asks the candidate to describe these experiences and categorize them according to the FSLA accomplishments that the activities were intended to influence. The resulting description serves to highlight strengths and gaps in a candidate's prior experience and can provide a foundation for individualized advising during the preparation program. If the resume is extended to internship experiences in the preparation program, it also may include reflections on the experience and systematic efforts to link the experience with concepts emphasized in the program.

Personal Knowledge-Base Assignment. The personal knowledge-base task asks candidates to describe and organize their initial and developing knowledge about school leadership. The task focuses on knowledge that students can write about, primarily declarative, procedural, and schematic knowledge in the knowledge taxonomy offered by Shavelson and Huang (2003). The task asks candidates to describe what they know and believe is most important in providing leadership for each of the nine accomplishments in the FSLA and to note whether the knowledge relates to the accomplishment's success criteria or action repertoire.

Since most principal candidates enter preparation programs with considerable school experience and well-developed ideas about how schools should work, this task can help candidates make their prior, often tacit, knowledge more explicit and can provide an initial assessment of candidates' knowledge and beliefs as they enter the program. Regular updates can help both candidates and program faculties recognize how this prior learning is affected by and integrated with the more formal learning in preparation programs. The result is a description of a candidate's developing knowledge, organized to mirror the structure we proposed in Chapter 10 for the profession's knowledge.

Structured Reading Log. This task asks candidates to use the FSLA as an organizing framework for their reading notes and reflections. We have found a "double-entry" note-taking approach to be particularly informative. Candidates copy or scan compelling quotes from their professional reading into a data matrix that includes the various types of knowledge (ethical reasoning, legal reasoning, social science, craft knowledge, and personal knowledge) for each of the nine FSLA accomplishments. Associated with each quote, the candidate writes a reflection that describes why this quote is significant to them. Consequently, this task asks candidates to assess constantly how professional readings relate to the principal's responsibility to realize school accomplishments and allows program faculties to monitor the kinds of understandings that candidates develop about principal practice as they engage with their reading.

As candidates add quotations and reflections regarding references, concepts, frameworks, understandings, or strategies, they will begin to sort these entries into either the success criteria or response repertoire category. As these reading logs accumulate over the course of an entire program, they result in an organized database of notes, structured like that proposed in Table 10.1 for the profession's knowledge, which includes both quotations from readings and candidate reflections.

HELPING PRINCIPAL CANDIDATES
USE THEIR KNOWLEDGE

Like other professional education endeavors, the goal of principal preparation is not just acquisition of knowledge, but also the use of knowledge to solve applied problems. And, because the contexts of practice are varied and constantly changing, principal candidates succeed only when they are able to use what they know in a variety of situations.

Performance in Different Contexts

Advice from various learning theories encourages both learning in realistic contexts and explicit efforts to sample the range of variability in those contexts where performance ultimately is expected. Considerable evidence supports the conclusion that transfer of learning is increased when a sufficient range of examples is included in initial learning (Bransford, Vye, Kinzer, & Risko, 1990; Englemann & Carnine, 1982). Much professional education involves a similar logic, attempting to develop the skills and understandings to address a wide range of "cases" that the professional will encounter. For physicians, attorneys, and architects, these cases are normally individual clients who request service, but have varying difficulties, needs, and goals. Building professional skill typically involves studying and experiencing a large number of such cases, understanding both the kinds of thinking that apply to all cases and the kinds of thinking that apply to the specifics of each case.

Principal preparation programs have developed several strategies for helping candidates sample a range of daily problems of school leadership. A rich literature on problem-based learning (Barrows, 1985, 1986; Bridges, 1992; Ford, Martin, Muth, & Steinbrecher, 1997; Murphy, Martin, Ford, & Muth, 1996; Muth, 1999a; Muth, Murphy, & Martin, 1994; Rehm & Muth, 1998) and case-based teaching (Ashbaugh & Kasten, 1991; *Journal of Cases in Educational Leadership*, 1998–present; Kowalski, 2001) points to instructional procedures that help principal candidates build flexible, generalized ways to think about daily school problems. By presenting several cases and by discussing how various circumstances could affect how a principal might respond to a particular case, these approaches offer considerable promise in helping prospective school leaders develop understandings that can be applied in context.

For example, problem-based learning situates learning in a particular context and asks students to integrate knowledge from various sources that may be needed to address an ill-structured, practical problem. Typically, teams of students are placed in the role of problem solvers, finding and integrating the needed information. Problem-based learning supports transfer to professional practice settings precisely because it requires responses to authentic settings during original learning (Duffy & Cunningham, 1996). In addition, because problem-based principal education programs typically have engaged students with many different problems of practice during the course of a program, candidates sample a variety of situations and pressures that affect how and when knowledge can be applied successfully (Bridges & Hallinger, 1995; Muth, 1999b).

Case teaching and problem-based learning offer important means of providing the multiple examples that help principal candidates build generalizable understandings related to management of daily problems (what we called leadership in the action domain in Chapter 8). Similar strategies for multiple examples are needed to foster the use of expertise in the leadership domains of sustainable purposes and strategic focus, but, in order to do this, the time frame for each example must be expanded. While skills at the level of daily action are important, we reasoned in Chapter 11 that the most useful case—or instance of principal work—is a full year in the life of a school.

The full year creates the context within which more immediate problems are understood and framed: Day-to-day problems are addressed in the context of an annual agenda that reflects the school's past performance, its community's purposes, and the staff and student characteristics peculiar to that school community. A critical part of the principal's job is to define and frame the year-long context within which daily problems are addressed. Effective principals envision and plan for the year ahead of time, operate within a framework during the year, and then reflect on the year. A candidate simply cannot understand the work of the principalship without a view of the full annual cycle. Nor can a principal perform expertly without the ability to define sustainable purposes and strategic targets in different school communities and situations.

One reason that preparation for the principalship is so complex is that these "annual cases" of principals' work are more difficult to experience and study than the cases of medicine and law, which usually are more circumscribed, less protracted, and less complex. Even though a case in medicine may contain years of data, it focuses on one client. So, too, a legal case may have found its way over the years to the Supreme Court, but it is bounded by the client's pursuits. For principal candidates, the case is the annual cycle, and to build facility with the annual cycle of school leadership, preparation programs need to structure learning experiences that allow candidates to experience many different annual cases—a challenge, given that most preparation programs provide only 1 or 2 years of part-time study, while typical medical or legal education lasts for 3 or more years of full-time study.

A contribution of the accomplishment perspective is the possible use of written annual cases in preparation programs. By reading and critiquing existing cases, by working with principals to develop annual agendas and writing cases, and by writing or participating in the development of several annual cases, prospective principals should develop the flexible insights needed for leadership in constantly changing school circumstances. Most people instinctively understand the need to solve short-term problems—crises, for example, are immediate if not clear. Given the year-long nature of principals' work, however, preparation programs need to foster the understanding that problems occur in the context of an annual cycle, that the purposes and agenda for the school create the context for solving daily problems, and that framing and sustaining this annual context is critical to principal success. Annual cases, then, add an important dimension to consideration of daily problems by focusing on the community purposes and annual agenda that create the context within which more immediate problems are addressed. Spillane and colleagues (2001) make a similar argument, noting that the "micro-problems" of day-to-day leadership must be dealt with in the framework of "macro-leadership functions" associated with overall school success.

Continuous Learning for Knowledge Use

Another challenge of knowledge use brings our discussion back to how individual candidates structure their developing knowledge. Expert professional practice often requires more than applying previous learning in new contexts (Muth & Barnett, 2001). The problems that principals face often require new learning as well—continuously improving one's understanding of community values and purposes, developing a successively deeper repertoire of strategies, reflectively and effectively modifying previous efforts, and so on. Preparation that builds readiness for such career-long learning depends on cognitive frameworks or scaffolds that help principals integrate personal and formal knowledge, and relate new learning to existing knowledge and structure (Bransford & Schwartz, 1999).

Again, an accomplishment model like the FSLA appears to offer advantages. For example, it can serve as a mechanism for ongoing integration of new knowledge and as a stimulus for questions that lead to further learning. Principals' continuing learning could be facilitated through collaborations between school districts and universities that support the use of common frameworks for developing expertise, mentoring new principals, evaluating principal performance, and supporting ongoing learning.

When professional practice is at its best, ongoing learning improves both individual expertise and the effectiveness of the profession as a whole (Fulmer, 1994). Mechanisms exist for individuals to document their learning in ways that are accessible to others. The annual case of school leadership might serve as such a mechanism. If principals routinely developed annual cases of their leadership approaches, contexts, and results, the reflection might well support consolidation of individual learning. It also could serve as a means for information exchange within the profession, documenting the development of craft knowledge and stimulating further study of apparent successes.

Performance Tasks to Support Knowledge Use

The annual case of school leadership abounds with possibilities for learning activities and performance tasks that focus on the use of knowledge in varied circumstances. Three possibilities from our work include a school reflection, a case critique, and a school leadership entry plan. While these tasks are necessarily paper-and-pencil based, they complement and help integrate other more applied projects.

School Reflection. Many candidates enter principal preparation programs with somewhat incomplete understandings of their own schools. Although they may have taught in the school for a number of years and even held some leadership responsibilities, many aspects of the school often lie beyond their personal experience and awareness. In this context, a useful performance task in the early stages of a preparation program asks candidates to read two or three cases and prepare a reflective essay on questions that they would now like to ask about their own school. That is, after reading annual cases from other schools, what would the candidate like to ask the principal, other teachers, district supervisors, or union representatives? As they review these essays, faculty members can learn about the extent to which candidates understand the complexities of school operation and the extent to which they are already able to take the principal's perspective in thinking about the school.

Case Critique. As candidates progress in their preparation programs, they should have increasing knowledge of leadership theories, school-improvement strategies, and critical perspectives on school goals and practices, all of which provide the foundation for analysis and critique of annual cases. Prompts related to each of the four leadership domains we discussed in Chapters 6–9 can provide some structure to the candidate's task: Do the school's goals differentially benefit various student groups? What evidence is there that the school is adapting to and leading a balance of community priorities and values? Are the school's goals grounded in student learning and assessment of current school operations? Is it clear that the school was organized to reach those goals? How did the major problems highlighted in the case advance the school and help accomplish goals? What evidence is there for development of social capital in the school and community?

Whether this critique is done individually or in teams, and is presented orally or in writing, it provides candidates with repeated opportunities to apply more abstract concepts and theories to the leadership challenges associated with framing sustainable goals, implementing a strategic focus, and strengthening social capital.

Leadership Entry Plan. Designed for completion near the end of a preparation program, this performance task asks candidates to select one annual case, assume that she or he has been selected in June as the school's principal for the year immediately following the case, and develop a plan for entry into the school's principalship. The task requires the candidate to decide what else she or he needs to know about the school, develop hypotheses about what the school needs in order to move forward, decide how to get needed information, and plan a series of activities over the summer and at the start of the school year to position the school for improvement. Naturally, much more information is needed than typically is available in an annual case, but annual cases often contain more information than new principals have about their first school assignment.

PROGRAMS FOR PREPARING
ACCOMPLISHMENT-MINDED LEADERS

We have written elsewhere about several ways that principal preparation programs might be structured to foster school–university connections (Browne-Ferrigno & Muth, 2001), promote collaborative learning in cohort groups (Barnett & Muth, 2003), link learning to problems of practice (Murphy, Martin, & Muth, 1994), and provide meaningful clinical experiences (Fulmer, Muth, & Reiter, 2004). These recommendations notwithstanding, we expect that programs that are structured in many different ways could prepare candidates for accomplishment-minded practice. The accomplishment perspective has more to say about *what* principal education programs need to get done than about *how* to do it. Our focus on knowledge development, structuring, and application is intended as an invitation to colleagues to join in the search for yet more effective preparation models.

To prepare prospective principals for their responsibilities, principal education programs must focus on accomplishments that are similar to the accomplishments that we have described for P–12 schools. Like schools, principal education programs strive to support student (principal-candidate) learning, and they do this through the curriculum that they define, the instruction and learning experiences that they provide, and the climate that they create to support candidates. These core accomplishments, in turn, are supported by others: developing program resources, using those resources to support program operations, supporting faculty, and engaging in program improvement. Like the accomplishments that we have described for schools, accomplishments for principal preparation programs include success criteria that reflect both general professional standards and the particular values of faculty and surrounding school districts. Each of the accomplishments can be reached in several different ways, so they are statements about what must get done, not how to do it. And, the uncertainties of principal preparation require ongoing measurement of student learning in order to check both the strategic focus and daily actions of principal preparation programs.

Accordingly, while organizing learning experiences for principal candidates around the accomplishments in the FSLA seems to us a natural evolution from our work with problem-based learning (Muth et al., 2001), it is just as possible that preparation for accomplishment-minded practice could occur in programs that are structured around more traditional university courses, extended internships, case-based teaching, or critical inquiry. While methods of preparation might well vary, the expected results are similar: Principal candidates graduate with the expertise needed to realize school accomplishments in a variety of community contexts, applying professional knowledge to understand and influence community expectations—the ends of schooling—as well as to design leadership strategies that help schools meet those expectations.

References

Achilles, C. M., Reynolds, J. S., & Achilles, S. H. (1997). *Problem analysis: Responding to school complexity.* Larchmont, NY: Eye on Education.

Andrews, E., & Ballek, K. (2005). Eva R. Baca Elementary School, school year 2003–2004: An annual case of school leadership. Unpublished manuscript. University of Colorado at Denver and Health Sciences Center, University of Washington, Bothell.

Argyris, C., Putnam, R., & Smith, D. M. (1985). *Action science: Concepts, methods, and skills for research and intervention.* San Francisco: Jossey-Bass.

Aronowitz, S., & Giroux, H. (1991). *Postmodern education: Politics, culture and social criticism.* Minneapolis: University of Minnesota Press.

Ashbaugh, C., & Kasten, K. (1991). *Educational leadership: Case studies for reflective practice.* New York: Longman.

Baca-Anderson, J., & Ballek, K. (2005). Park View Elementary School, school year 2003–2004: An annual case of school leadership. Unpublished manuscript. University of Colorado at Denver and Health Sciences Center, University of Washington, Bothell.

Ballek, K., O'Rourke, A., Provenzano, J., & Bellamy, T. (2005). Seven keys in cultivating principals and teacher leaders. *Journal of Staff Development, 26*(2), 42–49.

Banks, J. (1993). Multicultural education: Historical development, dimensions, and practices. In L. Darling-Hammond (Ed.), *Review of research in education* (Vol. 19, pp. 3–49). Washington, DC: American Educational Research Association.

Baptiste, H. (1999). The multicultural environment of schools: Implications to leaders. In L. Hughes (Ed.), *The principal as leader* (2nd ed.). Upper Saddle River, NJ: Merrill.

Barnett, B. G., & Muth, R. (2003). Assessment of cohort-based educational leadership preparation programs. *Educational Leadership and Administration: Teaching and Program Development, 15,* 97–112.

Barnhardt, V. (1994). *The school portfolio.* Larchmont, NY: Eye on Education.

Barrows, H. (1985). *How to design a problem-based curriculum for the preclinical years.* New York: Springer.

Barrows, H. (1986). A taxonomy of problem based learning methods. *Medical Education, 20,* 481–486.

Barth, R. S. (2001). *Learning by heart.* San Francisco: Jossey-Bass.

Beck, L. (1993). *Reclaiming educational administration as a caring profession.* New York: Teachers College Press.

173

Bellamy, T. (1999). *The whole school framework: A design for learning.* Des Moines: New Iowa Schools Development Corporation.

Bellamy, T., Crawford, L., Huber-Marshall, L., & Coulter, G. (2005). The fail-safe schools challenge: Leadership possibilities from high reliability organizations. *Educational Administration Quarterly, 4*(3), 383–412.

Bellamy, T., Fulmer, C., Murphy, M., & Muth, R. (2003). A framework for school leadership accomplishments: A perspective on knowledge, practice, and preparation for principals. *Leadership and Policy in Schools, 2*(4), 241–261.

Bellamy, T., Fulmer, C. L., Murphy, M. J., & Muth, R. (2006). Conceptual foundations for principal leadership. In A. Danzig, K. Borman, B. Jones, & W. Wright (Eds.), *Learner centered leadership: Research, policy and practice* (pp. 77–107). Mahwah, NJ: Erlbaum.

Bellamy, T., Holly, P., & Sinisi, R. (1999). *Cycles of school improvement.* Oxford, OH: National Staff Development Council.

Bernstein, R. (1993). *The new constellation: The ethical-political horizons of modernity/postmodernity.* Cambridge: Polity Press.

Black, J. A., & English, F. W. (1986). *What they don't tell you in schools of education about school administration.* Lancaster, PA: Technomic.

Blase, J. (1989). Teachers' political orientation vis-à-vis the principal: The micropolitics of the school. In J. Hannaway & R. Crowson (Eds.), *The politics of reforming school administration* (pp. 113–126). New York: Falmer.

Blase, J. (1993). The micropolitics of effective school-based leadership: Teachers' perspectives. *Educational Administration Quarterly, 29,* 142–163.

Blase, J., & Blase, J. (1999). Principals' instructional leadership and teacher development: Teachers' perspectives. *Educational Administration Quarterly, 35*(3), 349–378.

Blythe, T., Allen, D., & Powell, B. (1999). *Looking together at student work.* New York: Teachers College Press.

Bohman, J. (1991). *New philosophy of social science: Problems of indeterminacy.* Cambridge, MA: MIT Press.

Boje, D. M. (2001). *Narrative methods for organizational & communications research.* Thousand Oaks, CA: Sage.

Bolman, L., & Deal, T. (1991). *Reframing organizations: Artistry, choice, and leadership.* San Francisco: Jossey-Bass.

Bossert, S. (1988). School effects. In N. Boyan (Ed.), *Handbook of research on educational administration* (pp. 341–352). New York: Longman.

Bossert, S., Dwyer, D., Rowan, R., & Lee, G. (1982). The instructional management role of the principal. *Educational Administration Quarterly, 18*(3), 34–64.

Bransford, J., Brown, A., & Cocking, R. (Eds.). (2001). *How people learn: Brain, mind, experience, and school.* Washington, DC: National Academy Press.

Bransford, J., & Schwartz, D. (1999). Rethinking transfer: A simple proposal with multiple implications. In A. Iran-Nejad & D. Pearson (Eds.), *Review of research in education* (Vol. 24, pp. 61–100). Washington, DC: American Educational Research Association.

Bransford, J., Vye, N., Kinzer, C., & Risko, V. (1990). Teaching thinking and content knowledge: Toward an integrated approach. In B. Jones & L. Idon (Eds.), *Dimensions of thinking and cognitive instruction: Implications for educational reform* (Vol. 1, pp. 381–413). Hillsdale, NJ: Erlbaum.

Braun, D., & Guston, D. (2003). Principal–agent theory and research policy. *Science and Public Policy*, *30*(5), 302–308.

Brent, B. O. (1998). Should graduate training in educational administration be required for principal certification? Existing evidence suggests the answer is no. *Teaching in Educational Administration Newsletter*, *5*(2), 1, 3–8.

Brethower, D. (1997). Specifying the human performance technology knowledgebase. *Performance Improvement Quarterly*, *10*(1), 74–96.

Bridges, E. M. (with Hallinger, P.). (1992). *Problem based learning for administrators*. Eugene, OR: ERIC Clearinghouse on Educational Management.

Bridges, E. M., & Hallinger, P. (1995). *Problem based learning in leadership development*. Eugene, OR: ERIC Clearinghouse on Educational Management.

Browne-Ferrigno, T., Barnett, B., & Muth, R. (2003). Cohort program effectiveness: A call for a national research agenda. In F. C. Lunenburg & C. S. Carr (Eds.), *Shaping the future: Policy, partnerships, and emerging perspectives*. 2003 yearbook of the National Council of Professors of Educational Administration (pp. 274–290). Lanham, MD: Scarecrow Education.

Browne-Ferrigno, T., & Muth, R. (2001, November). *Becoming a principal: Role transformation through clinical practice*. Paper presented at the annual meeting of the University Council for Educational Administration, Cincinnati, OH.

Bruffee, K. A. (1986). Social construction, language, and the authority of knowledge. *College English*, *48*(8), 773–790.

Bruffee, K. (1993). *Collaborative learning: Higher education, interdependence and the authority of knowledge*. Baltimore: Johns Hopkins University Press.

Bryk, A., Camburn, E., & Louis, K. (1999). Professional community in Chicago elementary schools: Facilitating factors and organizational consequences. *Educational Administration Quarterly*, *35*, 751–781.

Bryk, A., Lee, V., & Holland, P. (1993). *Catholic schools and the common good*. Cambridge, MA: Harvard University Press.

Bull, B., & McCarthy, M. (1995). Reflections on the knowledge base in law and ethics for educational leaders. *Educational Administration Quarterly*, *31*(4), 613–631.

Bullough, R. V., Jr., & Pinnegar, S. (2001). Guidelines for quality in autobiographical forms of self-study research. *Educational Researcher*, *30*(3), 13–21.

Bunker, K., Kram, K., & Ting, S. (2002). The young and clueless [Electronic version]. *Harvard Business Review*, *80*(12), 1–8.

Burt, R. (1992). *Structural holes*. Cambridge, MA: Harvard University Press.

Burt, R. (2000). The network structure of social capital. In R. Sutton & B. Staw (Eds.), *Research in organizational behavior* (Vol. 22, pp. 345–423). Greenwich, CT: JAI Press.

Cambron-McCabe, N. (1999). Confronting fundamental transformation of leadership preparation. In J. Murphy & P. Forsyth (Eds.), *Educational administration: A decade of reform* (pp. 217–227). Thousand Oaks, CA: Corwin Press.

Camerlo, B., & Ballek, K. (2005). South Park Elementary School, school year 2003–2004: An annual case of school leadership. Unpublished manuscript. University of Colorado at Denver and Health Sciences Center, University of Washington, Bothell.

Cameron, K. (1986). Effectiveness as paradox: Consensus and conflict in conceptions of organizational effectiveness. *Management Science, 32*(5), 539–553.

Campbell, E. (1999). Ethical school leadership: Problems of an elusive role. In P. Begley (Ed.), *Values and educational leadership* (pp. 151–164). Albany: State University of New York Press.

Campbell, R., Cunningham, L., Nystrand, R., & Usdan, M. (1990). *The organization and control of American schools* (6th ed.). New York: Merrill.

Chappelow, C. (1998). 360-degree feedback. In C. McCauley, R. Moxley, & E. Van Velsor (Eds.), *The Center for Creative Leadership handbook of leadership development* (pp. 29–65). San Francisco: Jossey-Bass.

Chase, W., & Simon, H. (1973). Perception in chess. *Cognitive Psychology, 4,* 55–81.

Chi, M., Feltovich, P., & Glaser, R. (1981). Categorization and representation of physics problems by experts and novices. *Cognitive Science, 5,* 121–125.

Chi, M., Glaser, R., & Rees, E. (1982). Expertise in problem solving. In R. Sternberg (Ed.), *Advances in the psychology of human intelligence* (Vol. 1, pp. 7–75). Hillsdale, NJ: Erlbaum.

Chrislip, D. (2002). *The collaborative leadership fieldbook.* San Francisco: Jossey-Bass.

Chrislip, D., & Larson, C. (1994). *Collaborative leadership: How citizens and civic leaders can make a difference.* San Francisco: Jossey-Bass.

Clandinin, D. J., & Connelly, F. M. (2000). *Narrative inquiry: Experience and story in qualitative research.* San Francisco: Jossey-Bass.

Clarke, M., Davis, A., Rhodes, L., & Delott-Baker, E. (1996). *Creating coherence: High achieving classrooms for minority students* (Final report, U. S. Department of Education OERI Field Initiated Studies Program, grant R117 E302 44). Denver: University of Colorado at Denver.

Cohen, D., & Prusak, L. (2000). *In good company: How social capital makes organizations work.* Cambridge, MA: Harvard Business School Press.

Coleman, J. (1988). Social capital and the creation of human capital. *American Journal of Sociology, 94* (Suppl. Organizations and Institutions: Sociological and Economic Approaches to the Analysis of Social Structure), S95–S120.

Coleman, J. (1990). *Foundations of social theory.* Cambridge, MA: Harvard University Press.

Coleman, J., & Hoffer, T. (1987). *Public and private schools: The impact of communities.* New York: Basic Books.

Commission on the Skills of the American Workforce. (1990). *America's choice: High skills or low wages.* Washington, DC: National Center on Education and the Economy.

Conger, J., & Benjamin, B. (1999). *Building leaders: How successful companies develop the next generation.* San Francisco: Jossey-Bass.

Conle, C. (2003). An anatomy of narrative curricula. *Educational Researcher, 32*(3), 3–15.

Cooper, B. S., & Randall, E. V. (Eds.). (1999). *Accuracy or advocacy: The politics of research in education.* Thousand Oaks, CA: Corwin Press.

Council of Chief State School Officers. (1996). *Interstate leaders licensure consortium: Standards for school leaders.* Washington, DC: Author.

Crandall, D. P., Eiseman, J. W., & Louis, K. S. (1986). Strategic planning issues that bear on the success of school improvement efforts. *Educational Administration Quarterly, 22*(3), 21–53.

Cremin, L. (1970). *American education: The colonial experience.* New York: Harper Torchbooks.

Cuban, L. (1992). Managing dilemmas while building professional communities. *Educational Researcher, 21,* 4–11.

Culbertson, J. (1964). The preparation of administrators. In D. E. Griffiths (Ed.), *Behavioral science and educational administration.* Sixty-third yearbook of the National Society for the Study of Education, Part II (pp. 303–330). Chicago: University of Chicago Press.

Day, D. (2001). Leadership development: A review in context. *Leadership Quarterly, 11*(4), 581–613.

Deal, T. E., & Peterson, K. D. (1999). *Shaping school culture: The heart of leadership.* San Francisco: Jossey-Bass.

deLeon, P. (1988). *Advice and consent: The development of the policy sciences.* New York: Russell Sage Foundation.

Denzin, N. K. (1994). The art and politics of interpretation. In N. K. Denzin & Y. S. Lincoln (Eds.), *Handbook of qualitative research* (pp. 500–515). Thousand Oaks, CA: Sage.

Dewey, J. (1929). *The sources of a science of education.* New York: Liveright.

Dewey, J. (1938). *Experience and education.* New York: Collier Books.

Donmoyer, R. (1996a). The concept of a knowledge base. In F. Murray (Ed.), *The teacher educator's handbook: Building a knowledge base for the preparation of teachers* (pp. 92–119). San Francisco: Jossey-Bass.

Donmoyer, R. (1996b). Educational research in an era of paradigm proliferation: What's a journal editor to do? *Educational Researcher, 25*(2), 19–25.

Donmoyer, R. (1999). The continuing quest for a knowledge base: 1976–1998. In J. Murphy & K. Louis (Eds.), *Handbook of research on educational administration* (2nd ed., pp. 25–43). San Francisco: Jossey-Bass.

Donmoyer, R. (2001). Paradigm talk reconsidered. In V. Richardson (Ed.), *Handbook of research on teaching* (4th ed., pp. 174–197). Washington, DC: American Educational Research Association.

Driscoll, M., & Kerchner, C. (1999). The implications of social capital for schools, communities, and cities: Educational administration as if a sense of place mattered. In J. Murphy & K. Louis (Eds.), *Handbook of research on educational administration* (2nd ed., pp. 385–404). San Francisco: Jossey-Bass.

Duffy, T. M., & Cunningham, D. J. (1996). Constructivism: Implications for the design and delivery of instruction. In D. H. Jonassen (Ed.), *Handbook of research for educational communications and technology* (pp. 170–198). New York: Macmillan.

DuFour, R., & Eaker, R. (1998). *Professional learning communities at work: Best practices for enhancing student achievement.* Reston, VA: Association for Supervision and Curriculum Development.

Egan, D., & Schwartz, B. (1979). Chunking in recall of symbolic drawings. *Memory and Cognition, 7,* 149–158.

Elmore, R. (2000). *Building a new structure for school leadership.* Washington, DC: Albert Shanker Institute, American Federation of Teachers.

Emrick, J., & Peterson, S. (1977). *A synthesis of findings across five recent studies of educational dissemination and change.* San Francisco: Far West Laboratory for Educational Research and Development.

Englemann, S., & Carnine, D. (1982). *Theory of instruction: Principles and applications.* New York: Irvington.

English, F. (2003, Spring). About the policing function of ELCC/NCATE and the standardization of university preparation programs in educational administration. *AERA Division A Newsletter: School Leadership News,* pp. 5–8.

Epstein, J. (2001). *School, family, and community partnerships: Preparing educators and improving schools.* Boulder, CO: Westview.

Erickson, D. (1979). Research on educational administration: The state of the art. *Educational Researcher, 8*(3), 9–14.

Etzioni, A. (1967). Mixed-scanning: A "third" approach to decision making. *Public Administration Review, 27*(5), 385–392.

Etzioni, A. (1968). *The active society.* New York: Free Press.

Evans, R. (1996). *The human side of school change: Reform, resistance, and the real-life problems of innovation.* San Francisco: Jossey-Bass.

Evertson, C. (1989). Classroom organization and management. In M. Reynolds (Ed.), *Knowledge base for the beginning teacher* (pp. 59–70). Elmsford, NY: Pergamon.

Firestone, W., & Louis, K. (1999). Schools as cultures. In J. Murphy & K. Louis (Eds.), *Handbook of research on educational administration* (2nd ed., pp. 297–322). San Francisco: Jossey-Bass.

Florio-Ruane, S. (1989). Social organization of classes and school. In M. Reynolds (Ed.), *Knowledge base for the beginning teacher* (pp. 163–172). Elmsford, NY: Pergamon.

Ford, S., Martin, M., Muth, R., & Steinbrecher, E. (1997, February). The Denver Schools' Leadership Academy: Problem-based learning to prepare future school leaders. In J. Reyhner (Ed.), *Partnerships in education: Preparing teachers for the twenty-first century* (pp. 123–132). Flagstaff: Northern Arizona University.

Forrester, J. (2002). The principal–agent model and budget theory. In A. Kahn & B. Hildreth (Eds.), *Budget theory in the public sector* (pp. 123–138). Westport, CT: Quorum.

Forsyth, P., & Murphy, J. (1999). A decade of changes: Analysis and comment. In J. Murphy & P. Forsyth (Eds.), *Educational Administration: A decade of reform* (pp. 253–272). Thousand Oaks, CA: Sage.

Forsyth, P., & Tallerico, M. (1993). *City schools: Leading the way.* Newbury Park, CA: Corwin Press.

Frederickson, G. (1991). Toward a theory of the public for public administration. *Administration and Society, 22*(4), 395–417.

Fredericksen, N., Glaser, R., Lesgold, A., & Shafto, M. (Eds.). (1990). *Diagnostic monitoring of skill and knowledge acquisition.* Hillsdale, NJ: Erlbaum.

Freidson, E. (1970). *Profession of medicine: A study of the sociology of applied knowledge.* New York: Harper & Row.

Freidson, E. (1986). *Professional powers: A study of the institutionalization of formal knowledge.* Chicago: University of Chicago Press.

Freire, P. (1970). *Pedagogy of the oppressed.* New York: Herder & Herder.

Fukuyama, F. (1999). *Social capital and civil society.* Paper delivered at the International Monetary Fund Conference on Second Generation Reforms. Retrieved December 22, 2005, from http://www.imf.org/external/pubs/ft/seminar/1999/reforms/fukuyama.htm

Fullan, M. (1993). *Change forces: Probing the depths of educational reform.* London: Falmer.

Fullan, M. (2001). *Leading in a culture of change.* San Francisco: Jossey-Bass.

Fulmer, C. L. (1994). Redefining teaching and learning in educational administration. *Journal of School Leadership, 4,* 451–460.

Fulmer, C. L., Muth, R., & Reiter, K. F. (2004). Design elements for meaningful clinical practice experiences: The core of preparation programs. In C. Carr & C. L. Fulmer (Eds.), *Educational leadership: Knowing the way, going the way, showing the way* (pp. 190–199). Lanham, MD: Scarecrow Education.

Furman, G. C. (1998). Postmodernism and community in schools: Unraveling the paradox. *Educational Administration Quarterly, 34*(3), 298–328.

Furman, G. C., & Starratt, R. J. (2002). Leadership for democratic community in schools. In J. Murphy (Ed.), *The educational leadership challenge: Redefining leadership for the 21st century* (pp. 105–133). Chicago: University of Chicago Press.

Gaddy, B., Hall, W., & Marzano, R. (1996). *School wars: Resolving our conflicts over religion and values.* San Francisco: Jossey-Bass.

Garcia, J., & Ballek, K. (2005). Irving Elementary School, school year 2003–2004: An annual case of school leadership. Unpublished manuscript. University of Colorado at Denver and Health Sciences Center, University of Washington, Bothell.

Geertz, C. (1980). Blurred genres: The reconfiguration of social thought. *The American Scholar, 49*(2), 165–179.

Getzels, J. W. (1979). Problem-finding and research in educational administration. In G. L. Immegart & W. L. Boyd (Eds.), *Problem-finding in educational administration* (pp. 5–22). Lexington, MA: D. C. Heath.

Getzels, J. W. (1985, September). Problem finding and the enhancement of creativity. *NASSP Bulletin,* 55–61.

Getzels, J. W., Lipham, J. M., & Campbell, R. F. (1968). *Educational administration as a social process: Theory, research, practice.* New York: Harper & Row.

Gharahedaghi, J., & Ackoff, R. (1994). Mechanisms, organisms, and social systems. In H. Tsouke (Ed.), *New thinking in organizational behavior* (pp. 188–208). Oxford: Butterworth-Heinemann.

Gilbert, T. (1978). *Human competence.* New York: McGraw-Hill.

Giroux, H. (1997). *Pedagogy and the politics of hope.* Boulder, CO: Westview Press.

Glickman, C. (1985). *Supervision of instruction: A developmental approach.* Boston: Allyn & Bacon.

Goldring, E., & Greenfield, W. (2002). Understanding the evolving concept of leadership in education: Roles, expectations, and dilemmas. In J. Murphy (Ed.), *The educational leadership challenge: Refining leadership for the 21st century.* One hundred-first yearbook of the National Society for the Study of Education, Part I (pp. 1–19). Chicago: University of Chicago Press.

Goleman, D. (1998). *Working with emotional intelligence.* New York: Bantam Books.

Goleman, D., Boyatzis, R., & McKee, A. (2002). *Primal leadership: Realizing the power of emotional intelligence.* Cambridge, MA: Harvard Business School Press.

Goodlad, J. (1975). *The dynamics of educational change: Toward responsive schools.* New York: McGraw-Hill.

Goodlad, J. (1990). The occupation of teaching in schools. In J. Goodlad, R. Soder, & K. Sirotnik (Eds.), *The moral dimensions of teaching* (pp. 3–34). San Francisco: Jossey-Bass.

Goodlad, J. (1996). Democracy, education, and community. In R. Soder (Ed.), *Democracy, education, and the schools* (pp. 87–124). San Francisco: Jossey-Bass.

Goodlad, J. (1997). Reprise and a look ahead. In J. Goodlad & T. McMannon (Eds.), *The public purpose of education and schooling* (pp. 155–167). San Francisco: Jossey-Bass.

Goodlad, J., & McMannon, T. (Eds.). (1997). *The public purpose of education and schooling.* San Francisco: Jossey-Bass.

Goodlad, J., Soder, R., & Sirotnik, K. (Eds.). (1990). *The moral dimension of teaching.* San Francisco: Jossey-Bass.

Goodlad, S. (Ed.). (2001). *The last best hope: A democracy reader.* San Francisco: Jossey-Bass.

Greenfield, W. (1987). Moral imagination and interpersonal competence: Antecedents to instructional leadership. In W. Greenfield (Ed.), *Instructional leadership: Concepts, issues, and controversies* (pp. 56–73). Newton, MA: Allyn & Bacon.

Griffiths, D. E. (1959). *Administrative theory.* New York: Appleton-Century-Crofts.

Griffiths, D. E. (Guest Ed.). (1991). Nontraditional theory and research [Special issue]. *Educational Administration Quarterly, 27*(3).

Griffiths, D. E., Stout, R. T., & Forsyth, P. B. (1988). *Leaders for America's schools: The report and papers of the National Commission on Excellence in Educational Administration.* Berkeley, CA: McCutchan.

Gronn, P. (2002). Distributed leadership. In K. Leithwood, P. Hallinger, K. Seashore-Louis, G. Furman-Brown, P. Gronin, W. Milford, & K. Riley (Eds.), *Second international handbook of educational leadership and administration* (pp. 653–697). Dordrecht, Netherlands: Kluwer.

Gudmundsdottir, S. (2001). Narrative research on school practice. In V. Richardson (Ed.), *Handbook of research on teaching* (4th ed., pp. 226–240). Washington, DC: American Educational Research Association.

Gulick, L., & Urwick, L. (1937). *Papers on the science of administration*. New York: Institute for Public Administration.

Gutmann, A. (2000). Why should schools care about civic education? In L. McDonnell, P. Timpane, & R. Benjamin (Eds.), *Rediscovering the democratic purposes of education* (pp. 73–90). Lawrence: University of Kansas Press.

Gutmann, A. (2001). Democratic education in difficult times. In S. Goodlad (Ed.), *The last best hope: A democratic reader* (pp. 216–230). San Francisco: Jossey-Bass.

Haller, E. J., Brent, B. O., & McNamara, J. H. (1997). Does graduate training in educational administration improve schools? *Phi Delta Kappan, 70*(3), 222–227.

Haller, E., & Strike, K. (1986). *An introduction to educational administration: Social, legal, and ethical perspectives*. New York: Longman.

Hallinger, P., & McCary, C. (1990). Developing the strategic thinking of instructional leaders. *Elementary School Journal, 91*(2), 89–108.

Halverson, R. (2003). Systems of practice: How leaders use artifacts to create professional community in schools. *Education Policy Analysis Archives, 11*(37). Retrieved January 15, 2004, from http://epaa.asu.edu/epaa/v11n37/

Hargreaves, A. (1986). *Two cultures of schooling: The case of middle schools*. London: Falmer.

Hart, A. (1995). Reconceiving school leadership: Emergent views. *Elementary School Journal, 96*, 9–28.

Hart, A. M., & Murphy, M. J. (1990). New teachers react to redesigned teacher work. *American Journal of Education, 98*, 224–250.

Heck, R. H., & Hallinger, P. (1999). Next generation methods of study of leadership and school improvement. In J. Murphy & K. Louis (Eds.), *Handbook of research on educational administration* (2nd ed., pp. 141–162). San Francisco: Jossey-Bass.

Heifetz, R. A. (1994). *Leadership without easy answers*. Cambridge, MA: Belknap Press, Harvard University Press.

Hess, F. (2003). *A license to lead? A new leadership agenda for America's schools*. Washington, DC: Progressive Policy Institute.

Hiebert, J., Gilmore, R., & Stigler, J. (2002). A knowledge base for the teaching profession: What would it look like and how can we get one? *Educational Researcher, 31*(5), 3–15.

Hill, P. (2002). What principals need to know about teaching and learning. In M. Tucker & J. Codding (Eds.), *The principal challenge: Leading and managing schools in an era of accountability* (pp. 43–76). San Francisco: Jossey-Bass.

Hills, J. (1978). Problems in the production and utilization of knowledge in educational administration. *Educational Administration Quarterly, 14*(1), 1–12.

Hills, J., & Gibson, C. (1992). A conceptual framework for thinking about conceptual frameworks. *Journal of Educational Administration, 30*(4), 4–21.

Hodgkinson, C. (1991). *Educational leadership: The moral art*. Albany: State University of New York Press.

Hodgkinson, H. (2000). Educational demographics: What teachers should know. *Educational Leadership, 58*(4), 6–11.

Holland, P. (1998). Processes and techniques in supervision. In G. Firth & E. Pajak (Eds.), *Handbook of research on school supervision* (pp. 397–408). New York: Simon & Schuster Macmillan.

Holt, M. (1993). Dr. Deming and the improvement of schooling: No instant pudding. *Journal of Curriculum and Supervision, 9*, 6–23.

Horn, R. A. (2001). Promoting social justice and caring in schools and communities: The unrealized potential of the cohort model. *Journal of School Leadership, 11*(4), 313–334.

House, E. R. (1998). *Schools for sale: Why free market policies won't improve schools and what will*. New York: Teachers College Press.

Hoy, A., & Hoy, W. (2003). *Instructional leadership: A learning-centered guide*. Boston: Allyn & Bacon.

Hoy, W. (Ed.). (1994). PRIMUS: *The University Council of Educational Administration document base*. New York: McGraw-Hill.

Hubbard, R., & Power, B. (1993). The art of classroom inquiry: A handbook for teacher-researchers. Portsmouth, NH: Heinemann.

Hunter, M. (1976). Teacher competency: Problem, theory, and practice. *Theory into Practice, 15*(2), 162–171.

Immegart, G. L., & Boyd, W. L. (Eds.). (1979). *Problem-finding in educational administration*. Lexington, MA: D. C. Heath.

Jenlink, P. (2001). Beyond the knowledge base controversy: Advancing the ideal of scholar-practitioner leadership. In T. J. Kowalski & G. Perreault (Eds.), *21st century challenges for school administrators* (pp. 65–88). Lanham, MD: Scarecrow Press.

Jesse, D., Davis, A., & Pokorney, N. (2004). High achieving middle schools for Latino students in poverty. *Journal of Education for Students Placed at Risk, 9*(1), 23–45.

Journal of Cases in Educational Leadership. (1998–present). Tempe, AZ: University Council for Educational Administration. Retrieved July 10, 2006, from http://www.ucea.org/html/cases/

Kingdon, J. W. (1995). *Agendas, alternatives, and public policies* (2nd ed.). New York: Longman.

Knapp, M., & McLaughlin, M. (2003). *Leading for learning sourcebook: Concepts and examples*. Seattle: University of Washington Center for the Study of Teaching and Policy.

Kowalski, T. (2001). *Case studies on educational administration* (3rd ed.). New York: Longman.

Kozol, J. (1991). *Savage inequalities: Children in America's schools*. New York: Crown.

Labaree, D. (1997). *How to succeed in school without really learning: The credentials race in American education*. New Haven, CT: Yale University Press.

Labaree, D. (2000). No exit. Public education as an inescapably public good. In

L. Cuban & D. Shipps (Eds.), *Reconstructing the common good in education* (pp. 110–123). Stanford, CA: Stanford University Press.

Lajoie, S. (2003). Transitions and trajectories for studies of expertise. *Educational Researcher, 32*(8), 21–25.

Langer, E. (1989). *Mindfulness.* Cambridge: Perseus.

Langer, E., & Moldoveanu, M. (2000). The construct of mindfulness. *Journal of Social Issues, 56*(1), 1–9.

Larson, C., & Murtadha, K. (2002). Leadership for social justice. In J. Murphy (Ed.), *The educational leadership challenge: Redefining leadership for the 21st century* (pp. 134–161). Chicago: University of Chicago Press.

Leithwood, K., & Duke, D. (1999). A century's quest for a knowledge base. In J. Murphy & K. Louis (Eds.), *Handbook of research on educational administration* (2nd ed., pp. 45–72). San Francisco: Jossey-Bass.

Leithwood, K., & Montgomery, D. (1982). The role of the elementary principal in program improvement. *Review of Educational Research, 52,* 309–339.

Leithwood, K., & Montgomery, D. (1986). *Improving principal effectiveness: The principal profile.* Toronto: Ontario Institute for Studies in Education.

Leithwood, K., & Steinbach, R. (1995). *Expert problem solving.* Albany: State University of New York Press.

Leo, J. (2005, October 24). Class(room) warriors. *U.S. News and World Report,* p. 75.

Lesgold, A., Rubinson, H., Feltovich, P., Glaser, R., Klopfer, D., & Wang, Y. (1988). Expertise in complex skill: Diagnosing x-ray pictures. In M. Chi, R. Glaser, & M. Farr (Eds.), *The nature of expertise* (pp. 311–342). Hillsdale, NJ: Erlbaum.

Levine, A. (2005). *Educating school leaders.* New York: Education Schools Project, Teachers College.

Levine, D., & Lezotte, L. (1990). *Unusually effective schools: A review and analysis of research and practice.* Madison, WI: National Center for Effective Schools Research and Development.

Lightfoot, S. (1978). *Worlds apart.* New York: Basic Books.

Likert, R. (1967). *The human organization.* New York: McGraw-Hill.

Lincoln, Y. S., & Guba, E. G. (1985). *Naturalistic inquiry.* Beverly Hills, CA: Sage.

Lindblom, C. E., & Cohen, D. K. (1979). *Usable knowledge: Social science and social problem solving.* New Haven, CT: Yale University Press.

Lindsey, R., Robbins, D., & Terrell, R. (1999). *Cultural proficiency: A manual for school leaders.* Thousand Oaks, CA: Sage.

Linn, R., & Baker, E. (1996). Can performance assessments be psychometrically sound? In J. Baron & D. Wolf (Eds.), *Performance-based student assessment: Challenges and possibilities* (pp. 84–103). Ninety fifth yearbook of the National Society for the Study of Education. Chicago: University of Chicago Press.

Lipsey, M., & Wilson, D. (1993). The efficacy of psychological, educational, and behavioral treatment. *American Psychologist, 48*(12), 1181–1209.

Lipsky, M. (1980). *Street-level bureaucracy.* New York: Russell Sage Foundation.

Little, J. (1982). Norms of collegiality and experimentation: Workplace conditions of school success. *American Educational Research Journal, 19*(3), 325–340.

Little, J. (1988). Assessing the prospects for teacher leadership. In A. Lieberman (Ed.),

Building a professional culture in schools (pp. 78–106). New York: Teachers College Press.

Little, J. (1990). The persistence of privacy: Autonomy and initiative in teachers' professional relations. *Teachers College Record, 91*(4), 509–536.

Lortie, D. (1975). *Schoolteacher: A sociological study.* Chicago: University of Chicago Press.

Louis, K., Kruse, S., & Bryk, A. (1995). Professionalism and community: What is it and why is it important in urban schools? In K. Louis & S. Kruse (Eds.), *Professionalism and community: Perspectives on reforming urban schools* (pp. 3–22). Thousand Oaks, CA: Sage.

Louis, K., Marks, H., & Kruse, S. (1996). Teachers' professional community in restructuring schools. *American Educational Research Journal, 33*, 757–798.

Louis, M. R. (1980). Surprise and sense making: What newcomers experience in entering unfamiliar organizational settings. *Administrative Science Quarterly, 25*, 226–251.

Luegg, C., Bulkley, K., Firestone, W., & Garner, W. (2001). The contextual terrain facing school leaders. In J. Murphy (Ed.), *The educational leadership challenge: Redefining leadership for the 21st century* (pp. 20–41). Chicago: University of Chicago Press.

Lutz, F. W., & Iannaccone, L. (1978). *Public participation in local school districts: The dissatisfaction theory of democracy* (Politics of Education Series). Lexington, MA: Lexington Books.

Lutz, F. W., & Merz, C. (1992). *The politics of school/community relations.* New York: Teachers College Press.

Malen, B. (1994). The micropolitics of education: Mapping the multiple dimensions of power relations in school politics. *Journal of Education Policy, 9*(5/6), 147–167.

Malen, B., Murphy, M. J., & Hart, A. W. (1987). Restructuring teacher compensation systems: An analysis of three incentive strategies. In K. Alexander & D. Monk (Eds.), *Attracting and compensating for America's teachers—Eighth annual yearbook of American Education Finance Association* (pp. 91–142). Cambridge, MA: Ballinger.

Malen, B., Ogawa, R., & Kranz, J. (1990). What do we know about school-based management? In W. Clune & J. Witte (Eds.), *Choice and control in American education* (Vol. 2, pp. 289–342). Bristol, PA: Falmer Press.

Markow, D., & Scheer, M. (2003). *The MetLife survey of the American teacher: An examination of school leadership.* New York: MetLife.

Marks, H. (2000). Student engagement in instructional activity: Patterns in the elementary, middle, and high school years. *American Educational Research Journal, 37*(1), 153–184.

Marks, H., & Louis, K. (1999). Teacher empowerment and the capacity for organizational learning. *Educational Administration Quarterly, 35*(5), 707–750.

Martin, W., & Willower, D. (1981). The managerial behavior of high school principals. *Educational Administration Quarterly, 17*(1), 69–90.

Martinelli, K., & Muth, R. (1989). Improving educational problem solving. *Planning and Changing, 20*, 76–87.

Marzano, R. (2003). *What works in schools: Translating research into action.* Alexandria, VA: Association for Supervision and Curriculum Development.

Mather, S., & Hopkins, P. (2005). Bryn Mawr Elementary School, school year 2004–2005: An annual case of school leadership. Manuscript in preparation. University of Colorado at Denver and Health Sciences Center, University of Washington, Bothell.

Mazzoni, T. L. (1995). State policymaking and school reform: Influences and influentials. In J. D. Scribner & D. H. Layton (Eds.), *The study of educational politic.* The 1994 commemorative yearbook of the Politics of Education Association (pp. 53–74). Washington, DC: Falmer.

McCarthy, M. (1999a). The "changing" face of the educational leadership professoriate. In J. Murphy & P. Forsyth (Eds.), *Educational administration: A decade of reform* (pp. 192–214). Thousand Oaks, CA: Sage.

McCarthy, M. (1999b). The evolution of educational leadership preparation programs. In J. Murphy & K. Louis (Eds.), *Handbook of research on educational administration* (2nd ed., pp. 119–139). San Francisco: Jossey-Bass.

McLaughlin, M. (1993). What matters most in teachers' workplace context? In J. Little & M. McLaughlin (Eds.), *Teachers' work: Individuals, colleagues, and context* (pp. 79–103). New York: Teachers College Press.

Merton, R. K. (1967). *On theoretical sociology: Five essays, old and new.* New York: Free Press.

Mohrman, S., Lawler, E., & Mohrman, A. (1992). Applying employee involvement in schools. *Educational Evaluation and Policy Analysis, 14*(4), 347–360.

Murphy, J. (1990). Principal instructional leadership. In L. S. Lotto & P. Thurston (Eds.), *Advances in educational administration: Changing perspectives on the school* (Vol. 1, Part B, pp. 163–200). Greenwich, CT: JAI Press.

Murphy, J. (1992). *The landscape of leadership preparation: Reframing the education of school administrators.* Newbury Park, CA: Corwin Press.

Murphy, J. (Ed.). (2002a). *The educational leadership challenge: Redefining leadership for the 21st century.* One hundred-first yearbook of the National Society for the Study of Education, Part I. Chicago: University of Chicago Press.

Murphy, J. (2002b). Reculturing the profession of education: New blueprints. *Educational Administration Quarterly, 38*(2), 176–191.

Murphy, M. J., Martin, W. M., Ford, S., & Muth, R. (1996, October). *Problem-based learning: An idea whose time has come.* Paper presented at the annual meeting of the University Council for Educational Administration, Louisville, KY.

Murphy, M., Martin, M., & Muth, R. (1994, October). *Matching performance standards with problems of practice: Problem-based learning in a standards environment.* Symposium presentation on problem-based learning, performance standards, and portfolios at the annual meeting of the University Council for Educational Administration, Philadelphia, PA.

Muth, R. (1999a, August). *Developing a philosophy of problem-based learning for educational administration programs.* Paper presented at the annual conference of the National Council of Professors of Educational Administration, Jackson Hole, WY.

Muth, R. (1999b, August). *Integrating a learning-oriented paradigm: Implications for practice*. Paper presented at the annual meeting of the National Council of Professors of Educational Administration, Jackson Hole, WY.

Muth, R., Banks, D., Bonelli, J., Gaddis, B., Napierkowski, H., White, C., & Wood, V. (2001). Toward an instructional paradigm: Recasting how faculty work and students learn. In T. J. Kowalski & G. Perreault (Eds.), *Twenty-first century challenges for school administrators*. Ninth annual yearbook of the National Council of Professors of Educational Administration (pp. 29–53). Lanham, MD: Scarecrow Press.

Muth, R., & Barnett, B. (2001). Making the case for professional preparation: Using research for program improvement and political support. *Educational Leadership and Administration: Teaching and Program Development, 13*, 109–120.

Muth, R., Bellamy, G. T., Fulmer, C. L., & Murphy, M. J. (2004). A model for building knowledge for professional practice. In C. Carr & C. L. Fulmer (Eds.), *Educational leadership: Knowing the way, going the way, showing the way* (pp. 83–103). Lanham, MD: Scarecrow Education.

Muth, R., Murphy, M. J., & Martin, W. M. (1994). Problem-based learning at the University of Colorado at Denver. *Journal of School Leadership, 4*, 432–450.

Myers, V. M., & Kline, C. E. (2001/2002). Secondary school intervention assistance teams: Can they be effective? *High School Journal, 85*(2), 33–43.

National Commission on Excellence in Education. (1983). *A nation at risk: The imperative for educational reform*. Washington, DC: U.S. Department of Education.

National Policy Board for Educational Administration. (2002). *Standards for advanced programs in educational leadership for principals, superintendents, curriculum specialists, and supervisors*. Arlington, VA: Author.

New England Association of Schools and Colleges. (2001). *Manual for school evaluation*. Bedford, MA: Author.

Newlon, J. (1934). *Educational administration as social policy*. New York: Scribner.

No Child Left Behind Act of 2001. Pub. L. No. 107-110.

Noddings, N. (1999). Care, justice, and equity. In M. Katz, N. Noddings, & K. Strike (Eds.), *Justice and caring: The search for common ground in education* (pp. 7–20). New York: Teachers College Press.

North Central Association Commission on Accreditation and School Improvement. (2001). *Standards and criteria for elementary, middle level, secondary, and unit schools*. Tempe, AZ: Author.

Ogawa, R., & Bossert, S. (2000). Leadership as an organizational quality. In *The Jossey Bass reader on educational leadership* (pp. 38–58). San Francisco: Jossey-Bass.

Ogawa, R., Crowson, R., & Goldring, E. (1999). Enduring dilemmas of school organization. In J. Murphy & K. Louis (Eds.), *Handbook of research on educational administration* (2nd ed., pp. 277–296). San Francisco: Jossey-Bass.

Osborne, D., & Plastrik, P. (2000). *The reinventor's fieldbook: Tools for transforming your government*. San Francisco: Jossey-Bass.

Osborne, W., & Wiggins, T. (1989). Perceptions of tasks in the school principalship. *Journal of Personnel Evaluation in Education, 2*, 367–375.

Oser, F. (1994). Moral perspectives on teaching. In L. Darling-Hammond (Ed.), *Review of research in education* (Vol. 20, pp. 57–127). Washington, DC: American Educational Research Association.

Osterman, K. (2000). Students' need for belonging in the school community. *Review of Educational Research, 70*, 323–367.

Owen, K., & Ballek, K. (2005). Beulah Heights Elementary School, school year 2002–2003: An annual case of school leadership. Manuscript in preparation. University of Colorado at Denver and Health Sciences Center, University of Washington, Bothell.

Polanyi, M. (1962). *Personal knowledge: Towards a post-critical philosophy.* Chicago: University of Chicago Press.

Popham, W. (1987). The shortcomings of Champagne teacher evaluations. *Journal of Personnel Evaluation in Education, 1*, 25–28.

Portin, B., Schneider, P., DeArmond, M., & Gundlach, L. (2003). *Making sense of leading schools: A study of the school principalship.* Seattle: University of Washington, Center on Reinventing Public Education. Retrieved October 1, 2003, from http://crpe.org/pubs.shtml#leadership

Productivity Commission. (2003). Social capital: Reviewing the concept and its policy implications. Canberra, Australia: AusInfo. Retrieved December 22, 2005, from http://www.pc.gov.au/research/commres/socialcapital/keypoints.html

Public Agenda Foundation. (2001). *Trying to stay ahead of the game: Superintendents and principals talk about school leadership.* New York: Author.

Public School Forum of North Carolina. (1987). *The condition of being an educator: An analysis of North Carolina's public schools.* Raleigh: Public School Forum of North Carolina.

Putnam, R. (1993). *Making democracy work: Civic traditions in modern Italy.* Princeton, NJ: Princeton University Press.

Putnam, R. (2000). *Bowling alone: The collapse and revival of American community.* New York: Simon & Schuster.

Putnam, R., & Feldstein, L. (2003). *Better together: Restoring the American community.* New York: Simon & Schuster.

Quality Counts at 10: A decade of standards-based reform. (2006, January). Bethesda, MD: Education Week.

Rahim, H., & Hopkins, P. (2005). Van Asselt Elementary School, school year 2004–2005: An annual case of school leadership. Manuscript in preparation. University of Colorado at Denver and Health Sciences Center, University of Washington, Bothell.

Rallis, S. F. (1990). Professional teachers and restructuring schools: Leadership challenges. In B. Mitchell & L. Cunningham (Eds.), *Educational leadership and changing contexts of families, communities, and schools.* Eighty-ninth yearbook of the National Society for the Study of Education, Part II (pp. 184–209). Chicago: University of Chicago Press.

Ravitch, D., & Viteritti, J. (Eds.). (2001). *Making good citizens: Education and civil society.* New Haven, CT: Yale University Press.

Reason, J. (2000). Human error: Models and management [Electronic version]. *British Medical Journal, 320*(7237), 1–6.

Rehm, R., & Muth, R. (1998). Toward a theory of problem-based learning for the preparation of educational administrators. In R. Muth & M. Martin (Eds.), *Toward the year 2000: Leadership for quality schools*. Sixth annual yearbook of the National Council of Professors of Educational Administration (pp. 289–299). Lancaster, PA: Technomic.

Reid, W. (1978). *Thinking about the curriculum*. London: Routledge & Kegan Paul.

Richardson, V. (1996). The case for formal research and practical inquiry in teacher education. In F. Murray (Ed.), *The teacher educator's handbook: Building a knowledge base for the preparation of teachers* (pp. 715–737). San Francisco: Jossey-Bass.

Riehl, C. (2000). The principal's role in creating inclusive schools for diverse students: A review of normative, empirical, and critical literature on the practice of educational administration. *Review of Educational Research, 70*(1), 55–81.

Riessman, C. K. (1993). *Narrative analysis*. Newbury Park, CA: Sage.

Robinson, V. M. (1993). *Problem-based methodology: Research for the improvement of practice*. Oxford: Pergamon Press.

Robinson, V. M. (1996). Problem-based methodology and administrative practice. *Educational Administration Quarterly, 32*(3), 427–451.

Robinson, V. M. (1998). Methodology and the research-practice gap. *Educational Researcher, 27*(1), 17–26.

Rogers, E. (1967). *Bibliography on the diffusion of innovations*. East Lansing: Michigan State University, Department of Communications.

Rose, L., & Gallup, A. (2005). The 37th annual Phi Delta Kappa/Gallup poll of the public's attitudes toward the public schools. *Phi Delta Kappan, 87*(1), 41–57.

Sammons, P. (1999). *School effectiveness: Coming of age in the twenty-first century*. Exton, PA: Swets & Zeitlinger.

Sarason, S. (1972). *The creation of settings and future societies*. San Francisco: Brookline Books.

Scheerens, J., & Bosker, R. (1997). *The foundations of educational effectiveness*. New York: Elsevier.

Schein, E. (1992). *Organizational culture and leadership* (2nd ed.). San Francisco: Jossey-Bass.

Scheurich, J., & Skrla, L. (2003). *Leadership for equity and excellence: Creating high achieving classrooms, schools, and districts*. Thousand Oaks, CA: Corwin Press.

Scott, W. R. (2001). *Institutions and organizations* (2nd ed.). Thousand Oaks, CA: Sage.

Search Institute. (1993). *Healthy communities, healthy youth*. Minneapolis, MN: Author.

Secretary's Commission on Achieving Necessary Skills. (1991). *What work requires of schools*. Washington, DC: U.S. Department of Labor.

Senge, P. (1990). *The fifth discipline: The art and practice of the learning organization*. New York: Doubleday.

Senge, P., Cambron-McCabe, N., Lucas, T., Smith, B., Dutton, J., & Kleiner, A. (2000). *Schools that learn: A fifth discipline fieldbook for educators, parents, and everyone who cares about education.* A Fifth Discipline Resource. New York: Currency.

Sergiovanni, T. (1992). Moral authority and the regeneration of supervision. In C. Glickman (Ed.), *Supervision in transition* (pp. 203–214). Alexandria, VA: Association for Supervision and Curriculum Development.

Sergiovanni, T. J. (2001). *The principalship: A reflective practice perspective.* Needham Heights, MA: Allyn & Bacon.

Shapiro, J., & Stefkovich, J. (2001). *Ethical leadership and decision making in education: Applying theoretical perspectives to complex dilemmas.* Mahwah, NJ: Erlbaum.

Shavelson, R. (1972). Some aspects of the correspondence between content structure and cognitive structure in physics instruction. *Journal of Educational Psychology, 63,* 225–234.

Shavelson, R., & Huang, L. (2003). Responding responsibly. *Change, 35*(1), 10–19.

Shavelson, R., & Towne, L. (2002). *Scientific research in education.* Washington, DC: National Academy Press.

Shulman, L. (1986). Paradigms and research programs in the study of teaching: A contemporary perspective. In M. Wittrock (Ed.), *Handbook of research on teaching* (3rd ed., pp. 3–36). New York: Macmillan.

Shulman, L. (1998). Theory, practice, and the education of professionals. *Elementary School Journal, 98*(5), 511–526.

Silver, P. (1978). Some areas of concern in administrator preparation. In P. Silver & D. Spuck (Eds.), *Preparatory programs for educational administrators in the United States.* Columbus, OH: University Council for Educational Administration.

Silver, P. (1982). Administrator preparation. In H. Mitzel (Ed.), *Encyclopedia of educational research* (5th ed., Vol. 1, pp. 49–59). New York: Free Press.

Silver, P. (1983). Toward a redefinition of professionalism in educational administration. In P. Silver (Ed.), *Professionalism in educational administration* (pp. 8–25). Victoria, Australia: Deakin University Press.

Simon, H. (1981). *The sciences of the artificial* (2nd ed.). Cambridge, MA: MIT Press.

Sirotnik, K. (1990). Society, schooling, teaching, and preparing to teach. In J. Goodlad, R. Soder, & K. Sirotnik (Eds.), *The moral dimensions of teaching* (pp. 296–327). San Francisco: Jossey-Bass.

Slavin, R. E., Madden, N. A., Karweit, N. L., Dolan, L., & Wasik, B. A. (1996). *Every child, every school: Success for all.* Newbury Park, CA: Corwin Press.

Smith, M., & O'Day, J. (1991). Systemic school reform. In S. Fuhrman & B. Malen (Eds.), *The politics of curriculum and testing.* 1990 yearbook of the Politics of Education Association (pp. 233–267). Bristol, PA: Falmer.

Smylie, M., & Hart, A. (1999). School leadership for teacher learning and change: A human and social capital development perspective. In J. Murphy & K. Louis (Eds.), *Handbook of research on educational administration* (2nd ed., pp. 421–443). San Francisco: Jossey-Bass.

Snowden, P. E., & Gorton, R. A. (1998). *School leadership and administration:*

Important concepts, case studies and simulations (5th ed.). New York: McGraw-Hill.

Soder, R. (Ed.). (1996). *Democracy, education, and the schools.* San Francisco: Jossey-Bass.

Soder, R. (2001). *The language of leadership.* San Francisco: Jossey-Bass.

Solomon, D., Watson, M., & Battistich, V. (2001). Teaching and schooling effects on moral/prosocial development. In V. Richardson (Ed.), *Handbook of research on teaching* (4th ed., pp. 566–603). Washington, DC: American Educational Research Association.

Sosik, J., & Lee, D. (2002). Mentoring in organizations: A social judgment perspective for developing tomorrow's leaders. *Journal of Leadership Studies, 8*(4), 17–33.

Spillane, J. P., Halverson, R., & Diamond, J. B. (2001). Investigating school leadership practice: A distributed perspective. *Educational Researcher, 30*(3), 23–28.

Spillane J., & Louis, K. (2002). School improvement processes and practices: Professional learning for building instructional capacity. In J. Murphy (Ed.), *The educational leadership challenge: Redefining leadership for the 21st century.* One hundred-first yearbook of the National Society for the Study of Education, Part I (pp. 83–104). Chicago: University of Chicago Press.

Spring, J. (2002). *Political agendas for education: From the religious right to the green party* (2nd ed.). Mahwah, NJ: Erlbaum.

Stanton-Salazar, R. (1997). A social capital framework for understanding the socialization of racial minority children and youth. *Harvard Educational Review, 67*(1), 1–40.

Steinberg, L. (1996). *Beyond the classroom: Why school reform has failed and what parents need to do.* New York: Simon & Schuster.

Sternberg, R. (2003). What is an "expert student"? *Educational Researcher, 32*(8), 5–9.

Stevenson, H. W., & Stigler, J. W. (1992). *The learning gap: Why our schools are failing and what we can learn from Japanese and Chinese education.* New York: Simon & Schuster.

Stolovitch, H., & Keeps, E. (1992). What is human performance technology? In H. Stolovitch & E. Keeps (Eds.), *Handbook of human performance technology: A comprehensive guide for analyzing and solving performance problems in organizations* (pp. 1–13). San Francisco: Jossey-Bass.

Swidler, A. (1986). Culture in action: Symbols and strategies. *American Sociological Review, 51*(2), 273–286.

Taylor, D. L., Tashakkori, A., & Crone-Koshel, L. (2001). A model of planning for school improvement and obstacles to implementation. *Journal of School Leadership, 11*(6), 493–510.

Thompson, S. (Ed.). (1993). *Principals for our changing schools: Knowledge and skill base.* Lancaster, PA: Technomic.

Tucker, M., & Codding, J. (Eds.). (2002). *The principal challenge: Leading and managing schools in an era of accountability.* San Francisco: Jossey-Bass.

Tyack, D. B. (1974). *The one best system: A history of American urban education.* Cambridge, MA: Harvard University Press.

Tyack, D., & Hansot, E. (1982). *Managers of virtue: Public school leadership in America, 1820–1980.* New York: Basic Books.

Tye, B. (2000). *Hard truths: Uncovering the deep structure of schooling.* New York: Teachers College Press.

U.S. Department of Education. (2000). *Smaller learning communities fact sheet.* Washington, DC: Author.

Valente, W., & Valente, C. (2001). *Law in the schools.* Upper Saddle River, NJ: Merrill Prentice Hall.

Vander Ark, T. (2003). America's high school crisis: Policy reforms that will make a difference. *Education Week, 22*(29), 52, 41.

Wang, M., Haertel, G., & Walberg, H. (1993). Toward a knowledge base for school learning. *Review of Educational Research, 63*(3), 249–294.

Waters, T., Marzano, R., & McNulty, B. (2003). *Balanced leadership: What 30 years of research tells us about the effect of leadership on student achievement.* Aurora, CO: Mid-continent Research for Education and Learning.

Weber, J. (1997). Leading the instructional program. In S. Smith & P. Piele (Eds.), *School leadership: Handbook for excellence* (2nd ed., pp. 191–224). Eugene, OR: Eric Clearinghouse on Educational Management.

Weick, K. E. (1987). Organizational culture as a source of high reliability. *California Management Review, 29,* 112–127.

Weick, C., & Roberts, K. (1993). Collective mind in organization: Heedful interrelating on flight decks. *Administrative Science Quarterly, 38,* 357–381.

Weick, K., & Sutcliffe, K. (2001). *Managing the unexpected: Assuring high performance in an age of complexity.* San Francisco: Jossey-Bass.

Weick, K., Sutcliffe, K., & Obstfeld, D. (1999). Organizing for high reliability: Process of collective mindfulness. *Research in Organizational Behavior, 21,* 81–123.

West, K., & Ballek, K. (2005). Goodnight Elementary School, school year 2003–2004: An annual case of school leadership. Manuscript in preparation. University of Colorado at Denver and Health Sciences Center, University of Washington, Bothell.

West, L., & Staub, F. (2003). *Content-focused coaching: Transforming mathematics lessons.* Portsmouth, NH: Heinemann.

Wheatley, M., & Kellner-Rogers, M. (1995). Breathing life into organizations [Electronic version]. *Journal for Quality & Participation, 18*(4), 6–9.

Wiggins, G. (1998). *Educative assessment: Designing assessments to inform and improve student performance.* San Francisco: Jossey-Bass.

Wiggins, G., & McTighe, J. (1998). *Understanding by design.* Alexandria, VA: Association for Supervision and Curriculum Development.

Wiggins, G., & McTighe, J. (2005). *Understanding by design* (2nd ed.). Alexandria, VA: Association for Supervision and Curriculum Development.

Wilson, R. (2005, December 16). Education schools want to make sure prospective teachers have the right "dispositions." *The Chronicle of Higher Education,* pp. A8–A11.

Wirt, F., & Kirst, M. (1997). *The political dynamics of American education.* Berkeley, CA: McCutchan.

Witziers, B., Boskers, R., & Kruger, M. (2003). Educational leadership and student achievement: The elusive search for an association. *Educational Administration Quarterly, 39*(3), 398–425.

Wolcott, H. (1978). *The man in the principal's office*. New York: Holt, Rinehart & Winston.

Woolcock, M. (1998). Social capital and economic development: Toward a theoretical synthesis and policy framework. *Theory and Society, 27*, 151–208.

Index